The Routledge Course in Business Chin

求实商务汉语

The Routledge Course in Business Chinese has been specifically designed for students in the fourth year of language learning or above who wish to progress their language training and prepare to tackle real-life business situations confidently and effectively.

Designed to prepare students for the world of business, *The Routledge Course in Business Chinese* presents timeless business knowledge through topics ranging from frequently occurring business activities, economic systems and phenomena, to issues of common interest. Topics include: the stock market, international trade and economic recession and inflation.

Business knowledge is presented as a means to facilitate language learning, while the content-based materials enhance cultural awareness. The course focuses primarily on developing advanced language skills with particular emphasis on formal styles and business terminology.

Students are supported and guided through the course as they develop the skills they need to continue learning for themselves. Students are encouraged and inspired to explore and keep up to date with new developments in China's economy through their own efforts, thus developing an independent learning style and connecting classroom learning to the real world.

Key features

- focuses on practical language skills and language-learning skills
- foundation in the common core of the language reinforced through task-based exercises to encourage language use
- provides timeless topics as a foundation and encourages students to acquire recent information to supplement this through their own efforts thus guiding them to make the necessary connections between the classroom and the real world.

By the end of this rewarding course students will have the language skills and learning skills required to deal effectively with a range of business situations and the skills to prepare themselves for any future business encounters.

Qinghai Chen is a pioneer of Business Chinese teaching and research in the United States and is currently on the advisory committee of the Center for International Business Chinese Education and Resources Development at the Shanghai University of Finance and Economics (SHUFE) and the board of the Inter-University Program of Chinese Language Studies (IUP). He has also directed the University of Michigan Chinese Language Program for ten years.

Le Tang teaches Chinese at Stanford University and heads the Summer Intensive Chinese Program at the Monterey Institute of International Studies (MIIS).

Qiuli Zhao teaches Business Chinese at the University of Michigan.

Visit www.routledge.com/cw/chen for free access to supplementary materials for instructors and students, including a sample syllabus, audio files of all the main texts and reading articles in the exercises, photos, exercise keys, and more.

THE ROUTLEDGE COURSE IN
Business Chinese
求实商务汉语

Qinghai Chen
Le Tang and Qiuli Zhao

Routledge
Taylor & Francis Group

LONDON AND NEW YORK

First published 2013
by Routledge
2 Park Square, Milton Park, Abingdon, Oxon OX14 4RN

Simultaneously published in the USA and Canada
by Routledge
711 Third Avenue, New York, NY 10017

Routledge is an imprint of the Taylor & Francis Group, an informa business

British Library Cataloguing in Publication Data
A catalogue record for this book is available from the British Library

Library of Congress Cataloging in Publication Data
Chen, Qinghai.
    The Routledge course in business Chinese / Qinghai Chen, with Le Tang and Qiuli Zhao.
        p. cm.
    Includes bibliographical references and index.
    1. Chinese language—Textbooks for foreign speakers—English.   2. Chinese language—
Business Chinese.   I. Tang, Le.   II. Zhao, Qiuli.   III. Title.   IV. Title: Course in
business Chinese.
    PL1129.E5C414 2013
    495.1′82421—dc23

                                                                          2012002333

ISBN: 978-0-415-66802-6 (hbk)
ISBN: 978-0-415-66803-3 (pbk)
ISBN: 978-0-203-10720-1 (ebk)

Typeset in Scala
by Graphicraft Limited, Hong Kong

Printed and bound in Great Britain by
CPI Group (UK) Ltd, Croydon, CR0 4YY

目录
Contents

前言

Introduction

Features of the course

The Routledge Course in Business Chinese 《求实商务汉语：语言训练与学习指导》 is intended to consolidate and expand learners' existing foundations, which typically means three or more years of Chinese language study in a US university or college on a five-hour-per-week basis. It differs from many other Chinese textbooks at this level in that it provides language training in business contexts, and it teaches language for business as well as general purposes. The textbook begins with a warm-up lesson to prepare learners for their work in the course. Each of the twelve lessons that comes after the warm-up is comprised of the following four parts: 1) text 1, a short article; 2) text 2, a brief dialogue; 3) exercises; 4) learning guide. For details on the structure of the course, please refer to the warm-up lesson.

As a Business Chinese textbook, *The Routledge Course in Business Chinese* 《求实商务汉语》 is unique in two special features. First, its main texts are based on common business knowledge, which should be both familiar and useful to learners. As it is based on common knowledge, its content is relatively stable and will not be greatly affected by the fast-changing world. At the same time, it can stay current as its business topics can be updated through task-based activities every time it is used. It is hoped that this feature will allow the textbook to remain in active use for many years. Second, this textbook prepares learners for self-sustained continuous learning. The learning guides throughout the book cover learning strategies as well as important characteristics of formal-style Chinese in business contexts. All the issues are crucial for the further development of learners at this proficiency level. In this sense, *The Routledge Course in Business Chinese* 《求实商务汉语》 will not just contribute to learners' present studies but also benefit their future careers.

The Routledge Course in Business Chinese 《求实商务汉语》 is not meant to be a course of business knowledge, although it is content-based and oriented toward cultural literacy. While business knowledge in the texts serves as a means of facilitating learning and teaching, the training provided is focused on language skills with emphases on formal styles and business terminology. Much weight falls on the comprehension of Business Chinese texts and the acquisition of relatively formal language in oral applications. Writing in formal Chinese is not explicitly required. This is in accordance with the result of a national survey on Business Chinese courses at US universities and colleges, which ranks writing at the very bottom in both needs analysis and instructional design.

The Routledge Course in Business Chinese 《求实商务汉语》 is supported by a companion website (www.routledge.com/cw/chen) with free access to a *pinyin* version, an English version, and an audio file of all the main texts and reading articles in the exercises. The website also includes photos, exercise keys, and other supplementary materials.

Suggested use of the textbook

As mentioned above, *The Routledge Course in Business Chinese* 《求实商务汉语：语言训练与学习指导》 was developed with a target audience in mind. Even so, it can easily be adapted to a class of students with heterogeneous backgrounds. While approaches vary, one possibility is to give individualized assignments to different categories of students. Highly proficient Chinese-speaking students, for example, can be challenged with more demanding and comprehensive tasks, such as updating a business topic with a search for recent information in a written report or oral presentation. On the other hand, *The Routledge Course in Business Chinese* 《求实商务汉语》 is designed to suit a series of two 3-credit courses offered in two regular semesters. It can be adapted for use in just one semester, however, depending on the course's attributes, students' proficiency levels, and the instructor's preferences. Making selective use of course materials, including what is provided at the companion website as well as in the book itself, is also possible. Emphasis, for example, can be placed on particular topics or a certain language aspect, such as reading or speaking. Of course, the final instructional design rests in the hands of teachers, who can tailor requirements and the materials in the book to suit the needs of their classrooms.

Language is learned rather than taught. With this understanding, a learner's manual is provided in the form of the Business Chinese Warm-up, a preparatory lesson at the very beginning of the course. An important responsibility of the instructor is to help students with a thorough study of this lesson and make sure that they are well prepared for the challenges of the course. It is suggested that the first class meeting be devoted to this warm-up alone, and that this class include a presentation of the lesson and a discussion on the course syllabus, as prepared by the instructor. Those parts of the book that are presented in English, such as the learning guides, can be left to student self-study, provided that instructors conduct check-ups on a regular basis and arrange help sessions when a need arises. Also, we suggest that assessment of student achievement is better centered on practical applications than on linguistic forms.

Finally, it should be reiterated that learners with *The Routledge Course in Business Chinese* 《求实商务汉语》 are expected to advance on a dual track: language ability and language-learning ability. The ultimate goal of this course is to bring learners to a new starting point, from which they can move on to continuous learning by themselves. We can claim the success of the course only when students have acquired self-sustainability in Chinese learning and are able to tackle language tasks in the real business world.

Qualifications of authors

The authors of this textbook have all received advanced professional training in teaching Chinese as a foreign or second language.

Dr. Qinghai Chen (陈青海), the main author of this book, is a lifelong language professional. With a PhD in instructional science (language acquisition), he has had vast teaching experience in both China and the United States. As a pioneer of Business Chinese teaching and research in the US since 1992, he has authored a significant number of publications and conference presentations, and chaired several national events for Business Chinese instructors. He served on the board of the Chinese Language Teachers Association

(CLTA) from 2006 to 2009, and is currently on the advisory committee of the Center for International Business Chinese Education and Resources Development at the Shanghai University of Finance and Economics (SHUFE) and the board of the Inter-University Program of Chinese Language Studies (IUP). He has directed the University of Michigan Chinese Language Program for ten years.

Le Tang (唐 乐), with an MA in Teaching Chinese as a Foreign Language from Renmin University (China), became a member of the University of Michigan Chinese faculty in 2008. Before that she headed a CET language program in Beijing and taught at Middlebury College Summer Chinese School as well as Wake Forest University. Business Chinese is one of the courses she has taught or coordinated. She is currently teaching Chinese at Stanford University and heading the Summer Intensive Chinese Program at the Monterey Institute of International Studies (MIIS).

Qiuli Zhao (赵秋篱) joined the University of Michigan in 2008 with a Masters of Teaching Chinese as a Foreign Language from Beijing Language and Culture University (China). She has been teaching Business Chinese at the University of Michigan since then. She presented on task-based approaches in Business Chinese classrooms at the third Business Chinese workshop in 2010.

Acknowledgments

The development of Business Chinese as a college language course has been a collective endeavor in the United States for the past two decades. Dozens of colleagues have made their contributions through course design, teaching practice, the development of materials, publications, and/or field coordination. The University of Michigan Center for International Business Education (CIBE) has sponsored three Business Chinese workshops since 2003, which have provided a regular platform for exchange among Business Chinese instructors. The development of *The Routledge Course in Business Chinese* 《求实商务汉语：语言训练与学习指导》 has directly benefited from valuable issues raised and discussed on these and other occasions.

This development project has received partial funding from the US Federal Government's Title VI Fund through the University of Michigan. This funding was used in the support of a number of activities such as business context consultation, text translation, and photo preparation. The funding for creating audio files and the general illustration of people characters came from the publisher Taylor & Francis Group/Routledge, while facility and personnel support was provided by the U-M Language Resource Center (LRC), and other costs, such as the illustrations in individual lessons, were covered by the U-M Center for Chinese Studies (CCS).

Business content consultation at an early stage of development was received from Xiaolei Wang, a PhD candidate recommended by SHUFE. Translation of the main texts from Chinese into English was undertaken by Robyn Wang, a former student of the U-M Ross School of Business, who referred to assignments completed by the 2010 U-M class on Chinese Translation and Presentation. In addition to the three authors, participants in the recording project were U-M graduate students Ercha A, Jingchen Wu, Yueyang Zhong, Boyang Chai, Yuhua Wang, Liu Ming, and U-M audio engineer Phillip Cameron. Photos were mainly taken by Bingkang Xiang but were also contributed by Xiangrong Chen, Xiaoxian Zeng, Zixiang Cao, and Jennie Chen Volet. The illustrations of people characters were made by Yuxin Kong. English editing was conducted by Emily Goedde, a U-M PhD candidate, and Brian Goedde, a freelance writer.

Finally, *The Routledge Course in Business Chinese* 《求实商务汉语》 would not be what it is without the pertinent and thought-provoking comments from the four anonymous reviewers, or without the timely and patient guidance of Routledge editors Sonja Van Leeuwen, Andrea Hartill, Samantha Vale Noya and Sarah Mabley.

The authors of this book are indebted to all those mentioned above and would particularly like to extend their heartfelt thanks to U-M CIBE director Bradley Farnsworth for his long-term generous support to Business Chinese education. The authors also want to express their appreciation to users of this textbook in advance. We look forward to comments and suggestions from them.

致商务汉语教学同行

To fellow instructors of Business Chinese

本人在美国高校从事高年级商务汉语教学逾二十载。值此《求实商务汉语：语言训练与学习指导》出版之际，谨将有关心得跟同行们分享如下。

一、商务汉语课的性质

商务汉语是一种为特殊目的而开设的汉语语言课程，从语言教学的角度而言，其性质和目的与普通汉语课无异，只是在内容上使用了商务题材的载体而已。所谓的"商务"内容，无论是狭义还是广义，通常在高年级的教学中才能得到充分的体现。事实上，学生的"商务"汉语能力并非只能通过商务汉语课来习得，同样地，他们从商务汉语课所获得的语言能力也应能转换到其他领域去应用。如果学生在商务汉语课上只是增加了一些知识而并无语言能力的实质性提高，这样的商务汉语课只算得上是走过场的语言课，有人称之为"无源之水"和"无本之木"。

其实，商务汉语的"源"和"本"还应包括对语言学习能力的培养，在授之以"鱼"的同时授之以"渔"，使学生获得在今后继续自行学习的能力。一切汉语课，尤其是商务汉语课，都应将汉语学习的可持续性作为自己的努力方向。

二、高年级商务汉语课的特点

典型的高年级商务汉语课的学生，其语言能力正处于从中级向高级过渡的阶段，他们所面临的是与高年级普通汉语课学生相同的任务：一是熟悉正式语体，二是扩大词汇量并掌握正确的词语用法和搭配，三是理解和接受与语言学习相关的文化和专业知识。然而，普通汉语课强调的是全面的语言基础，而商务汉语课却必须注重实用性并有可能突出语言运用的某一个或几个方面。再换一个角度，把高年级的商务汉语课跟低年级的商务汉语课相比：低年级的商务汉语课不可避免地要同时承担低年级普通汉语课打好语言基础的任务，而高年级的商务汉语课则必须与现实的"商务"世界相联系，帮助学生提高运用汉语去解决实际问题的能力，包括通过汉语获取信息的能力和使用汉语完成特定任务的能力。

高年级商务汉语课所通常具有的另一个特点是：在同一个班上学习的学生背景迥异，实际语言能力严重参差不齐。因此，如何在同一门课里让不同的学生都受到适当的挑战并都在各自原有的基础上有所得益，是一个在日常教学中时刻存在的问题。

三、理想的高年级商务汉语教材

高年级商务汉语课必须与时俱进，跟上时代的脉搏。但经验证明，越是企图通过课文内容来具体反映当时现实世界的教材越不具有时效性，因为一切事实和数据在飞速发展的商务世界面前都会很快过时。随着教材的效用迅速降低，教师将不得不整天忙于补充、更新和更换书中的内容而难以将精力集中到教学上来。正因为如此，理想的商务汉语教材必须是相对稳定的，时效性的问题应留到教学的过程中由学生和教师共同合作去解决。

高年级商务汉语课的特点也要求教材具有鲜明的实践性，体现学以致用，学用结合。教材中的语言训练必须最终落实到任务型的要求，而实践任务的确定、提出和执行不但关系到语言能力的培养，也是确保课程时效性的关键，应受到编写者的充分重视。

高年级的商务汉语教材还应旗帜鲜明地开展对语言学习能力的培养，如对汉语主要特点的归纳和提示，对学习方法的介绍和示范，等等。该方面的内容应紧密配合语言能力从中级向高级发展的需要，对动机强烈、高度认真的学生尤其具有不可忽视的意义。

最后，高年级商务汉语教材必须是从美国高校目前的汉语教学实际出发的，无论在形式、内容还是难度上都要兼顾各种不同的教学对象，方便教师酌情处理。

《求实商务汉语》正是根据上述高年级商务汉语课的特点和理想编写的。书中的短文（课文一）语体较为正式，均系大商务概念的基本知识，既符合一般学生的兴趣和需要又能保持相对稳定。各课中的对话（课文二）使用连贯的人物反映了美国学生在华学习的各种经历，为正式语体在口语中的应用提供了生动的范例。书中的练习部分形式多样且难度各异，不但满足了语言学习的一般需要，而且着意加强了任务型的要求。至于每课中的学习指导，其特点是简明扼要，完全从加强学生自学能力的实际效果出发。凡此种种尝试，皆以"务本"和"求实"为指导思想，希望能为美国的商务汉语教学带来一丝新鲜的活力。

四、试用本教材的效果和体会

《求实商务汉语》曾在密歇根大学四年级商务汉语课的近四十名学生中试用，其中有母语非汉语的学生，也有母语为汉语的学生，甚至有少数在汉语国家或地区高中毕业的学生。他们普遍对本教材表示欢迎，并分别在语言能力上取得了不同程度、不同性质的进步。事实证明，本教材的预期效果是可以实现的，课程时效性的问题和提高语言实用能力的问题是可以通过实践任务的途径获得解决的。我们对用好本教材的体会是：第一，要在起始阶段组织学生认真学习书中的热身课并对全学期的实践任务作出安排，让学生明确要求，充满期待。第二，要鼓励自学，安排学生之间的互动和合作，将教师的"陪练"作用最大限度地集中在组织和引导上。第三，要在考核和评分中突出对预习及语言实用的要求，并酌情对不同背景和能力的学生实行区别对待，重在他们从各自原有基础上的提高。第四，要花大力气上好前三课，尤其是上好第一课，以便为全书的学习树立信心，建立规范。总而言之，要想方设法地使课程成为对所有学生都行之有效的一种真正意义上的助学系统。

语言教学中的各种变量使我们不可能也不应该在一种教材的使用中追求刻板的模式。对于《求实商务汉语》，我们也主张"教无定法"和"教亦多术"。教材本身只是为语言教学提供了一个带有理想色彩的平台，相信同行们的教学实践和批评指正将会给我们带来诸多宝贵的启迪。愿美国高校高年级的商务汉语教学能在本书的推动下更上一层楼。

美国密歇根大学　陈青海

本书人物

People in the dialogues

马　可（男）：美国 BBA 大学生，暑假在上海一家咨询公司实习，并在上海大学选修一门经济课。
Mark Smith (male): An American BBA student who is doing a summer internship at a consulting company in Shanghai while simultaneously taking an economics course at Shanghai University.

王静文（女）：马可的朋友，美国华裔 MBA 学生，曾经在中国学习和工作过。
Jingwen Wang (female): An American-Chinese MBA student who has studied and worked in China. Mark's friend.

张永安（男）：王静文的舅舅，上海中学教师。
Yong'an Zhang (male): A middle-school teacher in Shanghai. Jingwen's uncle.

方海明（女）：马可实习公司的总经理，海归，曾经是马可父亲的学生。
Haiming Fang (female): General Manager of the consulting company where Mark is doing his internship. She was once a student of Mark's father and has now returned to China.

林汉华（男）：马可选修的经济课教授。
Hanhua Lin (male): Professor of Mark's economics class.

钱　亮（男）：马可实习公司的年轻中国同事。
Liang Qian (male): A young worker that Mark works with at the consulting company.

李瑛瑛（女）：和马可一起修课的中国大学生。
Yingying Li (female): Mark's classmate in the economics class.

本书人物

李瑛瑛
林汉华
马可
王静文
张永安
方海明
钱亮

商务汉语热身

Business Chinese warm-up

What is Business Chinese?

"Business Chinese" refers to the Chinese language as applied in business contexts. Here, the word "business" is used in its broadest sense and covers the multiple fields of economics, finance, international trade, business administration, and so on. Business Chinese is by no means a "variation" of Chinese as claimed by some language educators and textbook authors, since its applications do not change any attributes or rules of the language. By taking this course, you are simply moving forward along a regular trajectory for Chinese language study, and most probably are moving from the upper intermediate level to the advanced level.

Nevertheless, Business Chinese does bring new challenges to language learners. Despite its pragmatic nature, one of its characteristics is its formal style, which is in many ways different from the casual or less formal styles you have so far been exposed to. The formal style, however, is not a unique feature of "Business" Chinese; it is a universal challenge for language learners as they strive for advanced proficiency. The only difference Business Chinese makes is that it uses business-context materials as the means of learning and teaching. The same instructional goals can be reached by other means, such as literary Chinese, medical Chinese, legal Chinese, and so on.

Besides its formal style, the other two main elements of Business Chinese are 1) business terms and expressions, and 2) business and cultural knowledge. As a language course, Business Chinese focuses on language skills. It is not meant to be a knowledge-based course even while it enhances cultural awareness through its content-based materials. Although you are studying Chinese in business contexts, your improved language ability and language-learning ability will be transferable to language use in other fields.

> QUESTION: Why are you taking this Business Chinese course?
>
> 问题：你为什么要学习商务汉语？

What can you expect from this textbook?

The Routledge Business Chinese Course《求实商务汉语：语言训练与学习指导》is not a textbook of news reports and articles. All its main texts are based on common business knowledge which should be familiar to you. Since you are dealing with common knowledge, you will find that the language in the book occurs in the real world. Similarly, since business fundamentals hardly change, the language representing them will remain relatively stable over a long period of time. This means that what you are going to learn from this Chinese textbook will not just be useful in your life now, but will also be useful for many years to come.

Additionally, unlike Business Chinese textbooks that focus on a single business field such as international trade, this textbook has developed a wide knowledge base with topics ranging from frequently occurring business activities, economic systems and phenomena, to issues of common interest. Such a textbook will help you by being better adaptable to future work and study.

You can expect from this textbook an improved ability for continued learning. We obviously cannot teach you everything in this language course, nor is it possible for us to predict your future needs. For this reason, this course is not limited to helping you acquire what is in the texts. Rather, it goes a step further to guide you, as you become effective self-managed learners. In other words, this textbook not only provides you with what to learn, but also teaches you how to learn. Our purpose is to enable you to continue to learn by yourselves whenever a specific need arises in the future.

Finally, you might feel curious about the title of this book, and particularly about the first word 求实. Here this phrase means "seeking a solid foundation." We believe that successful language acquisition hinges on a strong foundation, and that is the main goal of this course.

QUESTION: How will this textbook meet your personal expectations for the course?
问题：这本教材是否符合你对商务汉语课的期待？

How is this course structured?

The course starts with a warm-up section to prepare you for the tasks in this textbook. This is the preparatory lesson you are going over now. The twelve lessons following the warm-up maintain a unified format with four parts each: text 1, text 2, exercises, and a learning guide.

Text 1 is a short information-based article characterized by formal words and expressions, composite structures, and long sentences. It is provided in both simplified and traditional Chinese, with the traditional-character version being directly transcribed from the simplified-character version. The article is followed by a word list, a comprehension check, notes, and language tips. Please do not feel intimidated by the number of entries in the word list. Some items are not necessarily new to you, and even in items that appear to be "new," you may find familiar characters. Moreover, you will be given helpful tips on vocabulary expansion from the learning guides in the first few lessons. These guides will help your confidence grow as you progress and develop an enhanced learning ability. A matching audio file of this article can be accessed on the course's companion website (www.routledge.com/cw/chen).

Text 2 is a brief dialogue reflecting an American student's summer activities in Shanghai. It is directly related to the topic of the lesson. The characters in the dialogues are consistent throughout the twelve lessons, and their illustrations are provided after the book's introduction as well as in individual lessons. The language in the dialogue tends to be formal in discussing business contents, but carries various kinds of oral features at the same time. The dialogue is also supported by a word list, a comprehension check, notes, and language tips. A matching audio file can be accessed on the course's website.

Exercises are divided into eight types and are designed to facilitate your acquisition of formal language and business terminology, and to allow you the opportunity for language application. Business and cultural knowledge—another key element of Business Chinese— is purposely not covered since this textbook is not meant to be a knowledge-based course. It will be more efficient to acquire knowledge through your native language or with your improved Chinese abilities in the future. Writing skills, especially writing in formal language, is not explicitly required. You will be challenged, however, to collect and process relevant business information, and complete real-world tasks. Exercises in this book are more task-based than form-focused in order to encourage language use. Some items will challenge you to seek solutions on your own (through personal efforts or team work), such as bringing the topic of the lesson up to date. For items such as reading comprehension and discussion, audio files can be accessed on the course's companion website (www.routledge.com/cw/chen).

Learning guide is a concise introduction to key issues in Chinese-language study, accompanied by examples from previous lessons as well as a small dose of practice. The dual purpose of this part is to help you with your present studies and to turn you into better learners of Chinese. Whether the topic in the discussion is related to an important characteristic of the language or a useful learning strategy, you will gain knowledge about Chinese or Chinese acquisition rather than new language itself. It is this kind of knowledge that enlightens you how you can effectively improve your Chinese study. A secondary function of this part, whether you like it or not, is to serve the purpose of review, as it will continually cite examples from previous lessons.

Please remember the companion website at www.routledge.com/cw/chen, where you can find various kinds of supplementary and supporting materials for the course. It is a good idea to browse the site before you begin your work.

Things may be difficult for you at the beginning of the course. However, if you work hard under your teacher's guidance and do a good job on the first three lessons, the remaining lessons will start to help themselves. In particular, to ensure a successful start, you cannot "overdo it" on Lesson 1.

ACTIVITY: Browse a lesson in the book and exchange your impressions with a classmate. Be prepared to report your shared findings and feelings to the class.

活动：翻看本教材中的一课，然后跟一位同学交流一下对这本教材的印象。准备好向全班同学报告你们的发现和感想。

What is expected of learners?

There is a great temptation for a Business Chinese textbook to advertise itself as a course to take learners to a destination where they can handle Chinese language for business purposes in a professional manner. Few people, however, would take such a claim seriously. This simply sounds too unrealistic for one or two 3-credit-hour college courses taken over one or two semesters. It is a fact that no class can teach everything in a language or a profession, especially as learners' needs are always transforming in this ever-changing world. For serious language learners, learning is a continuous lifelong commitment. In addition, language is learned rather than taught. What is of primary importance for you now is to acquire the ability of continuing to learn on your own, whenever there is a new need.

For these reasons, we, the authors of this textbook, do not claim a destination of any kind. Instead, we aim to prepare you for a new "starting" point, from which you will be able to move on without a teacher by your side. To get to that point, you are expected to direct your efforts along the following 3A's route:

1   Absorbing the language in this textbook
Although this Business Chinese textbook, like any other language textbook, cannot cover all language applications in all business contexts, its meticulously prepared texts have provided essential information about common business topics in relatively formal language, along with samples of oral applications in business-relevant interpersonal communication. Acquisition of as many words, expressions, sentence patterns, etc. as possible from these texts will help to pave your way to the real business world and reinforce your language foundation for further development at the same time.

2   Adjusting your learning habits
Learning without a sense of achievement can be uninteresting and painful. When using this textbook, if you work hard but don't reach your desired level of achievement, you may want to rethink your approach. You may have been successful as a beginner but have started to fall behind at higher levels. Now it is time to see if you need a change in your learning habits. Take flash cards as an example. You have been using them for years, so why are they no longer as helpful? Indeed, there is nothing wrong with flash cards. The issue is that at higher levels of learning, the mechanisms in the language that holds words, expressions, sentences, and paragraphs together meaningfully become increasingly sophisticated. When the Chinese "tree" you have to comprehend or create gets bigger, the way you treat its "leaves" and "branches" has to change accordingly. Rote memorization is still indispensable, but it now has to extend beyond words to phrases, sentences, and discourses, and must become part of a comprehensive approach. In other words, you can no longer simply rely on flash cards of isolated vocabulary items. Instead, you have to adjust your habits by targeting the "tree" and making more and better use of your inference ability.

3   Acquiring the ability of continuing to learn
As users of this textbook, you are advised to always keep in mind that you must become an effective learner if you are serious about a China-related career. It is not just because learning of the language will never end; it is also because you will have to count on yourself in the future, as you complete real-world language tasks and for that purpose learn new things in the language. When you learn something new from this textbook, it should not just be that new thing you learn. You should also ascertain how you might learn new things like it in the future. In this sense, the more you take advantage of this textbook, the better learner you will become.

QUESTION: What are your expectations for yourself in taking this course?

问题：上这一门课你对自己有什么要求？

第一课 股票市场与房地产市场

Lesson 1 *The stock market and real estate market*

课文一 Text 1

中国最早的证券交易所成立于1905年，于1949年被关闭。现在大陆的两家证券交易所分别位于上海和深圳，是先后于1990年和1991年成立的。它们简称为"上交所"和"深交所"，通常也被称为"沪市"和"深市"。1992年，中国股市的股票交易价格被全部放开。

根据股票上市地点和投资者的不同，中国发行的股票分为A股、B股、H股、N股和S股。A股由大陆公司发行，供大陆机构、组织或个人以人民币认购和交易。B股是境外投资者向大陆公司投资而形成的股份，以人民币标明面值，以外币认购和交易。该种股票在上海和深圳两个证券交易所上市，从2001年开始已对大陆的个人居民开放。H股也称国企股，指注册地在内地、上市地在香港的外资股，主要供国际资本投资。而N股和S股是指在中国大陆注册、但分别在纽约和新加坡上市的外资股。

中国股市的历史不长，但发展的速度很快。今天，中国的股民数已经达到1.5亿，股市的总市值也已达到27万亿元人民币，成为全球第三，而且全部实现了网上交易。

中國最早的證券交易所成立於1905年，於1949年被關閉。現在大陸的兩家證券交易所分別位於上海和深圳，是先後於1990年和1991年成立的。它們簡稱為"上交所"和"深交所"，通常也被稱為"滬市"和"深市"。1992年，中國股市的股票交易價格被全部放開。

根據股票上市地點和投資者的不同，中國發行的股票分為A股、B股、H股、N股和S股。A股由大陸公司發行，供大陸機構、組織或個人以人民幣認購和交易。B股是境外投資者向大陸公司投資而形成的股份，以人民幣標明面值，以外幣認購和交易。該種股票在上海和深圳兩個證券交易所上市，從2001年開始已對大陸的個人居民開放。H股也稱國企股，指註冊地在內地、上市地在香港的外資股，主要供國際資本投資。而N股和S股是指在中國大陸註冊、但分別在紐約和新加坡上市的外資股。

中國股市的歷史不長，但發展的速度很快。今天，中國的股民數已經達到1.5億，股市的總市值也已達到27萬億元人民幣，成為全球第三，而且全部實現了網上交易。

词语表 Words and expressions

(* Refer to notes or language tips following the word list.)

1	股票		gǔpiào	share; stock; a certificate of these
2	市场	市場	shìchǎng	market
3	房地产	房地產	fángdìchǎn	real estate; real property; 房产和地产
4	证券	證券	zhèngquàn	security; bond
5	交易		jiāoyì	business transaction; deal; (做)买卖
6	所		suǒ	place; office; often as a suffix
7	成立		chénglì	establish; set up
8	关闭	關閉	guānbì	close; shut down
9	分别		fēnbié	respectively
10	位于*	位於	wèiyú	be located at; 在
11	简称*	簡稱	jiǎnchēng	be called for short; abbreviation
12	通常		tōngcháng	generally
13	称*	稱	chēng	call; be called; (被)叫做
14	股市		gǔshì	stock market; 股票市场
15	价格	價格	jiàgé	price; 价钱
16	全部		quánbù	all
17	根据	根據	gēnjù	according to

18	上市		shàngshì	*go on the market*
19	投资	投資	tóuzī	*invest*
20	者		zhě	*person (of a category); often as a suffix*
21	发行	發行	fāxíng	*issue*
22	供*		gōng	*provide sb with the convenience of doing sth*
23	机构	機構	jīgòu	*organization; institution*
24	组织	組織	zǔzhī	*organization*
25	人民币*	人民幣	rénmínbì	*Renminbi (RMB)*
26	认购	認購	rèngòu	*offer to buy; subscribe*
27	境外*		jìngwài	*outside of border; overseas*
28	形成		xíngchéng	*form; take shape*
29	股份		gǔfèn	*share; stock*
30	标明	標明	biāomíng	*mark; indicate*
31	面值		miànzhí	*face value*
32	外币	外幣	wàibì	*foreign currency;* 外国货币
33	该*	該	gāi	*this; that; the above-mentioned*
34	居民		jūmín	*resident; inhabitant*
35	开放	開放	kāifàng	*open up*
36	国企	國企	guóqǐ	*state-owned enterprise;* 国有企业
37	指*		zhǐ	*refer to*
38	注册	註冊	zhùcè	*register; registration*
39	内地*		nèidì	*inland; interior (of a country)*
40	外资	外資	wàizī	*foreign capital;* 外国资本
41	国际	國際	guójì	*international*
42	资本	資本	zīběn	*capital*
43	发展	發展	fāzhǎn	*develop; development*
44	速度		sùdù	*speed*
45	股民		gǔmín	*stock investor*
46	达到	達到	dádào	*reach (a figure)*
47	亿	億	yì	*a hundred million*
48	总	總	zǒng	*overall*
49	市值		shìzhí	*market value;* 市场价值
50	实现	實現	shíxiàn	*realize; realization*

专有名词 Proper nouns

1	大陆*	大陆	Dàlù	*mainland China*
2	深圳		Shēnzhèn	*Shenzhen, a city in southern China*
3	新加坡		Xīnjiāpō	*Singapore*

理解考核 Comprehension check

对错选择 True or false

		True	False
1	股票买卖必须在交易所进行。	☐	☐
2	中国二十世纪八十年代没有证券交易所。	☐	☐
3	B 股在中国大陆的居民可以购买以后就跟 A 股一样了。	☐	☐
4	N 股在中国大陆注册，在新加坡上市。	☐	☐
5	现在中国的股票交易都在网上进行。	☐	☐

注释 Notes

1 大陆，内地，境外，港澳台

中国大陆 (mainland China) refers to regions under the jurisdiction of the PRC central government. This term is often used as relative to 台湾 (Taiwan). 内地 (Inland) is the term used for PRC regions excluding 香港 (Hong Kong) and 澳门 (Macao). 境外 (Outside of border) is commonly understood as everywhere in the world that is not part of 内地. In this sense, 港澳台 (Hong Kong, Macao, and Taiwan) should all be regarded as 境外. Chinese speakers may show some variation in their actual usage of these terms. In this article, for example, 大陆 (such as in "大陆公司" and "大陆机构、组织或个人") is used in the sense of 内地, so "注册地在内地" and "在中国大陆注册" actually mean the same thing.

2 沪，深

沪 represents 上海, while 深 is short for 深圳, a big, modern city in the far south of mainland China across the border from Hong Kong. 深圳 began its development in 1980 when it became the first Special Economic Zone (经济特区). Actually, China's many place names, especially those of provinces (省), municipalities under the central government's direct jurisdiction (直辖市), ethnic minority autonomous regions (自治区), and special administrative zones (特别行政区), have one or two short forms in addition to their full names. These short forms frequently appear in official documents, formal writings, and in media language for the purpose of brevity.

3 人民币

The official currency in mainland China is the RMB or *rénmínbì* (based on its pronunciation in Chinese), which is represented by a ¥, ￥ or ￥ before an amount, such as ¥96.18; however, it is referred to as the CNY (Chinese Yuan) when exchange occurs.

语言提示 Language tips

1 于: 1) same as 在 when before a time or place word, but much more formal. 2) means 在 but forms a prosodic word with the preceded verb, such as in: 成立于: be set up in; 位于: be located at; 建于: be built in

- 中国最早的证券交易所成立于1905年，于1949年后被关闭。
- 现在大陆的两家证券交易所分别位于上海和深圳。

奥巴马(Obama)于1961年生于美国，于2008年当选为美国总统。
密歇根大学位于美国密歇根州，建于1817年，是美国最大的公立大学之一。

2 (被)称为: same as (被)叫做, but formal; (被)简称为: be called sth for short; 简称: abbreviated form of a name

- 它们简称为"上交所"和"深交所"，通常也被称为"沪市"和"深市"。
- H股也称国企股，指注册地在内地、上市地在香港的外资股。

芝加哥(Chicago)的风很大，所以这个城市被称为"风城"。
PRC是中华人民共和国在英文中的简称。

3 供: for (sb to do sth)

- A股由大陆公司发行，供大陆机构、组织或个人以人民币认购和交易。
- H股 ... 主要供国际资本投资。

这里的名画都标明了价格，供人们选购。
市场上可供学生学习的汉语课本越来越多。

4 该: this; that; the above-mentioned

- B股是境外投资者向大陆公司投资而形成的股份，....。该种股票 ... 从2001年开始已对大陆的个人居民开放。

微软公司(Microsoft)成立于1975年。比尔·盖茨是该公司的两个创始人之一。
北京大学是中国最有名的大学之一，该校的教师和学生都非常优秀。

5 指: refer to; may also be in the form of 是指 or 指的是

- H股也称国企股，指注册地在内地、上市地在香港的外资股。
- N股和S股是指 ... 分别在纽约和新加坡上市的外资股。

留学生指在外国学习的学生。
股民是指在股市认购和交易股票的人。

课文二 Text 2

　　房地产市场从事房产和地产的交易，也常被称为"房市"或"楼市"。和股市一样，房市也是目前中国市场经济的重要组成部分。马可一直对中国的房市感兴趣，现在他又要去上海了，就跟王静文谈起了这个话题。

王静文：嘿，马可，听说你又要去中国了！

马　可：是啊，下个星期就动身了。这次除了要在一家咨询公司实习三个月以外，我还会在上海大学选修一门中国经济课。

王静文：太好了！我舅舅最近还问起你呢。

马　可：张老师搬家了吗？他以前跟我说过，想换到郊区去住，买一套大一点儿的房子，既能改善居住条件，又是一项不错的投资，一举两得。

王静文：他们已经买了一套二手房，一直在装修，这个星期就要搬进去了。

马　可：真的吗？中国的老百姓怎么买房子？

王静文：跟在美国一样，不用一次性付清房款，可以办按揭。

马　可：什么是"按揭"？

王静文："按揭"就是英语里的 mortgage。

马　可：哦，那就是跟银行贷款，先付个首付，再分期付还。

王静文：对，我舅舅就是办了"按揭"买房的。

马　可：听说中国的房市发展得很快啊。

王静文：可不是吗？虽说中国的房地产才市场化了十几年，中间也出现过各种问题，可是现在都已经成了中国的支柱产业了。

马　可：我还听说，这些年中国的房价上涨得很厉害，很多人买不起房子。这是真的吗？

王静文：这个问题在大中城市比较突出，所以中国政府一直在对房市进行调控。

马　可：调控？

王静文：就是想出各种办法来给房市降温。这一点就跟美国不一样了。对了，有些问题你到了上海问我舅舅吧。

马　可：好，我一定去拜访张老师，上他那儿闹新房。

王静文：闹新房？我舅舅和舅妈不是新婚，哪儿来的"新房"让你闹啊！

马　可：哈哈，那就去参观一下他们的新居吧！

　　房地產市場從事房產和地產的交易，也常被稱為"房市"或"樓市"。和股市一樣，房市也是目前中國市場經濟的重要組成部分。馬可一直對中國的房市感興趣，現在他又要去上海了，就跟王靜文談起了這個話題。

王靜文：嘿，馬可，聽說你又要去中國了！

馬　可：是啊，下個星期就動身了。這次除了要在一家諮詢公司實習三個月以外，我還會在上海大學選修一門中國經濟課。

王靜文：太好了！我舅舅最近還問起你呢。

馬　可：張老師搬家了嗎？他以前跟我說過，想換到郊區去住，買一套大一點兒的房子，既能改善居住條件，又是一項不錯的投資，一舉兩得。

王靜文： 他們已經買了一套二手房，一直在裝修，這個星期就要搬進去了。

馬　可： 真的嗎？中國的老百姓怎麼買房子？

王靜文： 跟在美國一樣，不用一次性付清房款，可以辦按揭。

馬　可： 什麼是"按揭"？

王靜文： "按揭"就是英語裡的 mortgage。

馬　可： 哦，那就是跟銀行貸款，先付個首付，再分期付還。

王靜文： 對，我舅舅就是辦了"按揭"買房的。

馬　可： 聽說中國的房市發展得很快啊。

王靜文： 可不是嗎？雖說中國的房地產才市場化了十幾年，中間也出現過各種問題，可是現在都已經成了中國的支柱產業了。

馬　可： 我還聽說，這些年中國的房價上漲得很厲害，很多人買不起房子。這是真的嗎？

王靜文： 這個問題在大中城市比較突出，所以中國政府一直在對房市進行調控。

馬　可： 調控？

王靜文： 就是想出各種辦法來給房市降溫。這一點就跟美國不一樣了。對了，有些問題你到了上海問我舅舅吧。

馬　可： 好，我一定去拜訪張老師，上他那兒鬧新房。

王靜文： 鬧新房？我舅舅和舅媽不是新婚，哪兒來的"新房"讓你鬧啊！

馬　可： 哈哈，那就去參觀一下他們的新居吧！

词语表 Words and expressions

(* Refer to notes or language tips following the word list.)

1	从事	從事	cóngshì	*engage in; deal with;* 做
2	目前		mùqián	*now; presently;* 现在
3	经济	經濟	jīngjì	*economy*
4	组成	組成	zǔchéng	*form; make up*
5	动身	動身	dòngshēn	*set out (for a place)*

6	咨询	諮詢	zīxún	consult; consultation
7	实习	實習	shíxí	intern; internship
8	选修	選修	xuǎnxiū	take an elective or optional course
9	郊区	郊區	jiāoqū	suburbs
10	套		tào	classifier indicating a series or set of things
11	改善		gǎishàn	improve
12	居住		jūzhù	live; living
13	条件	條件	tiáojiàn	condition
14	项	項	xiàng	classifier for itemized things
15	一举两得*	一舉兩得	yī jǔ liǎng dé	obtain two benefits with one move
16	装修	裝修	zhuāngxiū	decorate; decoration
17	老百姓		lǎobǎixìng	ordinary people
18	一次		yīcì	one time
19	性*		xìng	suffix designating a specified quality, property, etc.
20	付清		fùqīng	pay off; clear (a bill)
21	款		kuǎn	fund; a sum of money
22	按揭*		ànjiē	mortgage
23	贷款	貸款	dàikuǎn	loan; 借钱
24	付		fù	pay
25	首付		shǒufù	down payment; first payment
26	分期		fēnqī	(pay) by installment
27	付还	付還	fùhuán	pay back
28	化*		huà	verb suffix –ize or –ify
29	支柱*		zhīzhù	pillar
30	产业*	產業	chǎnyè	industry
31	上涨	上漲	shàngzhǎng	rise; go up
32	突出		tūchū	outstanding; obvious
33	政府		zhèngfǔ	government
34	进行	進行	jìnxíng	proceed; carry out

35	调控	調控	tiáokòng	*regulation and control*
36	降温		jiàngwēn	*lower the temperature;* 降低温度
37	拜访	拜訪	bàifǎng	*pay sb a visit*
38	闹*	鬧	nào	*charivari*
39	新房*		xīnfáng	*bridal chamber*
40	参观	參觀	cānguān	*visit (a place); have a look around*
41	新居		xīnjū	*new residence*

理解考核 Comprehension check

回答问题 Answer the following questions

1 马可去中国做什么？

2 王静文的舅舅为什么买房子？他买的是什么样的房子？

3 中国人买房子的时候一般怎么付款？

4 中国的房市跟美国的房市有什么不同？

5 "新房"和"新居"的意思一样吗？

注释 Notes

1 按揭

Coined from the Cantonese pronunciation of the English word "mortgage," this word means the same as its English counterpart.

2 支柱产业

A "pillar industry" is a forerunning industry that grows relatively fast, guides and propels national economies, and exerts a wide and profound influence on regional economic development as well as other industries. In present-day China, mechanical-electronics, petrochemicals, automobile manufacturing, and the construction industry are considered pillar industries.

3 闹新房

Also called 闹洞房 or 闹房, this is a Chinese cultural tradition in which well-wishers charivari, or roast the bride and groom, in the bridal chamber on their wedding night.

语言提示 Language tips

1　既...又..., 一举两得: both . . . and . . . , gaining two things in one move

- 买一套大一点儿的房子，<u>既</u>能改善居住条件，<u>又</u>是一项不错的投资，<u>一举两得</u>。

  选修商务汉语课<u>既</u>能提高中文水平，<u>又</u>能了解中国的经济状况，<u>一举两得</u>。

  国家投资房地产市场，<u>既</u>能解决老百姓的住房问题，<u>又</u>有利于国民经济的发展，<u>一举两得</u>。

2　...化: verb suffix –ize or –ify
现代<u>化</u>: modernize; 全球<u>化</u>: globalize; 国际<u>化</u>: internationalize; 美国<u>化</u>: Americanize; 简<u>化</u>: simplify; 绿<u>化</u>: "greenify"; make (a place) green by planting trees and flowers

- 中国的房地产才市场<u>化</u>了十几年。

  <u>上海</u>是一个国际<u>化</u>的大都市。
  简体字是简<u>化</u>了的汉字。

3　...性: suffix designating a specified quality, property, etc.
周期<u>性</u>: periodic; 历史<u>性</u>: historic; 戏剧<u>性</u>: dramatic; 全国<u>性</u>: national

- ..., 不用一次<u>性</u>付清房款。

  在中国，春节是一个全国<u>性</u>的假日。
  他最近发现股市的涨跌带有周期<u>性</u>。

练习 Exercises

1　将左栏的动词和右栏的宾语配对，每个词语只能用一次。Match each verb in the left column with an appropriate object in the right column. Each item can be used only once.

1)	发行 ___	a)	条件
2)	拜访 ___	b)	网上交易
3)	标明 ___	c)	股票
4)	改善 ___	d)	面值
5)	实现 ___	e)	老师
6)	形成 ___	f)	证券交易所
7)	成立 ___	g)	房地产交易
8)	参观 ___	h)	股市
9)	投资 ___	i)	股份
10)	从事 ___	j)	新居

2　听写并用汉语解释下列词组。 Complete a dictation of the following phrases and explain them in Chinese.

1)	证券交易所	7)	二手房
2)	股票交易价格	8)	按揭
3)	境外投资者	9)	首付
4)	国企股	10)	房地产市场化
5)	外资股	11)	支柱产业
6)	股市的总市值	12)	闹新房

3　选词填空。 Fill in the blanks with the provided words and expressions.

1) 现代化，美化，国际化，全球化，绿化

   a) 在现代社会，很多学校走出国门实现了 _____。

   b) 改革开放以来，中国一直在努力进行 _____ 建设。

   c) 世界越来越小，_____ 的趋势不可避免。

   d) 我们要 _____ 环境，_____ 城市。

2) 历史性，国际性，全球性，一次性

   a) 人类在1969年第一次登上月球是一个 _____ 的事件。

   b) 政府希望大家少用 _____ 的产品。

   c) 这一次的股市下跌是 _____ 的。

   d) 中国的经济发展产生了 _____ 的影响。

3) 于，供，称为，该，指

   "上交所" _____ 上海证券交易所，又被 _____ "沪市"。_____ 交易所成立 _____ 1990年，是中国大陆的两家证券交易所之一，_____ 组织、机构及个人进行证券交易。

4　用指定的表达方式完成句子。 Complete the following sentences with the designated words or expressions.

1) 供

   a) 银行提供按揭，_____。

   b) 中国在改革开放以后恢复了证券交易所，_____。

2) 既...又...，一举两得

   a) 贷款买房，_____。

   b) 暑假实习，_____。

5 把下面的句子改成不太正式的语体。 Paraphrase the following sentences in a less formal style, paying special attention to the underlined words and phrases.

1) 中国最早的证券交易所<u>成立于</u>1905年，<u>该</u>交易所<u>于</u>1949年<u>被</u>关闭。

_____。

2) 王静文实习的公司主要<u>从事</u>房地产<u>业务</u>，<u>该</u>公司<u>早已于</u>香港上市。

_____。

3) H股也<u>称</u>国企股，<u>指</u>注册<u>地</u>在内地、<u>上市地</u>在香港的外资股，主要<u>供</u>国际资本投资。

_____

_____。

4) 房地产市场是<u>指从事</u>房产和地产<u>交易</u>的市场，<u>也</u>常<u>被称为</u>"房市"<u>或</u>"楼市"。

_____。

6 自行查找参考资料，解释与本课话题有关的词语。 Using available resources as a reference, explain the following terms, which are related to this lesson's topics.

1) 股市
   a) 牛市，熊市
   b) 开盘价，收盘价
   c) 反弹
   d) 崩盘

2) 房市
   a) 商品住宅
   b) 成交面积
   c) 经济适用房
   d) 廉租房

7 阅读理解与讨论。 Reading comprehension and discussion.

香港股市与内地股市的相关性

各个国家和地区股市之间的相关性受到经济、政治、社会等多方面因素的影响，有许多现象值得我们深思。

很多研究认为，香港股市与内地股市存在较大的相关性。持这种观点的理由是：1）香港地区与中国内地相邻，无时差影响。2）香港地区与内地的外贸依存度大，两地之间的贸易不断增加。3）内地有多家公司在内地和港交所同时上市。4）港币和人民币的汇率比较接近，参考价值较大。

　　但也有人认为，香港股市与内地股市的相关性较小，理由很简单：内地的股民在买卖股票时往往参考前一天美国股市的变化，不太关心同时交易的港股。

　　不管研究者的结论如何，近年来的事实是：香港股市发行新股所筹集的资金大部分投向了内地公司，中国股票在香港市场所占的份额在继续扩大。

相关	xiāngguān	related	贸易	màoyì	trade; business
政治	zhèngzhì	politics	不断	búduàn	continuous; continuously
方面	fāngmiàn	aspect	增加	zēngjiā	increase
因素	yīnsù	factor	汇率	huìlǜ	exchange rate
影响	yǐngxiǎng	influence	接近	jiējìn	close
现象	xiànxiàng	phenomenon	参考	cānkǎo	consult; refer to
值得	zhídé	deserve; be worth	价值	jiàzhí	value; worth
深思	shēnsī	deep thought; consideration	简单	jiǎndān	simple
存在	cúnzài	exist	往往	wǎngwǎng	often; frequently
持	chí	hold	变化	biànhuà	change
观点	guāndiǎn	viewpoint	结论	jiélùn	conclusion
理由	lǐyóu	reason; cause	筹集	chóují	raise (money)
相邻	xiānglín	adjacent	投向	tóuxiàng	throw at; direct toward
时差	shíchā	time difference	占	zhàn	take; occupy
外贸	wàimào	foreign trade	份额	fèn'é	share
依存度	yīcúndù	degree of dependence	扩大	kuòdà	enlarge; expand

选择填空 Select the correct answer for each blank.

I) 香港地区与内地的贸易不断增加，是因为 ＿＿＿＿＿。

    a) 两地的外贸依存度大

    b) 无时差影响

    c) 港币和人民币的汇率比较接近

2) 有研究认为，香港股市与内地股市相关性很大，<u>不是因为</u> ＿＿＿＿＿。

    a) 香港与内地的外贸依存度大

    b) 内地多家公司在内地和港交所同时上市

    c) 香港也使用人民币

3) 有人认为，香港股市与内地股市相关性较小，是因为 ＿＿＿＿＿。

    a) 内地公司股票很少在香港上市

    b) 内地股民不太关心香港股市的变化

    c) 内地股市与香港股市不是同时交易

4) 近年来的事实是，_____。

    a) 中国股票在香港股市所占的份额越来越大

    b) 中国股票在香港股市所占的份额越来越小

    c) 中国股票在香港股市所占的份额没有明显的变化

讨论 Discussion.

本文作者对香港股市与内地股市相关性的问题有什么看法？根据你了解的情况或所查的资料，你觉得香港股市与内地股市的相关性较大还是较小？What is the author's view on the relationship between Hong Kong and Inland China's stock markets? According to what you know or what you have found in research, do you think they are closely related or not?

8　实践活动。Tasks.

1) 上网查找参考资料，写出中国四个直辖市和五个自治区的名称及简称。Using the Internet as a resource, write out the names of China's four cities under the central government's direct jurisdiction and the five ethnic minority autonomous regions. Include their short forms in parentheses.

2) 做一个10分钟的口头报告，介绍"我所了解的中国股市"或"我所了解的中国房市"。先上网查看一条最近六个月之内与中国股市或房市有关的新闻，然后根据老师的要求为自己准备一个简单的提纲。在报告时要尽可能提供事实和例子。Give a ten-minute oral report on what you know about China's stock market or real estate market. You should search for a relevant news article from within the past six months and prepare a brief outline for yourself as per your teacher's instructions. Please make an effort to include facts and examples.

3) 参考马可的简历写一份你自己的中文简历。请注意：有些在西方被当作个人隐私的内容如年龄、性别和婚姻状况等常须出现在中文简历上，而传教之类的经历在目前的中国大陆可能具有负面的影响。Prepare your own Chinese language resume, using Mark's resume (available at the book's companion website) as a reference. Please remember that personal information regarded as private in the United States, such as age, gender, and marital status, are often required in a Chinese resume. Experience such as missionary work may be viewed negatively in present-day mainland China.

4) 如果你对一个不同的任务有兴趣，请结合本课的主题向老师提出建议，然后在老师的指导下完成这个任务。If you are interested in a different kind of task, you are encouraged to suggest your proposal and to complete it under your teacher's guidance.

学习指导 Learning guide

汉语的构词 Chinese word formation

For learners of Business Chinese, building vocabulary is a challenge. Sometimes, a word is hard to remember because the English annotation does not convey the exact sense. You will do better if you are familiar with one or more characters in the word and aware of the word's internal structure. Before we move on to suggest learning strategies for vocabulary expansion, it is necessary for you to have some basic knowledge of Chinese word formation.

One method of word formation in Chinese is the same as "conversion" in English. By "conversion," we mean that a word of a certain part of speech can be used as another part of speech without a change in its form. For example, the word 组织 can be both a noun and a verb in the same form:

A股供大陆机构、组织或个人认购和交易。(noun)
中国政府组织了这次交易会。(verb)

This may not sound unfamiliar to you, but you had best be careful, as equivalents in the two languages do not necessarily coincide in word formation. In English "organize" and "organization," equivalents of 组织, are not "conversion" but rather represent a different method of word formation called "derivation."

"Derivation" is the way a new word is formed when an affix (prefix or suffix) is added to a root word. This is how most English words are formed. In Chinese, however, the number of affixes is quite limited. In the two texts of this lesson, examples of suffixes include 交易所, 投资者, 一次性, 市场化, while 总市值, 老师 and 第三 are examples of prefixes.

The dominant method of word formation in Chinese is "compounding." This is the method by which the overwhelming majority of Chinese words, especially two-character compounds, are formed. Just like in English, compounding in Chinese can aid in learners' vocabulary expansion if the words are based on the same root. 股票, 股份, 股民, and 股市 are the best examples in this lesson. Since two-character compounds (or disyllabic words) are regarded as an important characteristic of formal-style Chinese, the following section deserves your special attention.

> QUESTION: What are the most common ways to form words in Chinese?

双音节复合词 Two-character compounds

Have you ever noticed that the majority of Chinese words are two-character (hence two-syllable) compounds? Although two-character compounds appear to be alike in form, they actually vary in internal structure. You will benefit from studying the following examples, almost all of which are taken from the two texts of this lesson:

- Synonyms (including near synonyms and words closely related in meaning)
  关闭，继续，城市
  监管，证券，装修

- Antonyms
  先后，买卖，高低

- Modifying + modified
  外币，首付，全球
  股民，面值，房款
  飞快，紧急，火红
  简称，力图，实习

- Verb + complement
  放开，标明，加强，改善，组成

- Verb + object (including those that may be analyzed as phrases)
  上市，投资，注册，贷款

- Subject + predicate
  金融，头痛，眼红，利多

Understanding the internal structure of a two-character compound will give you a better sense of the word and therefore you will be able to acquire it with relative ease. For example, if you know that 开放 is formed by synonyms but 放开 is a "verb + complement" structure, the additional meaning of the resultative complement 开 will make a stronger impression and be easier to remember. The list here is not complete, but it has covered the majority of two-character compounds in Chinese as far as internal structure is concerned. As for multi-character compounds, they usually involve more than one internal relationship. For example, in the word 房地产 (real estate property), 产 (property) is modified by the two-character compound 房地 (house and land). In this context, 房 and 地 are closely related in meaning, so they can be treated as "synonyms" in a loose sense.

> PRACTICE: Categorize the following two-character compounds according to their internal structures: 付清, 居住, 话题, 房价, 早晚, 形成, 搬家, 年轻, 动身, 调控, 新婚, 面熟.
>
> 1　Synonyms or antonyms
>
> 2　Modifying + modified
>
> 3　Verb + complement
>
> 4　Verb + object
>
> 5　Subject + predicate

第二课 外汇市场与汇率

Lesson 2 *The foreign exchange market and exchange rates*

课文一 Text 1

外汇交易市场是世界上最大的金融市场，买卖双方靠各种实时通讯工具连结，进行买卖。外汇交易的目的有投资和投机两类。中国加入世界贸易组织以后，外汇投资已经成为一个新的热点。

汇率是一国货币兑换另一国货币的比率，是以一种货币表示另一种货币的价格。汇率对经济的影响首先表现在进出口方面。一般来说，本币汇率下降有利于出口，不利于进口；若本币汇率上升，则有利于进口，不利于出口。第二，汇率的变化也会影响物价。汇率下降要引起进口商品在国内的价格上涨。相反，本币升值则有可能降低进口商品的价格。第三，汇率对短期资本流动有较大的影响。在本币对外贬值的趋势下，资本会外流，使本币汇率进一步下跌。而当本币对外升值时，资本将内流，使本币汇率进一步上升。

影响汇市的因素很多，但汇率的高低与变化归根到底是由供求关系决定的。目前，中国人民币的汇率制度是：以市场供求为基础，参考一篮子货币进行调节及有管理的浮动。

外匯交易市場是世界上最大的金融市場，買賣雙方靠各種實時通訊工具連結，進行買賣。外匯交易的目的有投資和投機兩類。中國加入世界貿易組織以後，外匯投資已經成為一個新的熱點。

匯率是一國貨幣兌換另一國貨幣的比率，是以一種貨幣表示另一種貨幣的價格。匯率對經濟的影響首先表現在進出口方面。一般來說，本幣匯率下降有利於出口，不利於進口；若本幣匯率上升，則有利於進口，不利於出口。第二，匯率的變化也會影響物價。匯率下降要引起進口商品在國內的價格上漲。相反，本幣升值則有可能降低進口商品的價格。第三，匯率對短期資本流動有較大的影響。在本幣對外貶值的趨勢下，資本會外流，使本幣匯率進一步下跌。而當本幣對外升值時，資本將內流，使本幣匯率進一步上升。

　　影響匯市的因素很多，但匯率的高低與變化歸根到底是由供求關係決定的。目前，中國人民幣的匯率制度是：以市場供求為基礎，參考一籃子貨幣進行調節及有管理的浮動。

词语表 Words and expressions

(* Refer to notes or language tips following the word list.)

I	外汇	外匯	wàihuì	*foreign exchange*
2	汇率	匯率	huìlǜ	*exchange rate*
3	金融		jīnróng	*finance*
4	双方	雙方	shuāngfāng	*both sides; both parties;* 两方
5	靠		kào	*depend on*
6	实时	實時	shíshí	*real time*
7	通讯	通訊	tōngxùn	*communication*
8	工具		gōngjù	*tool*
9	连结	連結	liánjié	*connect*
10	目的		mùdì	*purpose*
11	投机	投機	tóujī	*speculate in a risky adventure*
12	类	類	lèi	*type; category*
13	加入		jiārù	*join*
14	贸易	貿易	màoyì	*trade*
15	热点	熱點	rèdiǎn	*hot spot; center of attention*
16	货币	貨幣	huòbì	*money; currency*
17	兑换	兌換	duìhuàn	*exchange; convert (currencies)*
18	比率		bǐlǜ	*ratio; rate*

19	表示*		biǎoshì	*indicate*
20	首先		shǒuxiān	*before all others; first*
21	表现	表現	biǎoxiàn	*show; display*
22	进出口	進出口	jìnchūkǒu	*import and export;* 进口和出口
23	方面		fāngmiàn	*aspect*
24	本币	本幣	běnbì	*basic unit of a currency;* 本位货币
25	下降		xiàjiàng	*descend; decrease*
26	若*		ruò	*if;* 如果; 要是
27	上升		shàngshēng	*rise*
28	则*	則	zé	*then; in that case;* 那么
29	物价	物價	wùjià	*price of goods*
30	引起		yǐnqǐ	*bring about; cause*
31	相反		xiāngfǎn	*on the contrary*
32	升值		shēngzhí	*appreciation*
33	流动	流動	liúdòng	*flow*
34	贬值	貶值	biǎnzhí	*depreciation*
35	趋势*	趨勢	qūshì	*trend; tendency*
36	外流		wàiliú	*outflow*
37	下跌		xiàdiē	*(price, etc.) drop; decline*
38	内流		nèiliú	*inflow*
39	因素		yīnsù	*factor*
40	归根到底	歸根到底	guī gēn dào dǐ	*in the final analysis*
41	供求		gōngqiú	*supply and demand;* 供给和需求
42	关系	關係	guānxi	*relationship; relation*
43	制度		zhìdù	*system*
44	基础	基礎	jīchǔ	*foundation; base*
45	参考	參考	cānkǎo	*refer to (resources)*
46	调节	調節	tiáojié	*adjust; regulate*
47	管理		guǎnlǐ	*manage; control*
48	浮动*	浮動	fúdòng	*float; fluctuate*

专有名词 Proper nouns

世界贸易组织*	世界貿易組織	Shìjiè Màoyì Zǔzhī	*World Trade Organization (WTO)*

理解考核 Comprehension check

对错选择 True or false

		True	False
1	外汇交易只能在特定的场所进行。	☐	☐
2	汇率对经济的影响表现在多个方面。	☐	☐
3	本币升值会使进口减少，并使进口商品变得更贵。	☐	☐
4	影响汇率的因素很多，其中供求关系是最主要的。	☐	☐
5	在政府的外汇管制下，人民币的汇率不会浮动。	☐	☐

注释 Notes

1 世界贸易组织

This is the Chinese name of the World Trade Organization (WTO). It is often abbreviated as 世贸组织 or 世贸. China became an official member of the WTO on December 11, 2001. More information about the WTO is provided in Lesson 4.

2 一篮子货币

"A basket of currencies" means the combination of foreign currencies used as a reference in the determination of a foreign exchange rate. The weight of a certain foreign currency in the "basket" is usually based on its importance in the relevant country's international trade and investment. This is actually only one of the ways to set a foreign exchange rate. The exchange rates of the US dollar, Japanese yen, and Euro-zone currencies are fully floating.

语言提示 Language tips

1 以B表示A: show A in or with B

- 汇率 ... 是<u>以</u>一种货币<u>表示</u>另一种货币的价格。

  人们<u>以</u>"$"表示美元，<u>以</u>"￥"表示人民币。
  经济学常<u>以</u>GDP<u>表示</u>一个国家或者地区的经济情况。

2 若 ...，则 ...: same as 如果 ...，那么 ...，but more formal

- <u>若</u>本币汇率上升，<u>则</u>有利于进口，不利于出口。

  学生<u>若</u>付不起学费，<u>则</u>可以向银行贷款。
  <u>若</u>不重视教育，<u>则</u>国家的前景可想而知。

3 有利于 ...，不利于 ...: be good for ...，but be bad for ...

- 若本币汇率上升，则<u>有利于</u>进口，<u>不利于</u>出口。

  人民币升值<u>有利于</u>中国的进口。
  有些电视节目<u>不利于</u>孩子的成长。

4 在 ... 的趋势下: under the tendency of

- <u>在</u>本币对外贬值<u>的趋势下</u>，资本会外流。

  <u>在</u>全球化<u>的趋势下</u>，各国的对外贸易都有了巨大的发展。
  <u>在</u>人民币升值<u>的趋势下</u>，一些企业开始把在中国的工厂搬到其它
    国家。

5 而: a conjunction connecting two clauses that form a contrast in meaning

- 在本币对外贬值的趋势下，资本会外流 ...。<u>而</u>当本币对外升值时，
  资本将内流 ...。

  小地方自然环境较好，<u>而</u>大城市有更多的发展机会。
  一些国家觉得人民币升值太慢，<u>而</u>中国自己并不这样认为。

6 是由 ... 决定的: be decided by

- 汇率的高低与变化归根到底<u>是由</u>供求关系<u>决定的</u>。

  一个国家在世界上的影响<u>是由</u>它的经济实力<u>决定的</u>。
  房地产的价格<u>是由</u>市场上的供求关系<u>决定的</u>。

7 以A为B: take A as B; 把A作为B

- 人民币的汇率制度是：<u>以</u>市场供求<u>为</u>基础，参考一篮子货币进行调节
  及有管理的浮动。

  政府的工作应该<u>以</u>改善老百姓的生活<u>为</u>目的。
  中国目前<u>以</u>经济发展<u>为</u>中心。

课文二 Text 2

　　马可刚到上海就去了王静文的舅舅家，参观了他们的新居。王静文的舅舅和舅妈都很热情，请他周末去吃饭。星期六的下午，马可应邀而来。舅妈忙着在厨房做饭，马可就和舅舅在客厅坐下，边喝茶边聊了起来。

马　可：唉，昨天我去银行换钱，现在100美元只能换600多人民币。以前能换800多呢。

张永安：是啊，这些年人民币越来越值钱了。

马　可：听您这么说，中国老百姓是欢迎人民币升值了？

张永安：怎么说呢？人民币值钱，说明中国的经济实力强了，老百姓自然觉得自豪。而且，人民币升值也确实带来了一些好处。比方说，进口的汽车、家电什么的高档商品比以前便宜了，出国旅游和留学也比以前省钱了。我们也正计划着下次"黄金周"的时候来个出国自助游呢。

马　可：好处还真不少啊！

张永安：可是，有好处自然就有坏处，不是说汇率是把"双刃剑"吗？

马　可：这倒也是，我听说人民币升值对中国的外贸出口影响很大。

张永安：你说对了。这一升值，外贸出口企业的价格优势就没有了，有些规模小的企业顶不住压力就只好破产了。

马　可：企业倒闭，不是会影响到就业吗？

张永安：就是会影响就业。其实，除了企业倒闭以外，人民币升值也让外商到中国投资的时候越来越小心了，国外来中国旅游的人数也会受到影响。这么一来，你想想，全国得失去多少就业机会啊！

马　可：照您这么说，人民币升值，坏处比好处还多呢。

张永安：不过，再把话说回来，现在很多中国企业多少有一些问题。要是能通过人民币升值的冲击做一些改变，增强自己在国际上的竞争力，倒也未必不是一件好事。

马　可：那倒是，这就是中国人说的"祸福相依"吧？

张永安：嘿，你知道的还真不少啊！

馬可剛到上海就去了王靜文的舅舅家，參觀了他們的新居。王靜文的舅舅和舅媽都很熱情，請他週末去吃飯。星期六的下午，馬可應邀而來。舅媽忙著在廚房做飯，馬可就和舅舅在客廳坐下，邊喝茶邊聊了起來。

馬　可：唉，昨天我去銀行換錢，現在100美元只能換600多人民幣。以前能換800多呢。

張永安：是啊，這些年人民幣越來越值錢了。

馬　可：聽您這麼說，中國老百姓是歡迎人民幣升值了？

張永安：怎麼說呢？人民幣值錢，說明中國的經濟實力強了，老百姓自然覺得自豪。而且，人民幣升值也確實帶來了一些好處。比方說，進口的汽車、家電什麼的高檔商品比以前便宜了，出國旅遊和留學也比以前省錢了。我們也正計劃著下次"黃金周"的時候來個出國自助遊呢。

馬　可：好處還真不少啊！

張永安：可是，有好處自然就有壞處，不是說匯率是把"雙刃劍"嗎？

馬　可：這倒也是，我聽說人民幣升值對中國的外貿出口影響很大。

張永安：你說對了。這一升值，外貿出口企業的價格優勢就沒有了，有些規模小的企業頂不住壓力就只好破產了。

馬　可：企業倒閉，不是會影響到就業嗎？

張永安：就是會影響就業。其實，除了企業倒閉以外，人民幣升值也讓外商到中國投資的時候越來越小心了，國外來中

國旅遊的人數也會受到影響。這麼一來，你想想，全國
得失去多少就業機會啊！

馬　可：照您這麼說，人民幣升值，壞處比好處還多呢。

張永安：不過，再把話說回來，現在很多中國企業多少有一些問
題。要是能通過人民幣升值的衝擊做一些改變，增強自
己在國際上的競爭力，倒也未必不是一件好事。

馬　可：那倒是，這就是中國人說的"禍福相依"吧？

張永安：嘿，你知道的還真不少啊！

词语表 Words and expressions

(* Refer to notes or language tips following the word list.)

1	热情	熱情	rèqíng	*warmhearted and hospitable*
2	应邀而来	應邀而來	yìng yāo ér lái	*come as invited*
3	厨房	廚房	chúfáng	*kitchen*
4	客厅	客廳	kètīng	*sitting room*
5	聊		liáo	*chat*
6	换钱	換錢	huànqián	*change money*
7	值钱	值錢	zhíqián	*valuable*
8	欢迎	歡迎	huānyíng	*welcome*
9	实力	實力	shílì	*actual strength*
10	自然		zìrán	*naturally*
11	自豪		zìháo	*proud of sth*
12	确实	確實	quèshí	*indeed*; 真的
13	家电	家電	jiādiàn	*home appliance*; 家用电器
14	高档	高檔	gāodàng	*top grade*
15	省钱	省錢	shěngqián	*save money*
16	计划	計劃	jìhuà	*plan*; 打算
17	黄金周*	黃金週	Huángjīnzhōu	*Golden Week*
18	自助游*	自助遊	zìzhùyóu	*self-guided tour*

19	坏处	壞處	huàichu	*harm; disadvantage*
20	双刃剑	雙刃劍	shuāngrènjiàn	*double-edged sword*
21	优势	優勢	yōushì	*advantage*
22	规模	規模	guīmó	*scale; scope*
23	顶不住	頂不住	dǐng bu zhù	*cannot stand*
24	压力	壓力	yālì	*pressure; stress*
25	破产	破產	pòchǎn	*go bankrupt; bankruptcy*
26	倒闭	倒閉	dǎobì	*go out of business*
27	就业	就業	jiùyè	*obtain employment*
28	失去		shīqù	*lose*
29	照		zhào	*in accordance with;* 按照
30	通过	通過	tōngguò	*by means of*
31	冲击	衝擊	chōngjī	*attack; strike against*
32	增强	增強	zēngqiáng	*strengthen; enhance*
33	竞争	競爭	jìngzhēng	*competitive*
34	力		lì	*power; often as a suffix*
35	倒*		dào	*contrary to an expectation*
36	未必*		wèibì	*not necessarily;* 不一定
37	祸福相依*	禍福相依	huò fú xiāng yī	*mixed blessing*

理解考核 Comprehension check

回答问题 Answer the following questions

1 人民币升值给中国的老百姓带来了什么好处？

2 为什么说人民币升值对中国的外贸出口影响很大？

3 人民币升值对就业有什么影响？

4 人民币升值对中国企业来说是不是只有坏处没有好处？

5 "祸福相依"是什么意思？

注释 Notes

1 黄金周

In mainland China, a "Golden Week" is a seven-day break intended to stimulate domestic demand and promote consumption. There are two Golden Weeks in the year, one around Spring Festival and the other around National Day.

2 自助游

A self-guided tour is a new tourist program which allows flexibility in itinerary, transportation, room, board, etc. A travel agency makes arrangements based on customer choices.

3 祸福相依

Good fortune lies within the bad, and bad fortune lurks within the good. This idea has its origin in a quotation from 《道德经》, a work credited to Laozi, a Chinese philosopher in the fourth century BC. He is considered to be the father of Chinese Taoism.

语言提示 Language tips

1 这么一来：as a result

- 人民币升值也让外商 .... 这么一来, ... 全国得失去多少就业机会啊!

  他在郊区又买了一套二手房, 这么一来, 居住条件改善了很多。
  这家公司上个月在香港上市, 这么一来, 一定会发展得更快。

2 倒也未必：(contrary to what is thought) not necessarily

- 要是能通过人民币升值 ... 增强自己在国际上的竞争力, 倒也未必不是一件好事。

  有人担心经济发展得快会带来社会问题, 其实倒也未必, 还得看怎么发展。
  竞争让有些企业破产, 这倒也未必是坏事, 因为只有这样才能有更好的产品。

练习 Exercises

1 将左栏的动词和右栏的宾语配对，每个词语只能用一次。Match each verb in the left column with an appropriate object in the right column. Each item can be used only once.

1)	加入 ___	a)	经济课
2)	兑换 ___	b)	好处
3)	参考 ___	c)	一篮子货币
4)	引起 ___	d)	就业
5)	选修 ___	e)	竞争力
6)	带来 ___	f)	外币
7)	顶不住 ___	g)	世界贸易组织
8)	影响 ___	h)	压力
9)	增强 ___	i)	调节
10)	进行 ___	j)	物价上涨

2 听写并用汉语解释下列词组。Complete a dictation of the following phrases and explain them in Chinese.

1)	金融市场	7)	应邀而来
2)	实时通讯工具	8)	双刃剑
3)	本币	9)	外贸出口企业
4)	资本外流	10)	价格优势
5)	归根到底	11)	破产倒闭
6)	供求关系	12)	祸福相依

3 选词填空。Fill in the blanks with the provided words and expressions.

1) 由，则，为，若，以，而

   汇率是 _____ 一种货币表示另一种货币的价格。汇率的变化会影响进出口：_____ 本币汇率下降，则有利于出口；_____ 本币汇率上升，_____ 有利于进口。汇率的高低变化是以市场 _____ 基础，_____ 供求关系决定的。

2) 有利于，自助游，双刃剑，顶不住，进出口

汇率是一把 _____，人民币升值对外贸 _____ 既有好处又有坏处。人民币升值 _____ 进口，出国留学、_____ 也更便宜了；坏处是不利于出口，一些规模小的外贸出口企业 _____ 压力就只好破产了。

4 用指定的表达方式完成句子或对话。Complete the following sentences and dialogues with the designated words or expressions.

1) 有利于 . . . , 不利于 . . .

   a) 人民币升值 _____。

   b) 房价快速上涨 _____。

2) 在 . . . 的趋势下

   a) _____，全球兴起了"汉语热"。

   b) _____，中国的对外贸易有了很大的发展。

3) 是由 . . . 决定的

   a) 在计划经济下，产品的生产 _____；
      在市场经济下，产品的生产 _____。

   b) 一个国家是否强大 _____。

4) . . . , 这么一来 . . .

   a) 七十年代末，中国开始实行独生子女政策(one-child policy)，_____
     _____。

   b) 中国股市全部实现了网上交易，_____
     _____。

5) 倒也未必

   a) A: 听说股市风险很大，常常有人因为买股票而破产。

      B: 我觉得_____，也有很多人因为投资股票赚了大钱。

   b) A: 近几年中国经济的发展速度真让人自豪。

      B: _____，有时候经济发展太快会带来一些社会问题。

5 把下面的句子改成不太正式的语体。Paraphrase the following sentences in a less formal style, paying special attention to the underlined words and phrases.

1) <u>若</u>本币汇率上升，<u>则</u>有利于进口，<u>不利于</u>出口。

　　　　　　　　　　　　　　　　　　　　　　　　　　　　。

2) 发展经济<u>若</u>只考虑速度<u>而</u>不考虑<u>其他</u>因素，<u>则将</u>带来各种社会问题。

　　　　　　　　　　　　　　　　　　　　　　　　　　　　。

3) 在中国股市，<u>若</u>股票<u>价格上涨则以</u>红色表示，<u>而</u>股票<u>价格下跌则以</u>绿色表示。

　　　　　　　　　　　　　　　　　　　　　　　　　　　　

　　　　　　　　　　　　　　　　　　　　　　　　　　　　。

4) 中国<u>目前</u>的汇率制度<u>系以</u>市场供求<u>为</u>基础，<u>以</u>一篮子货币<u>为</u>参考。

　　　　　　　　　　　　　　　　　　　　　　　　　　　　。

5) 不少<u>以价格为优势</u>的中国外贸出口企业顶不住人民币升值的压力<u>而</u>破产。

　　　　　　　　　　　　　　　　　　　　　　　　　　　　。

6 自行查找参考资料，解释与本课话题有关的词语。Using available resources as a reference, explain the following terms, which are related to this lesson's topic.

1) 汇率自由化　　　　　　4) 国际货币的双向流动

2) 人民币国际化　　　　　5) 国际储备货币

3) 国际贸易的结算货币　　6) 外汇黑市

7 阅读理解与讨论。Reading comprehension and discussion.

人民币的汇率问题

随着中国对外贸易的迅速发展，人民币的汇率已成为国际上的一个热点。

美国政府认为中国一直在利用被低估的汇率来促进出口。正是中国出口的大幅增长造成了美国对华贸易的巨额逆差。因此，美国政府在要求中国增加从美国进口的同时，不断"劝说"中国政府调整汇率，让人民币升值。中国政府则认为，中国已经成为包括日本、韩国在内的周边国家的主要出口市场，也已成为欧洲和北美的重要出口市场。由此可见，人民币的币值没有被低估。

与此同时，世界上的经济专家对人民币的汇率问题各持己见。有人认为人民币被明显低估了。也有人认为不能只根据人民币和美元之间的汇率来讨论人民币升值的问题，因为事实上人民币对其他一些主要货币，如欧元和日元，是在升值的。

　　实际上，中国政府在2005年7月停止将人民币汇率和美元单一挂钩之后，已经开始实行参考一篮子货币进行调节的浮动汇率制度。对人民币汇率形成机制的进一步改革是符合中国本身利益的。可以预期的是，人民币将会逐步升值，最终形成由市场供求决定的汇率水平。

迅速	xùnsù	rapid; fast		与此同时	yǔ cǐ tóngshí	at the same time
利用	lìyòng	use; utilize		各持己见	gè chí jǐ jiàn	each sticking to his own view
低估	dīgū	underestimate				
促进	cùjìn	promote		明显	míngxiǎn	clear; obvious
大幅	dàfú	considerable		根据	gēnjù	according to
增长	zēngzhǎng	growth		讨论	tǎolùn	discuss
华	Huá	abbreviation for China		事实上	shìshí shang	in fact
巨额	jù'é	huge amount		实际上	shíjì shang	actually
逆差	nìchā	trade deficit		单一	dānyī	single; unitary
增加	zēngjiā	increase		挂钩	guàgōu	link up with
不断	bùduàn	continuously		实行	shíxíng	put into practice
劝说	quànshuō	persuade		机制	jīzhì	mechanism
调整	tiáozhěng	adjust		改革	gǎigé	reform
韩国	Hánguó	Republic of Korea		符合	fúhé	conform to
包括	bāokuò	include		本身	běnshēn	oneself; itself
周边	zhōubiān	vicinity		利益	lìyì	interest; benefit
欧洲	Ōuzhōu	Europe		预期	yùqī	anticipate
北美	Běiměi	North America		逐步	zhúbù	gradually
由此可见	yóu cǐ kě jiàn	can be seen from this		最终	zuìzhōng	final; eventually

选择填空 Select the correct answer for each blank.

1) 人民币的汇率，美国一直认为 _____，中国则认为 _____。

　　a) 比实际的价值低

　　b) 比实际的价值高

　　c) 符合实际价值

2) 美国认为，人民币目前的汇率对美国的出口 _____。

　　a) 没有影响

　　b) 有很好的影响

　　c) 有不好的影响

3) 世界上经济学家 _____。

　　a) 对人民币汇率问题的看法都一样

　　b) 都认为人民币的币值没有被低估

　　c) 有人认为讨论这个问题不能只看人民币和美元之间的汇率

4) 根据文中的说法，对日元来说，人民币事实上 _____。

    a) 已经贬值了

    b) 已经升值了

    c) 汇率没变

讨论 Discussion.

    本文提到了对人民币汇率问题的哪几种看法？根据你了解的情况或所查的资料，你支持哪种看法？为什么？What are the viewpoints mentioned in this article regarding the RMB's exchange rate? According to what you know or what you have found in research, which viewpoint would you like to support? Explain why that is so.

8 实践活动。Tasks.

1) 查出当天、一个月前及一年前人民币对美元和其他三种主要货币的汇率，并列表说明趋势。Find the exchange rates between the RMB, US dollar and three other major currencies from today, a month ago, and a year ago. Make a list to show fluctuation tendencies.

2) 做一个10分钟的口头报告，介绍"人民币汇率对中国经济的影响"或"人民币汇率对世界经济的影响"。先上网查看一条最近六个月之内与人民币汇率有关的新闻，然后根据老师的要求为自己准备一个简单的提纲。在报告时要尽可能提供事实和例子。Give a ten-minute oral report about the impact of the RMB's exchange rate on the Chinese or world economy. You should search for a relevant news article from within the past six months and prepare a brief outline for yourself as per your teacher's instructions. Please make an effort to include facts and examples.

3) 第7题中的阅读短文包含416个汉字和标点符号，请将其缩写成150个左右。缩写后的短文应保持原文的主要意思，并尽可能保留原文的语句。然后在文中的关键词语（不能超过四个）下划线。Condense the reading in Exercise 7 from 416 to about 150 characters, including punctuation marks. The short version should include the main points and as much original language as possible. After finishing, underline the key words (at most four) in it.

4) 如果你对一个不同的任务有兴趣，请结合本课的主题向老师提出建议，然后在老师的指导下完成这个任务。If you are interested in a different kind of task, you are encouraged to suggest your proposal and to complete it under your teacher's guidance.

学习指导 Learning guide

词汇量扩展（一）Vocabulary expansion (1)

As an experienced language learner, you must have developed some effective learning strategies. However, now that you are faced with the new challenge of formal language in business contexts, you will soon realize that mechanical memory work, although still indispensible, is no longer sufficient for vocabulary expansion. You now have to experiment with more effective ways by tapping into your cognitive ability and existing knowledge of Chinese. In this lesson and Lesson 3, a total of six vocabulary expansion strategies will be recommended.

Strategy 1: Guessing from familiar characters 认字猜词

The following words are formed with characters you are supposed to have learned in the past. How can familiar characters help you in guessing the meaning of a new word? The examples here will give you some ideas:

双方	two + side	both parties
实时	real + time	real-time
加入	add + enter	join
进出口	enter + exit + mouth	import and export 进口和出口
物价	thing + price	price of goods
商品	trade + article	goods (品 and 物 being synonyms)

PRACTICE: Make sense of the English definitions by looking into the meanings of the Chinese characters.

1	热点	hot + spot	hot spot
2	认购	_____+_____	offer to buy
3	内地	_____+_____	inland
4	动身	_____+_____	set off; leave
5	二手房	_____+_____+_____	second-hand housing
6	分期	_____+_____	(pay) in installments

Strategy 2: Getting hints from character components 望形生义

You should know that some Chinese character components, called semantic radicals, suggest meaning. If you examine these characters from the first two lessons: 资 (in投资), 购 (in认购), 货 (in货币), 贸 (in外贸), you will find that they all carry the component 贝/贝 (shell). This component contributes the meaning "money" to the words and characters in which it appears. The character 价/價 (in 价格, 价值, 房价, 物价), if not in its simplified form, would have carried this component and also made sense. Another radical that suggests the meaning of "money" comes from the character 金 (gold), as seen on the left side of 钱/錢. We are sure that you have learned many other semantic radicals. It is time for a review. You may want to prepare a list for yourself as a quick reference.

PRACTICE: Check the following words in Lesson 3 and see how their meaning is related to "money."

1 销售 _____

2 营销_____

3 促销_____

4 消费_____

Strategy 3: Reasoning by analogy 类推辨义

When you come across words and expressions sharing a certain character, you have a good chance of finding a likeness of meaning in their definitions. It is important to figure out this likeness because it will help you to reason out by analogy words and expressions containing the same character.

付还 pay back   Likeness in 付: pay; payment
付清 pay off
首付 down payment

房款 house-buying money   Likeness in 款: a sum of money
贷款 borrow money; loan
付款 pay (money)

PRACTICE: Find likenesses in each group and reason out the undefined item by analogy.

1 外汇 foreign exchange; 汇率 exchange rate   汇市 _____

2 资本 capital; 外资 foreign capital; 投资 invest   合资 _____

3 货币 currency; 外币 foreign currency   港币 _____

4 股票 stock; 股份 share; 股民 stockholder;   股金 _____
   股市 stock market

5 推动 push into action; 流动 flow; 浮动 float;   带动 _____
   动身 set off

第三课 市场营销

Lesson 3 *Marketing*

课文一 Text 1

实现企业目标的关键在于正确确定目标市场的需求，并且比竞争者更好地提供目标市场所需要的产品或服务。正因为如此，市场营销是以满足顾客的需求为出发点的。市场营销观念的四个支柱是：目标市场，顾客需要，整合营销，盈利能力。

信息是企业的耳目。企业需要通过市场调查来确定目标市场，了解其现状及发展趋势。一个企业只有掌握了丰富的信息，才能有计划地组织各项经营活动，获得最大利润。

影响较大的4P营销理论产生于20世纪60年代。它把营销要素分为四类，即产品(Product)、价格(Price)、渠道(Place)和促销(Promotion)。80年代以来，人们逐步认识到企业外部环境对营销的重要性，于是出现了一种大市场营销策略，在4P的基础上增加政治力量(Political Power)与公共关系(Public Relations)，形成了6P理论。

影响市场营销的因素很多。微观的如产品和服务的购买者、供应商、中间商、竞争者、企业内部的管理等。从宏观来看，人口、教育水平、收入水平、国家政治、社会环境、自然因素，等等，都会对企业的市场营销产生不同的影响。

實現企業目標的關鍵在於正確確定目標市場的需求，並且比競爭者更好地提供目標市場所需要的產品或服務。正因為如此，市場營銷是以滿足顧客的需求為出發點的。市場營銷觀念的四個支柱是：目標市場，顧客需要，整合營銷，盈利能力。

　　信息是企業的耳目。企業需要通過市場調查來確定目標市場，瞭解其現狀及發展趨勢。一個企業只有掌握了豐富的信息，才能有計劃地組織各項經營活動，獲得最大利潤。

　　影響較大的4P營銷理論產生於20世紀60年代。它把營銷要素分為四類，即產品(Product)、價格(Price)、渠道(Place)和促銷(Promotion)。80年代以來，人們逐步認識到企業外部環境對營銷的重要性，於是出現了一種大市場營銷策略，在4P的基礎上增加政治力量(Political Power)與公共關係(Public Relations)，形成了6P理論。

　　影響市場營銷的因素很多。微觀的如產品和服務的購買者、供應商、中間商、競爭者、企業內部的管理等。從宏觀來看，人口、教育水準、收入水準、國家政治、社會環境、自然因素，等等，都會對企業的市場營銷產生不同的影響。

词语表 Words and expressions

(* Refer to notes or language tips following the word list.)

I	营销	營銷	yíngxiāo	*marketing*
2	企业	企業	qǐyè	*enterprise*
3	目标	目標	mùbiāo	*target*
4	关键	關鍵	guānjiàn	*key point; the key (to sth)*
5	正确	正確	zhèngquè	*correct; correctly;* 对
6	确定	確定	quèdìng	*decide; confirm*
7	需求		xūqiú	*demand*
8	提供		tígōng	*provide; supply*
9	产品	產品	chǎnpǐn	*product*
10	服务	服務	fúwù	*service*
11	满足	滿足	mǎnzú	*satisfy*
12	顾客	顧客	gùkè	*customer*
13	出发	出發	chūfā	*set out; start*
14	点	點	diǎn	*point; spot; dot; often as a suffix*

15	观念	觀念	guānniàn	concept; idea; 看法
16	整合		zhěnghé	integrate
17	盈利		yínglì	earn a profit; profit; 赚钱
18	信息		xìnxī	information
19	耳目		ěrmù	ears and eyes
20	调查	調查	diàochá	investigation
21	了解	瞭解	liǎojiě	understand; know about
22	其*		qí	its; it
23	现状	現狀	xiànzhuàng	current situation
24	掌握		zhǎngwò	master
25	丰富	豐富	fēngfù	abundant; plentiful; 很多
26	各		gè	each; every
27	经营	經營	jīngyíng	run (a business)
28	获得	獲得	huòdé	obtain; acquire; 得到
29	利润	利潤	lìrùn	profit
30	理论	理論	lǐlùn	theory
31	产生	產生	chǎnshēng	come into being; emerge
32	要素		yàosù	essential factor; key element
33	渠道		qúdào	channel
34	促销	促銷	cùxiāo	promotion
35	逐步		zhúbù	gradually; step by step
36	环境	環境	huánjìng	environment
37	策略		cèlüè	tactics
38	政治		zhèngzhì	politics; political
39	力量		lìliàng	force; power
40	微观	微觀	wēiguān	microscopic
41	供应	供應	gōngyìng	supply; provide
42	商		shāng	merchant; businessman; dealer; often as a suffix
43	中间商	中間商	zhōngjiānshāng	middleman
44	宏观	宏觀	hóngguān	macroscopic
45	水平		shuǐpíng	level

理解考核 Comprehension check

对错选择 True or false

		True	False
1	一个企业想要在竞争中成功，就得为目标市场提供更好的产品与服务。	☐	☐
2	企业是在确定了目标市场之后才进行市场调查的。	☐	☐
3	从4P到6P的发展用了不到十年的时间。	☐	☐
4	大市场营销策略把市场营销看作是企业内部的事。	☐	☐
5	影响市场营销的因素包括企业内部的管理，也包括企业的外部环境。	☐	☐

语言提示 Language tips

1 在于: lie in

- 实现企业目标的关键<u>在于</u>正确确定目标市场的需求。

 中国开放市场的目的<u>在于</u>发展经济。
 物价涨跌的根本原因<u>在于</u>供求关系的变化。

2 S 所 V 的: Here 所 is used before the verb in a "subject + predicate" structure. It turns the phrase into a noun modifier.

- 实现企业目标的关键在于 . . . 比竞争者更好地提供<u>目标市场所需要的</u>产品或服务。

 <u>中国人民银行所发行的</u>货币称为"人民币"。
 这个学期<u>我所选修的</u>课都跟亚洲经济有关。

3 通过 . . . 来 V: In this phrase "通过 . . ." indicates the way of doing things while "来 V" indicates the purpose.

- 企业需要<u>通过市场调查来确定</u>目标市场，了解其现状及发展趋势。

 政府<u>通过发展生产来改善</u>人民的生活。
 不少公司<u>通过进入国外市场来获得</u>更大的利润。

4 其: As a pronoun, 其 can mean "his, her, its, or their," or "he, she, it, or they." It represents the aforementioned noun.

- 企业需要通过市场调查来确定<u>目标市场</u>，了解<u>其</u>现状及发展趋势。

 <u>信息</u>是企业的耳目，<u>其</u>重要性不言自明。
 从事外汇投资的人最关心<u>汇率</u>，每天都注意<u>其</u>高低与变化。

42

5　即: namely; mean; the same as; (也) 就是

- 4P . . . 把营销要素分为四类，<u>即</u>产品、价格、渠道和促销。

　　大陆的两家证券交易所，<u>即</u>"沪市"和"深市"，分别位于上海和深圳。

　　市场营销观念有四个支柱，<u>即</u>目标市场、顾客需要、整合营销和盈利能力。

6　等/等等: and so on; etc. While 等等 always indicates an incomplete list, 等 may be used after either an incomplete or a complete list.

- 影响市场营销的因素很多 . . . 如产品和服务的购买者、供应商、中间商 . . . <u>等</u>。
- 从宏观来看，人口、教育水平、收入水平 . . . <u>等等</u>，都会对市场营销产生不同的影响。
- 还有很多新的市场没有充分开发，比如说农村市场、老年市场，. . . <u>等等</u>。(L3-2)

　　外汇市场的买卖双方靠电话、电脑和传真机<u>等</u>实时通讯工具连接。
　　休伦(Huron)、安大略(Ontario)、密歇根(Michigan)、伊利(Erie)、苏必利尔(Superior)<u>等</u>五大湖都在密歇根州一带(yīdài, area around a particular place)。
　　中国发行的股票分为 A 股、B 股、H 股<u>等等</u>。

课文二 Text 2

　　马可在上海的实习进行得很顺利。他的团队成功地帮一家外国公司设计了一份在中国市场的营销计划，客户非常满意。于是周末大家聚在一起庆祝，公司的方总也来参加，并向大家表示祝贺。

方　总：马可，听说这次的营销计划你出了一些好点子。

马　可：方总您过奖了。中国的市场这么大这么新，这次我参加了对中国市场的调查和分析，应该说学到了不少才是。今天有机会，正好想请教一下方总对中国市场的看法。

方　总：你太客气了。其实你刚才说中国市场"大"和"新"，这话就说到点子上了。中国就是因为大，再加上开放的时间不长，还有很多新的市场没有充分开发，比如说农村市场、老年市场、旅游市场、文化市场，等等，只要能抢得先机，必定大有可为。

马　可：方总的意思我懂。这些市场都还是一块块新的"蛋糕"，等着人来切呢。

方　总：对，不过机会往往是跟挑战并存的。中国市场很特殊。一个外国企业要想成功进入中国市场，非得好好下一番功夫不可。

马　可：我在美国修过一门市场营销课。我的体会是，一个企业首先得在市场调查上下功夫。没有成功的市场调查，就不可能有成功的产品和营销策略。

方　总：你这样说我很同意。在中国市场上，外国企业必须了解中国的消费者需要什么样的产品，愿意花多少钱，喜欢去哪儿买，还必须知道怎么去吸引他们。所以，除了消费者以外，中国的投资环境和特殊的商务文化，也都需要好好研究和分析。这一次你参加设计的营销计划，我们就是在市场调查上下了一大番功夫的。

马　可：我现在真的明白为什么外国企业需要像我们这样的咨询公司了。

方　总：而我们公司也需要像你这样既熟悉西方又了解中国的老外啊。

马　可：方总，我昨天学了一个成语："功夫不负有心人"。这次实习我一定好好下功夫。

　　馬可在上海的實習進行得很順利。他的團隊成功地幫一家外國公司設計了一份在中國市場的營銷計劃，客戶非常滿意。於是週末大家聚在一起慶祝，公司的方總也來參加，並向大家表示祝賀。

方　總：　馬可，聽說這次的營銷計劃你出了一些好點子。

馬　可：　方總您過獎了。中國的市場這麼大這麼新，這次我參加了對中國市場的調查和分析，應該說學到了不少才是。今天有機會，正好想請教一下方總對中國市場的看法。

方　總：　你太客氣了。其實你剛才說中國市場"大"和"新"，這話就說到點子上了。中國就是因為大，再加上開放的時間不長，還有很多新的市場沒有充分開發，比如說農村市場、老年市場、旅遊市場、文化市場，等等，只要能搶得先機，必定大有可為。

馬　可：　方總的意思我懂。這些市場都還是一塊塊新的"蛋糕"，等著人來切呢。

方　總：　對，不過機會往往是跟挑戰並存的。中國市場很特殊。一個外國企業要想成功進入中國市場，非得好好下一番功夫不可。

馬　可：　我在美國修過一門市場營銷課。我的體會是，一個企業首先得在市場調查上下功夫。沒有成功的市場調查，就不可能有成功的產品和營銷策略。

方　總：　你這樣說我很同意。在中國市場上，外國企業必須瞭解中國的消費者需要什麼樣的產品，願意花多少錢，喜歡去哪兒買，還必須知道怎麼去吸引他們。所以，除了消費者以外，中國的投資環境和特殊的商務文化，也都需要好好研究和分析。這一次你參加設計的營銷計劃，我們就是在市場調查上下了一大番功夫的。

馬　可：　我現在真的明白為什麼外國企業需要像我們這樣的諮詢公司了。

方　總：　而我們公司也需要像你這樣既熟悉西方又瞭解中國的老外啊。

馬　可：　方總，我昨天學了一個成語："功夫不負有心人"。這次實習我一定好好下功夫。

词语表 Words and expressions

(* Refer to notes or language tips following the word list.)

1	顺利	順利	shùnlì	*smooth; without a hitch*
2	团队	團隊	tuánduì	*team*
3	成功		chénggōng	*success; successful*
4	设计	設計	shèjì	*design*
5	客户		kèhù	*client; customer*
6	聚		jù	*assemble; get together*
7	庆祝	慶祝	qìngzhù	*celebrate*
8	总	總	zǒng	*chief; short for "general manager"*
9	祝贺	祝賀	zhùhè	*congratulate; congratulation*
10	点子*	點子	diǎnzi	*idea; key point;* 想法; 主意
11	过奖	過獎	guòjiǎng	*(in response to a compliment) overpraise*
12	分析		fēnxī	*analyze; analysis*
13	请教	請教	qǐngjiào	*ask for advice; consult*
14	充分		chōngfèn	*adequate; ample*
15	农村	農村	nóngcūn	*countryside*
16	抢得	搶得	qiǎngdé	*vie for and win*
17	先机	先機	xiānjī	*preemptive opportunity*
18	必定		bìdìng	*be bound to; be sure to;* 一定
19	大有可为	大有可為	dà yǒu kě wéi	*promising*
20	蛋糕		dàngāo	*cake*
21	切		qiē	*cut*
22	往往		wǎngwǎng	*often; frequently;* 常常
23	挑战	挑戰	tiǎozhàn	*challenge*
24	并存*	並存	bìngcún	*coexist*
25	特殊		tèshū	*exceptional; special;* 特别
26	番		fān	*(measure word) time, as in* 一番功夫

27	功夫*		gōngfu	*time devoted to a task; same as* 工夫
28	修		xiū	*study (a course)*
29	体会	體會	tǐhuì	*knowledge from experience; realize*
30	消费	消費	xiāofèi	*consume*
31	吸引		xīyǐn	*attract*
32	商务	商務	shāngwù	*business affairs*
33	研究		yánjiū	*research*
34	熟悉		shúxī	*be familiar with*

俗语 Common sayings

功夫不负有心人*	功夫不負有心人	gōngfu bù fù yǒuxīnrén	*Efforts will not betray a person who is observant and conscientious.*

理解考核 Comprehension check

回答问题 Answer the following questions

1　为什么说中国的市场又"大"又"新"？

2　马可为什么说中国的市场是"新的蛋糕"？

3　马可觉得企业应该在什么方面下功夫？为什么？

4　方总觉得，外国企业要进入中国市场，需要研究分析哪些方面？

5　马可为什么说"功夫不负有心人"？

注释 Notes

1　功夫不负有心人/下功夫

功夫, also 工夫, stands for the time spent on a task, suggesting hard work. 下功夫 means to devote a lot of time and energy. 有心人 refers to a person with aspiration and determination. The saying 功夫不负有心人, therefore, teaches and encourages people to earn success through persistent effort. A similar common saying in Chinese is 天下无难事，只怕有心人.

语言提示 Language tips

1 出点子: make suggestions; offer advice

- 听说这次的营销计划你出了一些好点子。

  那家咨询公司给我们出过不少坏点子。
  这次装修房子，欢迎大家给我们出点子。

  说到点子上了: (a remark) gets to the heart of the matter

- 你刚才说中国市场"大"和"新"，这话就说到点子上了。

  你说人口问题对中国的发展有很大影响，这就说到点子上了。
  关于这个问题，他说了不少，可是都没说到点子上。

2 A 跟 B 并存: A and B coexist.

- 机会往往是跟挑战并存的。

  经济的快速发展总是跟各种社会问题并存的。
  在中国，古老的传统跟现代的文化并存。

3 非（得）...不可: must do sth; have to do sth

- 一个外国企业要想成功进入中国市场，非得好好下一番功夫不可。

  这次实习，我非得好好下功夫不可。
  你们那儿的房市非降温不可。

练习 Exercises

1 将左栏的主语部分和右栏的谓语部分配对，每个词语只能用一次。 Match each topic in the left column with an appropriate comment in the right column. Each item can be used only once.

1)	中国 _____	a)	成立于 1990 年
2)	资本 _____	b)	影响物价
3)	大家 _____	c)	加入世贸组织
4)	房价 _____	d)	破产
5)	汇率变化 _____	e)	产生营销策略
6)	市场调查 _____	f)	并存
7)	企业 _____	g)	上涨得很快
8)	机会与挑战 _____	h)	觉得自豪
9)	上交所 _____	i)	聚在一起庆祝
10)	马可 _____	j)	外流

2 听写并用汉语解释下列词组。Complete a dictation of the following phrases and explain them in Chinese.

1) 目标市场
2) 整合营销
3) 盈利能力
4) 发展趋势
5) 获得最大利润
6) 企业外部环境
7) 营销计划
8) 老年市场
9) 抢得先机
10) 大有可为
11) 投资环境
12) 商务文化

3 选词填空。Fill in the blanks with the provided words and expressions.

1) 投资环境，吸引客户，商务文化，抢得先机，大有可为，充分开发

目前，中国很多市场还没有 ＿＿＿＿，如果一个企业能 ＿＿＿＿，一定会 ＿＿＿＿。外商进入中国市场时，需要了解消费者，懂得如何 ＿＿＿＿，同时，也需要了解 ＿＿＿＿ 与 ＿＿＿＿。

2) 才是，请教，客气，应该，点子，过奖

A：小王，这次的工作你出了不少好 ＿＿＿＿ 啊！

B：刘经理，您 ＿＿＿＿ 了，＿＿＿＿ 说我学到了不少 ＿＿＿＿。以后还有不少问题要向您 ＿＿＿＿ 呢。

A：你太 ＿＿＿＿ 了。有事情尽管找我，我们可以一起讨论。

B：太感谢了！

4 用指定的表达方式完成句子或对话。Complete the following sentences and dialogues with the designated words or expressions.

1) 通过 ... 来 V

a) A：在中国，老百姓是怎么买房子的？

B：＿＿＿＿＿＿＿＿＿＿＿＿＿＿＿＿＿＿＿＿＿。

b) A：为什么企业在进入一个市场前先要进行市场调查？

B：＿＿＿＿＿＿＿＿＿＿＿＿＿＿＿＿＿＿＿＿＿。

2) 出点子/说到点子上

a) 我很想投资，可是我对股市不太了解，＿＿＿＿＿＿＿＿＿＿＿＿＿＿＿＿＿＿＿。

b) 他说来说去都是没用的话，＿＿＿＿＿＿＿＿＿＿＿＿＿＿＿＿＿＿＿。

3) 等/等等

    a) 人民币升值也带来了一些好处，比方说，_____。

    b) 各个国家和地区股市之间的相关性受到 _____
多方面因素的影响。

4) A 跟 B并存

    a) 北京的街头，_____。你既能看到故宫(gùgōng,
The Forbidden City)、天坛 (tiāntán, The Temple of Heaven)，又能看到鸟巢
(niǎocháo, "Bird's Nest")、水立方(shuǐlìfāng, "Water Cube")。

    b) 在生活中 _____，就看我们每个人怎么面对。

5) 非（得）... 不可

    a) 要改善人民生活，_____。

    b) 你最懂装修了，这次装修，_____。

5 把下面的句子改成不太正式的语体。Paraphrase the following sentences in a less formal style, paying special attention to underlined words and phrases.

1) 企业由市场调查来确定目标市场，了解其现状及发展趋势。

    _____。

2) 近年来中国股市发展较快，其总市值已达 27 万亿元人民币，成为全球第三。

    _____。

3) 4P产生于20世纪60年代，该理论把营销要素分为四类，即产品、价格、渠道和促销。

    _____。

4) 中国人所说的"按揭"，即英文中的"mortgage"，指向银行贷款，先付首付，再分期付还。

    _____。

5) 实现企业目标的关键在于以顾客需求为出发点，更好地提供目标市场所需的产品或服务。

    _____。

6) 市场调查的目的在于掌握企业所需的信息。一个企业若掌握了丰富的信息，则有利于组织各项经营活动。

    _____。

6　自行查找参考资料，解释与本课话题有关的词语。 Using available resources as a reference, explain the following terms, which are related to this lesson's topic.

1) 市场定位　　　4) 供不应求

2) 市场份额　　　5) 买方市场/卖方市场

3) 供过于求　　　6) 消费者心理动机

7　阅读理解与讨论。 Reading comprehension and discussion.

宜家家居 (IKEA) 与整合营销传播

　　传统的4P营销理念是以产品为出发点的。随着生产力的发展和市场的信息化，市场的主动权从企业转移到了消费者手中。因此，在二十世纪九十年代出现了一种称为 4C 的整合营销传播理念，要求企业考虑以下四个方面：消费者的需求和欲望 (Consumer wants and needs)，消费者的成本和费用 (Cost)，消费者购买的便利性 (Convenience)，企业与消费者的沟通(Communication)。这种理念把消费者当作了营销策略的中心。宜家家居(IKEA)正是充分考虑了目标消费者的需要和感受，才得以一直在家居市场的激烈竞争中处于领先地位的。

　　宜家家居于1999年进入中国市场后，将城市白领作为主要目标客户，其销售额每年都实现了两位数的增长。他们的做法是：第一，降低购物成本和提高消费者满意度。第二，重视接触点的管理，让购买家具更为快乐。第三，通过"数据库→沟通计划→执行→消费者回应→→数据库→沟通计划→执行→消费者回应"的循环过程，保持与消费者的良好沟通。第四，重视品牌的定位和塑造，建立及加强消费者的信赖感。第五，努力承担社会责任，使企业成为世界级公民。这些整合营销传播的特色就是宜家成功的原因。

整合	zhěnghé	integrated	度	dù	degree
传播	chuánbō	dissemination	重视	zhòngshì	place importance on
理念	lǐniàn	concept; philosophy	接触	jiēchù	get in touch with
生产力	shēngchǎnlì	productivity	数据	shùjù	data; statistics
主动	zhǔdòng	voluntarily; actively	库	kù	warehouse; storehouse
权	quán	right; entitlement	执行	zhíxíng	carry out
转移	zhuǎnyí	shift; transfer	回应	huíyìng	feedback
考虑	kǎolǜ	think over; consider	循环	xúnhuán	move in circles; circulate
成本	chéngběn	cost	过程	guòchéng	process
沟通	gōutōng	communication	保持	bǎochí	keep (up)
当作	dàngzuò	look on as; take as; treat as	良好	liánghǎo	good; fine
感受	gǎnshòu	feeling; impression	品牌	pǐnpái	brand
得以	déyǐ	so that; so as to	定位	dìngwèi	position; orientate
激烈	jīliè	violent; intense	塑造	sùzào	mold; make by molding
领先	lǐngxiān	be in the lead	加强	jiāqiáng	strengthen; enhance
白领	báilǐng	white-collar	信赖	xìnlài	count on; trust
销售	xiāoshòu	sell	感	gǎn	sense; feeling
额	é	specified amount	承担	chéngdān	bear; undertake
两位数	liǎngwèishù	double-digit	责任	zérèn	responsibility; duty
增长	zēngzhǎng	increase	级	jí	level; grade; rank
购物	gòuwù	shopping	公民	gōngmín	citizen
满意	mǎnyì	satisfaction	特色	tèsè	distinguishing feature

选择填空 Select the correct answer for each blank.

1) 4P营销理论以 ＿＿＿＿＿ 为出发点，"4C"认为 ＿＿＿＿＿ 是营销策略的中心。

    a) 国家政策

    b) 消费者

    c) 产品

2) 宜家进入中国后，其销售额的增长率可能是 ＿＿＿＿＿。

    a) 8%

    b) 12%

    c) 150%

3) 宜家在中国的主要目标客户是 ＿＿＿＿＿。

    a) 蓝领

    b) 金领

    c) 白领

讨论 Discussion.

宜家家居在中国使用什么样的营销策略？根据你了解的情况或所查的资料，请你谈谈宜家在美国的经营情况。What are IKEA's marketing strategies in China? According to what you know or what you have found in research, does IKEA have the same strategies in the United States?

8 实践活动。Tasks.

1) 在4P、4C理论之后，又有人提出了4R理论。请查出4R是指哪些营销要素，并将这三个理论进行对比，找出异同。Somebody raised a "4R's" theory after "4P's" and "4C's." Find out what marketing factors "4R's" stand for and make a succinct comparison among the three theories.

2) 做一个10分钟的口头报告，介绍一个在中国成功经营的美国公司的案例。在报告中要通过事实和例子说明该公司在中国的营销策略，并提出你自己的看法和建议。先查看最近六个月之内的资料，然后根据老师的要求为自己准备一个简单的提纲。Give a ten-minute case report about a US company that operates successfully in China. You should introduce the company's marketing strategy in China with facts and examples, including how well it has worked. You should also provide your own comments and suggestions for the company. Ideally you should base your report on information from within the past six months and prepare a brief outline for yourself as per your teacher's instructions.

3) 为你喜欢的一种产品设计一个音像广告。一般的广告采用以下的结构：a) 抓住观众的注意力，b) 表现产品的特色，c) 鼓励观众采取行动，但你可以加入自己的创意。把你的广告设计写出来（不要超过一页）跟班上的同学分享，并听取大家的意见。Design an audio-visual ad for a product of your choice. You are encouraged to be creative, although a typical ad follows a three-step format: a) catching the audience's attention, b) showing the product's unique features, and c) encouraging the audience to take action. Write out your design (limited to one page), and share it with your classmates for critiques.

4) 如果你对一个别的任务有兴趣，请结合本课的主题向老师提出建议，然后在老师的指导下完成这个任务。If you are interested in a different task, you are encouraged to suggest your proposal and to complete it under your teacher's guidance.

学习指导 Learning guide

词汇量扩展（二）Vocabulary expansion (2)

Strategy 4: Consolidating through contrasts 对比强化

Words with opposite meanings (antonyms) can be paired in language acquisition so that your knowledge of one can be easily extended to the other. When learned through contrast, new words are quickly consolidated in your comprehension and retention. The following examples, all from Lessons 1 and 2, should be familiar to you:

境内 within the boundaries; domestic　　境外 out of the boundaries; overseas

本币 basic unit of local currency　　外币 foreign currency

升值 increase in value; appreciate　　贬值 fall in value; depreciate

上升 go up; hoist　　下降 come down; fall

上涨 go up; rise　　下跌 come down; drop

外流 outflow　　内流 inflow

好处 benefit; advantage　　坏处 harm; disadvantage

PRACTICE: Find words in the first two lessons that are antonyms to the given words.

1) 得到 get　　＿＿＿＿ lose

2) 市区 city proper　　＿＿＿＿ suburb

3) 中资 Chinese capital　　＿＿＿＿ foreign capital

4) 下市 withdraw from the market　　＿＿＿＿ go on the market

5) 升温 warm up　　＿＿＿＿ cool down

6) 退出 withdraw　　　　　　　　_____ join

7) 必修 required (course)　　　　_____ elective (course)

8) 单方 single party　　　　　　 _____ both parties

9) 低档 low-grade　　　　　　　　_____ high-grade

10) 劣势 inferiority; weakness　　_____ superiority; strength

Strategy 5: Checking on the original complete form 探本溯源

Short forms (or abbreviations) serve the purpose of convenience in communication although they are not as formal. They vary widely in the ways they are formed. Once a short form is established through popular usage, it is classified and regarded as a special kind of compound word. You should never try to create a Chinese short form by yourself, but always watch out for and follow native speakers' practices. Examples of short forms are:

股市	股票交易市场	家电	家用电器
房市	房地产市场	港交所	香港证券交易所
汇市	外汇市场	国企	国有企业
本币	本位货币	世贸	世界贸易组织
股价	股票交易价格	入世	加入世界贸易组织

PRACTICE: Study the short forms of these three Chinese government offices.

1　证监会　中国证券监督管理委员会 China Securities Regulatory Commission

监督　　jiāndū　　　　supervise

管理　　guǎnlǐ　　　　manage

委员会　wěiyuánhuì　　commission; committee

2　银监会　中国银行业监督管理委员会 China Banking Regulatory Commission

银行　　yínháng　　　bank; banking

业　　　yè　　　　　 line of business; industry; often as a suffix

3　保监会　中国保险监督管理委员会 China Insurance Regulatory Commission

保险　　bǎoxiǎn　　　insurance

Strategy 6: Gaining help from the context 瞻前顾后

You can tell the meaning of a word or phrase from its context only if the context makes some sense to you. Oftentimes the context does make some sense since at your proficiency level you already have a good chance of finding familiar words, characters, and character components. In such cases, the meaning of a new word or phrase may reliably occur to you in the big picture. Here is an example of how the context can be helpful:

> 马可所在的咨询公司正协助一个美国公司在中国进行贸易洽谈。
> 马可答应过方总要"好好下功夫"，所以忙得不亦乐乎。(L4-2)

You may have never seen the phrase 不亦乐乎 before. However, you would not mistake it for "not being happy" since you know that a person who wants to 好好下功夫 (L3) can only be "extremely" busy and at the same time enjoys what he is doing. Unknowingly, you have decoded 不亦乐乎 in the context; the only thing left for you to do is to find out its pronunciation and to begin to use it. As for 协助 and 洽谈, you can use the context for their meanings too. However, you can also apply a guessing strategy since you already know 助 and 谈.

PRACTICE: Go over the paragraph and figure out the meanings of the underlined words.

国际贸易是指不同国家或地区之间的商品、服务和生产要素的交换活动。从特定某一个国家的角度来看，即被称为对外贸易，如"中国的对外贸易"等。(L4-1)

第四课 国际贸易

Lesson 4 *International trade*

课文一 Text 1

国际贸易是指不同国家或地区之间的商品、服务和生产要素的交换活动。从特定某一个国家的角度来看，即被称为对外贸易，如"中国的对外贸易"等。

国际贸易调节各国市场的供求关系，促进劳动力、资本、土地、技术等生产要素在世界范围内的充分利用，对参与贸易的国家及世界经济的发展都具有重要作用。然而，各国的语言、法律、经济政策以及风俗习惯不同，各国间的货币、度量衡、海关制度也存在差异。因此，与国内贸易相比，国际贸易更为复杂，商业风险也较大。

国际贸易主要由进口贸易和出口贸易组成，故亦称"进出口贸易"。一个国家在一定时期内（通常为一年）出口总额与进口总额之间的差额，称为"贸易差额"。如出口额大于进口额，叫做"贸易顺差"；反之，则为"贸易逆差"。若二者相当，即为"贸易平衡"。贸易顺差可以推进经济增长，增加就业，但大量的顺差往往会导致贸易纠纷。

世界贸易组织(WTO)是一个独立于联合国的永久性国际组织，负责管理世界经济和贸易秩序。它在调解成员争端方面具有更高的权威性。中国于2001年12月11日正式成为世贸组织成员。

國際貿易是指不同國家或地區之間的商品、服務和生產要素的交換活動。從特定某一個國家的角度來看，即被稱為對外貿易，如"中國的對外貿易"等。

　　國際貿易調節各國市場的供求關係，促進勞動力、資本、土地、技術等生產要素在世界範圍內的充分利用，對參與貿易的國家及世界經濟的發展都具有重要作用。然而，各國的語言、法律、經濟政策以及風俗習慣不同，各國間的貨幣、度量衡、海關制度也存在差異。因此，與國內貿易相比，國際貿易更為複雜，商業風險也較大。

　　國際貿易主要由進口貿易和出口貿易組成，故亦稱"進出口貿易"。一個國家在一定時期內（通常為一年）出口總額與進口總額之間的差額，稱為"貿易差額"。如出口額大於進口額，叫做"貿易順差"；反之，則為"貿易逆差"。若二者相當，即為"貿易平衡"。貿易順差可以推進經濟增長，增加就業，但大量的順差往往會導致貿易糾紛。

　　世界貿易組織(WTO)是一個獨立於聯合國的永久性國際組織，負責管理世界經濟和貿易秩序。它在調解成員爭端方面具有更高的權威性。中國於2001年12月11日正式成為世貿組織成員。

词语表 Words and expressions

(* Refer to notes or language tips following the word list.)

1	地区	地區	dìqū	*region*
2	生产	生產	shēngchǎn	*produce; production*
3	交换	交換	jiāohuàn	*exchange*
4	特定		tèdìng	*specific*
5	某*		mǒu	*certain; some*
6	角度*		jiǎodù	*perspective; angle*
7	促进	促進	cùjìn	*promote*
8	劳动力	勞動力	láodònglì	*labor; labor force*
9	技术	技術	jìshù	*technology*
10	范围	範圍	fànwéi	*range*
11	参与	參與	cānyù	*participate in*

12	具有		jùyǒu	have; 有
13	作用		zuòyòng	effect; role
14	法律		fǎlǜ	law
15	政策		zhèngcè	policy
16	风俗习惯	風俗習慣	fēngsú xíguàn	customs and habits
17	度量衡		dùliànghéng	length, capacity, and weight
18	海关	海關	hǎiguān	customs; customhouse
19	存在		cúnzài	exist; 有
20	差异	差異	chāyì	difference; 不同
21	复杂	複雜	fùzá	complicated
22	商业	商業	shāngyè	commerce; trade; business
23	风险	風險	fēngxiǎn	risk
24	故*		gù	so; therefore; 所以
25	亦*		yì	also; too; 也
26	总额	總額	zǒng'é	total (amount or value)
27	差额	差額	chā'é	difference; margin
28	顺差	順差	shùnchā	(in foreign trade) surplus
29	逆差		nìchā	(in foreign trade) deficit
30	相当	相當	xiāngdāng	match; be about equal to
31	平衡		pínghéng	balance
32	推进	推進	tuījìn	promote
33	增长	增長	zēngzhǎng	grow; growth
34	导致	導致	dǎozhì	lead to; result in
35	纠纷	糾紛	jiūfēn	dispute; issue
36	独立	獨立	dúlì	independent
37	永久		yǒngjiǔ	permanent
38	负责	負責	fùzé	be in charge of
39	秩序		zhìxù	order
40	调解	調解	tiáojiě	mediate
41	成员	成員	chéngyuán	member
42	争端	爭端	zhēngduān	controversial issue; conflict

| 43 | 权威 | 權威 | quánwēi | *authority* |
| 44 | 正式 | | zhèngshì | *officially* |

专有名词 Proper nouns

| | 联合国 | 聯合國 | Liánhéguó | *United Nations* |

理解考核 Comprehension check

对错选择 True or false

		True	False
1	中国与别的国家或地区之间的商品、服务和生产要素的交换活动即为"中国的对外贸易"。	☐	☐
2	国际贸易比国内贸易更复杂，风险更大。	☐	☐
3	贸易差额是指一个国家的贸易额与另一个国家的贸易额之间的差额。	☐	☐
4	贸易顺差既能促进经济增长，又可能导致贸易纠纷。	☐	☐
5	世界贸易组织是联合国的一个组成部分。	☐	☐

语言提示 Language tips

1 某: This is used for an indefinite person or thing, but it can also be used to avoid naming a known person or thing.

- 从特定某一个国家的角度来看，即被称为对外贸易，...

  汇率是某一国货币兑换另一国货币的比率。
  这份市场营销计划是某家外国咨询公司设计的。

2 从 ... 的角度来看: judged by sb or from a certain perspective

- 从特定某一个国家的角度来看，即被称为对外贸易，...

  从中国外贸出口的角度来看，人民币升值坏处比好处多。
  从宏观角度来看，国家政治会影响企业的市场营销。

3 与 ... 相比: compared with

- 与国内贸易相比，国际贸易更为复杂，商业风险也较大。

  与美国股市相比，中国股市的历史短多了。
  与其他公司相比，我们的服务更有竞争优势。

4 故: same as 所以, but formal

- 国际贸易主要由进口贸易和出口贸易组成，故亦称"进出口贸易"。

  汇率的变化对经济的影响有好有坏，故被说成是一把"双刃剑"。
  信息是企业的耳目，故对企业的发展有决定性的影响。

5 亦: same as 也, but formal

- 国际贸易主要由进口贸易和出口贸易组成，故亦称"进出口贸易"。

  上海证券交易所亦称"沪市"。
  最近美国的股市涨势明显，欧洲股市亦有上涨的趋势。

6 反之: a connective meaning "on the contrary; whereas; or otherwise"

- 如出口额大于进口额，叫做"贸易顺差"；反之，则为"贸易逆差"。

  货币贬值会引起进口商品的价格上涨；反之，货币升值则会使进口商
    品的价格下跌。
  经济不好时要让房市"升温"，反之，经济过热时得给房市"降温"。

课文二 Text 2

　　马可所在的咨询公司正协助一个美国公司在中国进行贸易洽谈。马可答应过方总要"好好下功夫"，所以忙得不亦乐乎。这天晚上，他正在上网，正好王静文也上网了，两个人就用Skype聊了起来。

王静文：你好，马可。最近在忙什么呢？
马　可：我下个月要和同事们一起参加一个美国客户跟中国贸易伙伴的洽谈，主要是向中国出口农产品。我正在这儿做准备呢。
王静文：得看不少资料吧？
马　可：可不是吗，我没想到国际贸易洽谈这么复杂。询价，报价，交货日期，付款方式，包装，运输，保险，佣金，一个环节都不能少。

王静文：好像还不止这些吧。有了问题怎么仲裁，怎么索赔，合同上也都得写清楚呀。

马　可：是啊，每个环节都不能大意。你看，我这个单子上都记着呢。这几天，我们一直在调查中方的情况。方总说："知己知彼，百战百胜。"你比较有经验，有什么要提醒我的吗？

王静文：我觉得，弄清对方的情况真的很重要。资金，信誉，对商品的需求，能接受的价格范围，有没有特殊要求什么的，都必须做到心中有底。

马　可：其实这些方面我们已经了解得差不多了。下个星期就要开始跟美方客户一起准备洽谈方案了。你对洽谈有什么建议吗？

王静文：通常卖方得先把能让步的底线定下来，让讨价还价有个范围。最好是多准备几套方案，到了谈判桌上随机应变。

马　可：有道理！那么，跟中国公司谈判要特别注意什么呢？

王静文：中国人都比较重面子，所以在洽谈的时候得注意给对方留面子，让人家也有成就感才好。可是这一点你不用担心。到时候只要看方总和你的中国同事怎么办，跟他们学着点儿就行。

马　可：没问题，保证不出洋相。

王静文：还有，签约的时候可得要喝酒啊！

马　可：你知道我不喝酒，到时候我就以茶代酒吧。

———————————

馬可所在的諮詢公司正協助一個美國公司在中國進行貿易洽談。馬可答應過方總要"好好下功夫"，所以忙得不亦樂乎。這天晚上，他正在上網，正好王靜文也上網了，兩個人就用Skype聊了起來。

王靜文：你好，馬可。最近在忙什麼呢？

馬　可：我下個月要和同事們一起參加一個美國客戶跟中國貿易夥伴的洽談，主要是向中國出口農產品。我正在這兒做準備呢。

王靜文：得看不少資料吧？

馬　可：可不是嗎，我沒想到國際貿易洽談這麼複雜。詢價，報價，交貨日期，付款方式，包裝，運輸，保險，傭金，一個環節都不能少。

王靜文：好像還不止這些吧。有了問題怎麼仲裁，怎麼索賠，合同上也都得寫清楚呀。

馬　可：是啊，每個環節都不能大意。你看，我這個單子上都記著呢。這幾天，我們一直在調查中方的情況。方總說："知己知彼，百戰百勝。"你比較有經驗，有什麼要提醒我的嗎？

王靜文：我覺得，弄清對方的情況真的很重要。資金，信譽，對商品的需求，能接受的價格範圍，有沒有特殊要求什麼的，都必須做到心中有底。

馬　可：其實這些方面我們已經瞭解得差不多了。下個星期就要開始跟美方客戶一起準備洽談方案了。你對洽談有什麼建議嗎？

王靜文：通常賣方得先把能讓步的底線定下來，讓討價還價有個範圍。最好是多準備幾套方案，到了談判桌上隨機應變。

馬　可：有道理！那麼，跟中國公司談判要特別注意什麼呢？

王靜文：中國人都比較重面子，所以在洽談的時候得注意給對方留面子，讓人家也有成就感才好。可是這一點你不用擔心。到時候只要看方總和你的中國同事怎麼辦，跟他們學著點兒就行。

馬　可：沒問題，保證不出洋相。

王靜文：還有，簽約的時候可得要喝酒啊！

馬　可：你知道我不喝酒，到時候我就以茶代酒吧。

词语表 Words and expressions

(* Refer to notes or language tips following the word list.)

I	协助	協助	xiézhù	*help*; 帮助
2	洽谈	洽談	qiàtán	*negotiate; negotiation*
3	答应	答應	dāying	*promise*
4	不亦乐乎*	不亦樂乎	bù yì lè hū	*awfully; extremely*
5	同事		tóngshì	*co-worker; colleague*
6	伙伴	夥伴	huǒbàn	*partners*
7	农产品	農產品	nóngchǎnpǐn	*agricultural product*
8	资料	資料	zīliào	*data; information*
9	询价	詢價	xúnjià	*inquire; inquiry*; 问价
10	报价	報價	bàojià	*quote*
11	交货	交貨	jiāohuò	*delivery of goods*
12	方式		fāngshì	*way (of doing sth)*
13	包装		bāozhuāng	*packaging*
14	运输	運輸	yùnshū	*transportation*
15	保险	保險	bǎoxiǎn	*insurance*

16	佣金	傭金	yòngjīn	*commission*
17	环节	環節	huánjié	*link*
18	不止		bùzhǐ	*exceed; not limited to;* 不只
19	仲裁	仲裁	zhòngcái	*arbitrate*
20	索赔	索賠	suǒpéi	*claim*
21	合同		hétong	*contract*
22	大意		dàyi	*be careless*
23	单子	單子	dānzi	*list*
24	经验	經驗	jīngyàn	*experience*
25	提醒		tíxǐng	*remind*
26	弄清		nòngqīng	*make clear; find out*
27	信誉	信譽	xìnyù	*reputation*
28	心中有底		xīnzhōng yǒu dǐ	*know what to expect;* 心中有数
29	方案		fāng'àn	*plan*
30	建议	建議	jiànyì	*suggest; suggestion*
31	让步	讓步	ràngbù	*concede*
32	底线	底線	dǐxiàn	*baseline; bottom line*
33	讨价还价	討價還價	tǎojià huánjià	*bargain*
34	谈判	談判	tánpàn	*negotiate; negotiation*
35	随机应变	隨機應變	suí jī yìng biàn	*adapt oneself quickly to changing condition*
36	面子*		miànzi	*face; feeling*
37	成就		chéngjiù	*achievement*
38	保证	保證	bǎozhèng	*guarantee*
39	出洋相*		chū yángxiàng	*make a fool of oneself*
40	签约	簽約	qiānyuē	*sign a contract*
41	以茶代酒		yǐ chá dài jiǔ	*drink tea instead of wine*

理解考核 Comprehension check

回答问题 Answer the following questions

1 国际贸易洽谈包括哪些环节？

2 在贸易洽谈前的准备工作中什么事情很重要？

3 为什么要为洽谈多准备几套方案？

4 跟中国公司谈判要特别注意什么？为什么？

5 签合同要喝酒的时候，要是不会喝酒怎么办？

注释 Notes

1 不亦乐乎

This saying originated in the 《论语》 (*Lún Yǔ*), or *The Analects*, a book that recorded the words and deeds of Confucius and his disciples. The complete original sentence is 有朋自远方来，不亦乐乎？(=有朋友从很远的地方来，不也是很快乐的吗？ "Isn't it a delight to have friends from afar?") Now, contrary to its original meaning, 不亦乐乎 is often used to express the extremity of something, as in 忙得不亦乐乎.

2 知己知彼，百战百胜 (*zhc jh zhc bh, bfi zhàn bfi shèng*)

This is another common saying with its origin in the Chinese classics, meaning that, if you know yourself and know your enemy, you will win every battle you fight. Refer to 《孙子兵法》 (*Sūnzǐ Bīngfǎ*), or *The Art of War*, by Sun Tzu.

3 面子

This word means "face" or "reputation," as seen in 爱面子: be anxious to save one's face; 要面子: be concerned about face-saving; 重面子: attach importance to face-saving; and 丢面子: lose face. But 面子 can also mean "feelings," such as in 给 . . . 面子 or 给 . . . 留面子: show due respect for sb's feelings.

4 出洋相

This phrase's literal meaning is "show a foreign appearance" or "look foreign," but it actually means "make a laughing stock of oneself" or "lose face."

语言提示 Language tips

1 把...定下来: make a decision about sth; get sth settled or fixed
   - 通常卖方得先把能让步的底线定下来，让讨价还价有个范围。

   经过长时间的讨论，我们终于把这份市场营销计划定下来了。
   公司进入市场之前，得先把目标客户定下来。

2 得/要...才好: It would be good only if ...
   - 中国人都比较重面子，...在洽谈的时候得注意给对方留面子...才好。

   进行贸易洽谈，要"知己知彼"才好。
   从事美中贸易很不容易，得既熟悉美国又了解中国才好。

练习 Exercises

1 将左栏的介词和右栏的词语配对，每个词语只能用一次。Match each preposition in the left column with an appropriate word or phrase in the right column. Each item can be used only once.

1)	在 ... _____	a)	定下来
2)	向 ... _____	b)	有影响
3)	对 ... _____	c)	的角度来看
4)	与 ... _____	d)	表示祝贺
5)	给 ... _____	e)	组成
6)	从 ... _____	f)	相比
7)	把 ... _____	g)	留面子
8)	由 ... _____	h)	的基础上

2 听写并用汉语解释下列词组。Complete a dictation of the following phrases and explain them in Chinese.

1)	对外贸易	7)	忙得不亦乐乎
2)	供求关系	8)	知己知彼，百战百胜
3)	生产要素	9)	随机应变
4)	度量衡	10)	重面子
5)	贸易纠纷	11)	成就感
6)	永久性国际组织	12)	出洋相

3　选词填空。 Fill in the blanks with the provided words and expressions.

1) 故，称，亦，即，若，则，反之

　　国际贸易由进口贸易和出口贸易组成，＿＿＿＿＿＿＿＿＿"进出口贸易"。如出口额大于进口额，叫做"贸易顺差"，＿＿＿＿＿，＿＿＿＿＿为"贸易逆差"。＿＿＿＿＿二者相当，＿＿＿＿＿为"贸易平衡"。贸易顺差会推进经济增长，但大量的顺差＿＿＿＿＿会导致贸易纠纷。

2) 讨价还价，随机应变，知己知彼，心中有底

　　贸易洽谈时应该做到＿＿＿＿＿。如果是卖方，一定要先弄清买方的情况，资金、信誉、对产品的需求什么的，都必须做到＿＿＿＿＿；同时得把价格的底线定下来，让＿＿＿＿＿有个范围。然后要多准备几套方案，到了谈判桌上可以＿＿＿＿＿。

4　用指定的表达方式完成句子或对话。 Complete the following sentences with the designated words or expressions.

1) 从 . . . 的角度来看

　　a) 影响市场营销的因素很多，＿＿＿＿＿＿＿＿＿＿＿＿＿＿＿＿＿＿。

　　b) ＿＿＿＿＿＿＿＿＿＿＿，中国利用被低估的汇率来促进出口；＿＿＿＿＿＿＿＿＿＿，人民币的币值没有被低估。

2) 与 . . . 相比

　　a) ＿＿＿＿＿＿＿＿＿＿＿＿＿＿＿＿＿，内地股市与香港股市的相关性较大。

　　b) ＿＿＿＿＿＿＿＿＿＿＿＿＿＿＿＿＿，中国市场还是一块块新的"蛋糕"，等着人来切呢。

3) . . . ，反之 . . .

　　a) 公司经营状况好则它的股票上涨，＿＿＿＿＿＿＿＿＿＿＿＿＿＿＿＿＿。

　　b) 良好的学习习惯有利于学习的进步，＿＿＿＿＿＿＿＿＿＿＿＿＿＿＿＿。

4) 把 . . . 定下来

　　a) 明天要和美方客户一起开会，＿＿＿＿＿＿＿＿＿＿＿＿＿＿＿＿。

　　b) 外国公司进入中国市场之前，＿＿＿＿＿＿＿＿＿＿＿＿＿＿＿＿。

5) 得/要 . . . 才好

　　a) 想在中国公司实习，＿＿＿＿＿＿＿＿＿＿＿＿＿＿＿＿＿。

　　b) 商务汉语这门课不太容易，＿＿＿＿＿＿＿＿＿＿＿＿＿＿＿＿。

5　把下面的句子改成不太正式的语体。 Paraphrase the following sentences in a less formal style, paying special attention to the underlined words and phrases.

1) 从特定某一国家的角度来看，国际贸易<u>亦称为</u>对外贸易，<u>如</u>"中国的对外贸易"等。

_____

_____。

2) <u>某外国公司计划于</u>明年进入中国市场，<u>故目前正对</u>其产品的目标市场进行调查。

_____

_____。

3) 国际贸易主要<u>由</u>进口贸易和出口贸易<u>组成</u>，<u>故亦称</u>"进出口贸易"。

_____

_____。

4) <u>若出口额</u>大于进口额，称为"贸易顺差"；<u>反之</u>，<u>则为</u>"贸易逆差"。<u>若二者相当即为</u>"贸易平衡"。

_____

_____。

5) <u>在</u>一国货币对外贬值的<u>趋势下</u>，资本将外流，<u>使该国</u>货币的汇率<u>进一步下跌</u>；<u>反之</u>，资本<u>将内流</u>，<u>使该国</u>货币的汇率<u>上升</u>。

_____

_____。

6　自行查找参考资料，解释与本课话题有关的词语。 Using available resources as a reference, explain the following terms, which are related to this lesson's topic.

1) 产品目录
2) 季节性商品
3) 优惠价
4) 意向书
5) 购货合同
6) 贸易保护主义
7) 政府补贴
8) 倾销

7　阅读理解与讨论。Reading comprehension and discussion.

世界贸易组织及其标识

　　世界贸易组织简称"世贸组织"或"世贸"，是一个独立于联合国的永久性国际组织，负责监督成员经济体之间各种贸易协议的执行。该机构总部设在瑞士日内瓦，于1995年1月1日正式开始运作，并于1996年1月1日正式取代关贸总协定秘书处。世贸组织管理众多贸易协定，监督各成员贸易立法，是多边贸易体制的法律基础和组织基础，也是通过谈判解决贸易争端的重要场所。截至2011年12月31日，该机构共有157个成员。因其成员间的贸易额占世界贸易总额的比重极大，世贸组织是最重要的国际经济组织之一，被称为"经济联合国"。

　　1997年10月9日，世贸组织启用新的标识。该标识由六道向上弯曲的弧线组成，上三道和下三道分别为红、蓝、绿三种颜色，意味着充满活力的世贸组织将在持久和有序地扩大世界贸易方面发挥关键作用。六道弧线组成的球形表示世贸组织是不同成员组成的国际机构。标识久看有动感，象征世贸组织充满活力。该标识由新加坡的杨淑女士设计，其中采用了中国传统书法的笔势。(请见本书相关网站。See companion website for this logo: www.routledge.com/cw/chen.)

监督	jiāndū	supervise	截至	jiézhì	by (a time)
经济体	jīngjìtǐ	economic entity	占	zhàn	make up; account for
协议	xiéyì	agreement	比重	bǐzhòng	proportion
执行	zhíxíng	execute; execution	启用	qǐyòng	start using
总部	zǒngbù	headquarters	标识	biāozhì	logo; emblem; sign
设	shè	set up	弯曲	wānqū	circuitous; bending
瑞士	Ruìshì	Switzerland	弧线	húxiàn	pitch arc
日内瓦	Rìnèiwǎ	Geneva	意味	yìwèi	mean
运作	yùnzuò	operate	充满	chōngmǎn	be full of
取代	qǔdài	replace	活力	huólì	vitality
关贸总协定	Guānmào zǒng xiédìng	GATT	持久	chíjiǔ	everlastingly
秘书处	mìshūchù	secretariat	有序	yǒuxù	orderly
众多	zhòngduō	many	发挥	fāhuī	play (a role)
协定	xiédìng	agreement	动感	dònggǎn	dynamic
立法	lìfǎ	legislation	象征	xiàngzhēng	symbol
多边	duōbiān	multilateral	设计	shèjì	design
体制	tǐzhì	system	采用	cǎiyòng	adopt
解决	jiějué	solve	笔势	bǐshì	style of brushwork
场所	chǎngsuǒ	place			

连线 Match the dates and events in the following list. Also refer to L4-1.

1)　1995年1月1日 ＿＿＿　　a)　中国加入世贸组织

2)　1996年1月1日 ＿＿＿　　b)　世贸组织共有153个成员

3)　1997年10月9日 ＿＿＿　　c)　世贸组织正式开始运作

4)　2001年12月11日 ＿＿＿　　d)　世贸组织正式取代关贸总协定秘书处

5)　2010年12月31日 ＿＿＿　　e)　世贸组织启用新的标识

讨论 Discussion.

世贸组织的主要职能是什么？根据你了解的情况或所查的资料，你认为这些年世贸组织工作得好不好？What are the WTO's main functions? According to what you know or what you have found in research, do you think the WTO has been doing a good job?

8　实践活动。Tasks.

1) 查出过去五年里美中之间的进出口贸易总额，说明顺差和逆差的情况，并指出数据所反映的趋势。Find out the import and export volumes between the United States and China from the past five years. Make a list to show surplus or deficit, and point out the tendencies shown in the data.

2) 做一个10分钟的口头报告，介绍一个中国（或美国）与别的国家的贸易争端的案例。在报告中要介绍这次争端的起因、过程及结果，并发表自己的看法。先查看最近六个月之内的资料，然后根据老师的要求为自己准备一个简单的提纲。Give a ten-minute oral report about a trade dispute between China (or the US) and another country. Regarding the dispute, you should explain its cause, process, and result, and provide your own comments. Ideally, you should base your report on information from within the past six months and prepare a brief outline for yourself as per your teacher's instructions.

3) 你在一家生产和出口玩具的中国公司实习。该公司即将跟一家美国公司进行贸易洽谈，让你准备一个提纲。现在你得把所有需要洽谈的问题一个一个列出来。注意不要超过一页。Suppose you are doing an internship at a toy manufacturer and exporter in China. The company is having you prepare an outline for a forthcoming negotiation with a US company. You now need to make a list of the issues to be covered at the meeting. Note that the outline should be limited to one page.

4) 如果你对一个不同的任务有兴趣，请结合本课的主题向老师提出建议，然后在老师的指导下完成这个任务。If you are interested in a different kind of task, you are encouraged to suggest your proposal and to complete it under your teacher's guidance.

学习指导 Learning guide

词性和句子成分 Parts of speech and sentence elements

In Chinese, as in English, sentence elements are made of words of specific parts of speech or phrases formed by these words, while a word's part of speech is determined by the way it works with other words in a phrase or sentence. Knowledge of parts of speech, therefore, plays a crucial role in recognizing a sentence's elements, especially its essential elements—the subject (basically a noun or a pronoun), the predicate (basically a verb, an adjective, or a noun), and the object (basically a noun or a pronoun).

Have you ever noticed that nouns, verbs, and adjectives can be identified by certain signs in the context? Here is a review of the most important signs that you have seen previously.

Signs of noun:	Preceded by an adjective	好<u>机会</u>　最大<u>利润</u>　不少<u>资料</u>
	Preceded by a numeral + classifier	一家<u>公司</u>　两种<u>货币</u> 是(一)把"<u>双刃剑</u>"
	Preceded by a 的 modifier	企业的<u>目标</u>　在上海的<u>实习</u> 新的<u>理论</u>　她对市场的<u>看法</u>
	Followed by 们	<u>股民</u>们　<u>顾客</u>们
Signs of verb:	Followed by 着, 了, 过	我正<u>计划</u>着来个自助游。 中国股市<u>实现</u>了网上交易。 房市<u>出现</u>过各种问题。
	Preceded by 正在, 会, 要, 将, 已经, 曾经, etc.	人民币将会<u>升值</u>。 股民已经<u>达到</u>1.5亿。
	Preceded by 得, 应该, 必须, 能, 可以, etc.	企业必须<u>了解</u>消费者的想法。 在买房时可以<u>办</u>按揭。
	Preceded by a 地 modifier	他们要更好地<u>提供</u>产品或服务。 公司有计划地<u>组织</u>经营活动。
	Preceded by 被 (+ agent)	那个股市于1949年被政府<u>关闭</u>。 价格被全部<u>放开</u>。
	Preceded by a 把 structure	我们再把话<u>说</u>回来。 你先得把能让步的底线<u>定</u>下来。
	Followed by a 得 modifier	房价<u>上涨</u>得很厉害。 这方面我们<u>了解</u>得差不多了。
	In a negative form	不<u>用</u>　买不<u>起</u>　去不<u>去</u>　没<u>想</u>到 有没<u>有</u>要求　非<u>下</u>功夫不可
	With an object	做<u>准备</u>　调节<u>供求关系</u>
Signs of adjective:	Preceded by an adverb of degree	发展的速度很<u>快</u>。 客户非常<u>满意</u>。
	Followed by a 得 modifier	马可<u>忙</u>得不亦乐乎。 这件事<u>复杂</u>得很。
	In a negative form	这两个问题不<u>一样</u>。 那里的环境<u>好</u>不<u>好</u>？

语序（一）Word order (1)

As a non-inflectional language, Chinese relies heavily on word order in specifying the relationships between words and phrases. For example, 经济发展 means "economical development," while 发展经济 becomes "develop the economy." Typically, elements in a sentence take the following order:

(Attribute → **Subject**)   //   (Adverbial → **Predicate** ← Complement) + (Attribute → **Object**)
       Topic   Comment

Here, a double slash is used to separate the topic and the comment, the two sections in a complete sentence. If the predicate is a verb, the basic structure Subject + Predicate + Object would coincide with the typical English word order SVO. Subject and object can have attributive modifiers; predicates, on the other hand, can be modified by preceding adverbials and/or succeeding complements. In certain cases this order may show variations.

Now let's go over three major sentence patterns in Chinese. In the following examples subjects are double-underlined, predicates single-underlined, objects dot-underlined, and the topics and comments in the sentences are separated by a double slash.

- Subject + verbal predicate + object (S + VP + O)
  不同国家的制度 // 存在各种差异。
  他们 // 下个月要参加一个贸易洽谈。
  马可 // 又看了一遍手里的资料。
  同事们 // 一下子把话都说清楚了。

- Subject + adjectival predicate (S + AP)
  中国的经济实力 // 强了。
  客户 // 非常满意。

- Subject + 是 + nominal predicative (S 是 NP).
  信息 // 是企业的耳目。
  世贸 // 是一个国际组织。

You should already know that a sentence element is not necessary a word or a phrase. It can be as complicated as a sentence structure itself, such as the object 我不喝酒 in the following sentence: 他们 知道 我不喝酒。

PRACTICE: Mark the subjects, predicates, and objects as per the above examples.

1　我 正在这儿做 准备 呢。

2　他 参加了 对中国市场的调查和分析。

3　马可的实习 进行得很顺利。

4　中国的市场 这么大这么新。

5　人民币 越来越值钱了。

6　市场营销 是 实现企业目标的关键。

REVIEW PRACTICE: Categorize the following two-character compounds according to their internal structures. (Refer to Li's learning guide if necessary.)

热情, 失去, 报价, 风险, 耳目, 目标, 独立, 供求, 弄清, 推进, 让步, 差异

1　Synonyms or antonyms

2　Modifying + modified

3　Verb + complement

4　Verb + object

5　Subject + predicate

第五课 企业管理

Lesson 5 *Business administration*

课文一 Text 1

　　企业管理是企业对生产经营活动进行组织、计划、指挥、监督和调节的总称。企业的具体业务活动，如人力资源管理、财务管理、生产管理、采购管理、营销管理等，通常由专门的职能部门来进行。

　　一般来说，企业管理经历了三个阶段：经验管理阶段，科学管理阶段及文化管理阶段。在企业发展的初期，因为规模较小，基本上靠人治，以经验管理为主。当企业规模较大时，人治显得力不从心，因而在管理中引进了规章制度，这就是科学管理。经验管理和科学管理都是从外部对员工进行控制，通过惩罚或奖励来实现。但人是有感情的，多数人喜欢挑战，愿意努力，积极向上。这样，当企业发展到一定的程度，就出现了以人为本的管理理念，即文化管理。尤其在当前的知识经济时期，尊重人性和实现个人价值变得更为重要。当然，文化管理并不排斥科学管理和经验管理。这三种管理方式的完美结合才是一个企业的成功之道。

　　许多中国企业已经认识到，由于中国的国情不同，在学习西方现代管理科学时必须把西方的管理模式中国化。因此，它们在管理过程中特别注意中国人的文化传统及心理行为特性。

　　企業管理是企業對生產經營活動進行組織、計劃、指揮、監督和調節的總稱。企業的具體業務活動，如人力資源管理、財務管理、生產管理、採購管理、營銷管理等，通常由專門的職能部門來進行。

　　一般來說，企業管理經歷了三個階段：經驗管理階段，科學管理階段及文化管理階段。在企業發展的初期，因為規模較小，基本上靠人治，以經驗管理為主。當企業規模較大時，人治顯得力不從心，因而在管理中引進了規章制度，這就是科學管理。經驗管理和科學管理都是從外部對員工進行控制，通過懲罰或獎勵來實現。但人是有感情的，多數人喜歡挑戰，願意努力，積極向上。這樣，當企業發展到一定的程度，就出現了以人為本的管理理念，即文化管理。尤其在當前的知識經濟時期，尊重人性和實現個人價值變得更為重要。當然，文化管理並不排斥科學管理和經驗管理。這三種管理方式的完美結合才是一個企業的成功之道。

　　許多中國企業已經認識到，由於中國的國情不同，在學習西方現代管理科學時必須把西方的管理模式中國化。因此，它們在管理過程中特別注意中國人的文化傳統及心理行為特性。

词语表 Words and expressions

(* Refer to notes or language tips following the word list.)

I	指挥	指揮	zhǐhuī	direct; command
2	监督	監督	jiāndū	supervise; watch over
3	总称	總稱	zǒngchēng	general term
4	具体	具體	jùtǐ	concrete; specific
5	业务	業務	yèwù	business
6	人力		rénlì	manpower
7	资源	資源	zīyuán	resource
8	财务	財務	cáiwù	finance; financial affair
9	采购	採購	cǎigòu	purchase (for an organization or enterprise); 买; 购买
10	专门	專門	zhuānmén	special; specially; specialized
11	职能	職能	zhínéng	function
12	部门	部門	bùmén	department of an organization
13	经历	經歷	jīnglì	go through; undergo an experience
14	阶段	階段	jiēduàn	phase; stage

15	科学	科學	kēxué	*science; scientific*
16	初期		chūqī	*beginning period*
17	基本		jīběn	*basic; essential*
18	人治		rénzhì	*rule by men*
19	显得	顯得	xiǎnde	*look; seem; appear;* 看起来
20	力不从心	力不從心	lì bù cóng xīn	*ability falling short of one's wishes*
21	引进	引進	yǐnjìn	*introduce from elsewhere; import*
22	规章	規章	guīzhāng	*rules; regulations*
23	员工	員工	yuángōng	*staff; personnel*
24	控制		kòngzhì	*control*
25	惩罚	懲罰	chéngfá	*punish; punishment*
26	奖励	獎勵	jiǎnglì	*award; reward with honor or money*
27	感情		gǎnqíng	*emotion; sentiment*
28	积极	積極	jījí	*active; positive*
29	程度		chéngdù	*degree; extent*
30	以人为本	以人為本	yǐ rén wéi běn	*people-oriented; person-centered*
31	理念		lǐniàn	*concept*
32	尤其*		yóuqí	*especially; particularly;* 特别
33	当前	當前	dāngqián	*present; current;* 目前
34	知识	知識	zhīshi	*knowledge*
35	尊重		zūnzhòng	*respect*
36	人性		rénxìng	*human nature; humanity*
37	价值	價值	jiàzhí	*value*
38	排斥		páichì	*exclude; reject*
39	完美		wánměi	*perfect; flawless*
40	结合	結合	jiéhé	*combine; combination*
41	国情	國情	guóqíng	*conditions of a country*
42	模式		móshì	*mode*
43	过程	過程	guòchéng	*process; course*
44	心理		xīnlǐ	*psychology; psychological*
45	行为	行為	xíngwéi	*behavior; act*
46	特性		tèxìng	*characteristic; special property*

理解考核 Comprehension check

对错选择 True or false

		True	False
I	企业的人力资源管理、财务管理、生产管理、采购管理、营销管理等通常是由专门的职能部门来负责的。	☐	☐
2	不管是经验管理还是科学管理，它们都是从外部对员工进行控制，通过奖惩来实现的。	☐	☐
3	企业管理到了文化管理阶段就不再需要经验管理和科学管理了。	☐	☐
4	由于国情不同，中国企业不能学习现代的西方管理模式。	☐	☐
5	管理中国企业应该特别注意中国人的文化传统和心理行为特性。	☐	☐

语言提示 Language tips

I 以 N 为 Adj: have N as Adj, where the Adj is often monosyllabic.

- 在企业发展的初期，因为规模较小，基本上靠人治，<u>以</u>经验管理<u>为</u>主。
- 当企业发展到一定的程度，就出现了<u>以</u>人<u>为</u>本的管理理念。

我们班的学生<u>以</u>本科生<u>为</u>主。
企业的发展应<u>以</u>长远目标<u>为</u>重。

2 因而: as a result; therefore; thus

- 当企业规模较大时，人治显得力不从心，<u>因而</u>在管理中引进了规章制度。

该国劳动力成本很低，<u>因而</u>吸引了不少外资。
这家公司拥有大量的专业人才和管理人才，<u>因而</u>很有实力。

3 尤其: especially; particularly

- 当企业发展到一定的程度，就出现了...文化管理。<u>尤其</u>在当前...，尊重人性...变得更为重要。

金融人才现在很受欢迎。<u>尤其</u>在中国，懂外语的金融人才很容易找到工作。
各地存在的差异，<u>尤其</u>是政策和法规方面的不同，我们得特别注意。

4 由于: owing to; as a result of

- 由于中国的国情不同，在学习西方现代管理科学时必须把西方的管理模式中国化。

  由于社会是不断进步的，管理理念也一直在发生变化。
  由于人民币升值，中国的出口企业都感到了压力。

课文二 Text 2

马可在上海除了实习，还选修了一门经济课，有时也参加一些学术活动。这天，他和经济课的同学李瑛瑛一起，去参加了一个人力资源管理的讲座。讲座完了以后，两个人坐在店里喝咖啡，谈得津津有味。

李瑛瑛: 你觉得今天的讲座怎么样？

马　可: 好极了，特别是那个百度的例子让我深受启发。以前我只知道百度是一个中文搜索引擎。别的什么都不知道。

李瑛瑛: 百度在中国家喻户晓。他们从2000年创立时的十几个人，到成为全球最大的中文搜索引擎，只用了五年的时间。

马　可: 听了今天的讲座，我明白了他们的成功不是偶然的。我对他们的人力资源管理特别佩服。

李瑛瑛: 我也是。我觉得他们在企业发展的不同阶段实行不同重点的人力资源管理，正是这一点确保了他们的成功。

马　可: 一个企业的发展要经过引入期、成长期、成熟期和衰退期。每个时期对人力资源的要求是不一样的。百度的人力资源管理以公司上市的时间为界，分为两个阶段，这是很英明的。

李瑛瑛: 是啊。在创业初期，他们基本上是开发产品和技术，需要的是专业技术人员和研发人员。到了成长期，关键就变成能不能把成熟的产品推向市场了。特别是上市以后，把握市场和提升企业品牌都变得更加重要，这时候对人才的需求也就不一样了。

马　可：　管理也必须更规范了。比如他们建立的《职业道德与行
　　　　　为规范》就很成功。

李瑛瑛：　对。从这个意义上来说，百度在人力资源管理上真正做
　　　　　到了与时俱进。

马　可：　嗨，你在百度有熟人吗？

李瑛瑛：　什么意思？

马　可：　想去那儿工作啊！

李瑛瑛：　那你赶巧了，百度的老总是我叔。

马　可：　真的吗？"君子成人之美。"那就多多拜托了。

李瑛瑛：　你呀，就"做梦娶媳妇儿"吧。我这是跟你开玩笑呢。

　　馬可在上海除了實習，還選修了一門經濟課，有時也參加一
些學術活動。這天，他和經濟課的同學李瑛瑛一起，去參加了一
個人力資源管理的講座。講座完了以後，兩個人坐在店裡喝咖
啡，談得津津有味。

李瑛瑛：　你覺得今天的講座怎麼樣？

馬　可：　好極了，特別是那個百度的例子讓我深受啟發。以前我
　　　　　只知道百度是一個中文搜尋引擎。別的什麼都不知道。

李瑛瑛：　百度在中國家喻戶曉。他們從2000年創立時的十幾個
　　　　　人，到成為全球最大的中文搜索引擎，只用了五年的時間。

馬　可：聽了今天的講座，我明白了他們的成功不是偶然的。我對他們的人力資源管理特別佩服。

李瑛瑛：我也是。我覺得他們在企業發展的不同階段實行不同重點的人力資源管理，正是這一點確保了他們的成功。

馬　可：一個企業的發展要經過引入期、成長期、成熟期和衰退期。每個時期對人力資源的要求是不一樣的。百度的人力資源管理以公司上市的時間為界，分為兩個階段，這是很英明的。

李瑛瑛：是啊。在創業初期，他們基本上是開發產品和技術，需要的是專業技術人員和研發人員。到了成長期，關鍵就變成能不能把成熟的產品推向市場了。特別是上市以後，把握市場和提升企業品牌都變得更加重要，這時候對人才的需求也就不一樣了。

馬　可：管理也必須更規範了。比如他們建立的《職業道德與行為規範》就很成功。

李瑛瑛：對。從這個意義上來說，百度在人力資源管理上真正做到了與時俱進。

馬　可：嗨，你在百度有熟人嗎？

李瑛瑛：什麼意思？

馬　可：想去那兒工作啊！

李瑛瑛：那你趕巧了，百度的老總是我叔。

馬　可：真的嗎？"君子成人之美。"那就多多拜託了。

李瑛瑛：你呀，就"做夢娶媳婦兒"吧。我這是跟你開玩笑呢。

词语表 Words and expressions

(* Refer to notes or language tips following the word list.)

1	学术	學術	xuéshù	*systematic learning; academic*
2	讲座	講座	jiǎngzuò	*lecture*
3	津津有味		jīnjīn yǒu wèi	*(to eat) with appetite and relish; (to read or listen) with great interest*
4	例子		lìzi	*example; instance*

5	深受启发	深受啟發	shēn shòu qǐfā	*be greatly inspired*
6	搜索		sōusuǒ	*search*
7	引擎		yǐnqíng	*engine*
8	家喻户晓	家喻戶曉	jiā yù hù xiǎo	*known to every family and household; widely known*
9	创立	創立	chuànglì	*found; form*
10	偶然*		ǒurán	*accidental; by chance*
11	佩服		pèifú	*admire*
12	实行	實行	shíxíng	*put into practice*
13	重点	重點	zhòngdiǎn	*emphasis; the focal (or key) point*
14	确保	確保	quèbǎo	*ensure; assure*
15	引入		yǐnrù	*introduce from elsewhere;* 引进
16	成熟		chéngshú	*ripe; mature*
17	衰退		shuāituì	*decay; recession*
18	界*		jiè	*boundary*
19	英明		yīngmíng	*wise; brilliant*
20	创业	創業	chuàngyè	*start an enterprise*
21	开发	開發	kāifā	*open up and develop*
22	研发	研發	yánfā	*research and development;* 研究开发
23	推		tuī	*push forward*
24	把握		bǎwò	*grasp; seize (an opportunity)*
25	提升		tíshēng	*upgrade*
26	品牌		pǐnpái	*brand*
27	人才		réncái	*person of talent*
28	规范	規範	guīfàn	*standard; norm*
29	建立		jiànlì	*build up; establish*
30	职业	職業	zhíyè	*profession; professional*
31	道德		dàodé	*morals; ethics*
32	意义*	意義	yìyì	*sense; meaning; significance*
33	与时俱进	與時俱進	yǔ shí jù jìn	*advance with the times*

34	熟人		shúrén	*acquaintance*
35	赶巧	趕巧	gǎnqiǎo	*it so happened that*
36	老总	老總	lǎozǒng	*general manager*
37	拜托	拜託	bàituō	*entrust sth to sb; request a favor*

俗语 Common sayings

1	君子成人之美*		jūnzǐ chéng rén zhī měi	*A gentleman is always ready to help others attain their goals.*
2	做梦娶媳妇儿*	做夢娶媳婦兒	zuòmèng qǔ xífur	*a marriage that only happens in one's dreams*

理解考核 Comprehension check

回答问题 Answer the following questions

1 "百度"是一家什么样的公司？他们的发展迅速吗？

2 李瑛瑛觉得是什么确保了"百度"的成功？

3 一个企业的发展要经历哪几个时期？

4 "百度"的人力资源管理分为几个阶段？是怎么分的？

5 李瑛瑛跟马可开了个什么玩笑？

注释 Notes

1 君子成人之美

A gentleman should help others to fulfill their honorable goals. Reflecting a high virtue advocated by Confucius and his disciples, this saying is quite popular among well-educated Chinese people.

2 做梦娶媳妇儿

This common saying carries a derogatory sense, referring to wishful thinking.

语言提示 Language tips

1　特别是: By citing an example, this expression lays emphasis on a specific aspect or issue while making a general statement. The synonymic 尤其是 sounds more formal.

■ . . . ，<u>特别是</u>那个百度的例子让我深受启发。

中国的不少方面，<u>特别是</u>劳动力和消费市场，对外国企业有吸引力。
那儿的房价一直在上升，<u>特别是</u>最近几年涨得非常厉害。

2　不是偶然的: While the meaning of the expression is self-explanatory, its tone can be made stronger by adding a 决 at the beginning.

■ 听了今天的讲座，我明白了他们的成功<u>不是偶然的</u>。

这次谈判双方都做了不少准备，所以谈得顺利<u>不是偶然的</u>。
小王学习努力，实习经验也不少，他找到这个好工作<u>决不是偶然的</u>。

3　以 . . . 为界，分为 . . . : with . . . as the boundary or demarcation line, be divided into . . .

■ 百度的人力资源管理<u>以</u>公司上市的时间<u>为界</u>，<u>分为</u>两个阶段，这是很英明的。

不少人以为中国<u>以</u>长江<u>为界</u>，<u>分为</u>南方和北方。
他们学校<u>以</u>一条河<u>为界</u>，<u>分为</u>南校区和北校区。

4　从这个意义上来说: judging or judged in this sense

■ <u>从这个意义上来说</u>，百度在人力资源管理上真正做到了与时俱进。

人类的生存离不开环境，<u>从这个意义上来说</u>，我们决不能让经济活动破坏环境。
企业是社会的重要组成部分，<u>从这个意义上来说</u>，企业的发展能促进社会的进步。

练习 Exercises

1　将左栏的定语和右栏的名词或名词短语配对，每个词语只能用一次。
Match each attributive modifier in the left column with an appropriate noun or noun phrase in the right column. Each item can be used only once.

1) 突出的 _____　　a) 实力

2) 雄厚的 _____　　b) 底线

3) 丰富的 _____　　c) 技术人员

4) 专门的 _____　　d) 管理策略

5) 积极的 ＿＿＿＿＿　　　　e) 职能部门

6) 英明的 ＿＿＿＿＿　　　　f) 态度

7) 让步的 ＿＿＿＿＿　　　　g) 信息

8) 专业的 ＿＿＿＿＿　　　　h) 问题

2　听写并用汉语解释下列词组。Complete a dictation of the following phrases and explain them in Chinese.

1) 人力资源管理　　　　7) 搜索引擎

2) 力不从心　　　　　　8) 企业成长期

3) 以人为本　　　　　　9) 与时俱进

4) 知识经济时期　　　10) 职业道德

5) 津津有味　　　　　11) 君子成人之美

6) 家喻户晓　　　　　12) 做梦娶媳妇

3　选词填空。Fill in the blanks with the provided words and expressions.

1) 当前，尤其，因而，显得，由于

　　＿＿＿＿＿ 企业的经验管理和科学管理都是从外部对员工进行控制，当企业发展到一定的程度就会力不从心，＿＿＿＿＿ 就出现了以人为本的文化管理。＿＿＿＿＿ 在 ＿＿＿＿＿ 的知识经济时期，文化管理 ＿＿＿＿＿ 更为重要。

2) 以人为本，家喻户晓，与时俱进，深受启发

　　"百度"是一家 ＿＿＿＿＿ 的中文搜索引擎。他们 ＿＿＿＿＿，在企业发展的不同阶段实行不同重点的人力资源管理，做到了 ＿＿＿＿＿。他们的成功使很多中国企业 ＿＿＿＿＿。

4　用指定的表达方式完成句子或对话。Complete the following sentences with the designated words or expressions.

1) 特别是

a) 在贸易洽谈以前要做很多准备，＿＿＿＿＿＿＿＿＿＿＿＿＿＿＿＿＿＿＿＿＿＿＿。

b) 国际贸易的风险比较大，＿＿＿＿＿＿＿＿＿＿＿＿＿＿＿＿＿＿＿＿＿＿＿＿＿。

2) 不是偶然的

    a) 他积极努力，是个喜欢挑战的人，＿＿＿＿＿＿＿＿＿＿＿＿＿＿。

    b) 这家公司进入中国时完全不考虑中国市场的特殊性，＿＿＿＿＿＿＿

    ＿＿＿＿＿＿＿＿＿＿＿＿＿＿＿＿＿＿＿＿＿＿＿＿＿＿＿＿。

3) 从这个意义上来说

    a) 人民币升值使很多外贸出口企业失去了价格优势，＿＿＿＿＿＿＿＿＿

    ＿＿＿＿＿＿＿＿＿＿＿＿＿＿＿＿＿＿＿＿＿＿＿＿＿＿＿＿。

    b) 中国股票在香港市场上所占的份额越来越大，＿＿＿＿＿＿＿＿＿＿＿

    ＿＿＿＿＿＿＿＿＿＿＿＿＿＿＿＿＿＿＿＿＿＿＿＿＿＿＿＿。

5 把下面的句子改成不太正式的语体。 Paraphrase the following sentences in a less formal style, paying special attention to the underlined words and phrases.

1) 很多企业<u>在其</u>发展<u>初期由于</u>规模较小，<u>基本上以</u>经验管理<u>为主</u>。

    ＿＿＿＿＿＿＿＿＿＿＿＿＿＿＿＿＿＿＿＿＿＿＿＿＿＿＿＿＿＿＿＿。

2) 中国经济<u>以</u>改革开放<u>为界</u>，<u>之前</u>实行计划经济，<u>之后</u>改为市场经济。<u>后者</u><u>以</u>促进经济发展，提高人民生活水平<u>为重</u>。

    ＿＿＿＿＿＿＿＿＿＿＿＿＿＿＿＿＿＿＿＿＿＿＿＿＿＿＿＿＿＿＿＿

    ＿＿＿＿＿＿＿＿＿＿＿＿＿＿＿＿＿＿＿＿＿＿＿＿＿＿＿＿＿＿＿＿。

3) <u>在</u>经营规模不断扩大的<u>趋势下</u>，经验管理显得<u>力不从心</u>，<u>因而引进</u>了使用规章制度的管理，<u>即</u>科学管理。

    ＿＿＿＿＿＿＿＿＿＿＿＿＿＿＿＿＿＿＿＿＿＿＿＿＿＿＿＿＿＿＿＿

    ＿＿＿＿＿＿＿＿＿＿＿＿＿＿＿＿＿＿＿＿＿＿＿＿＿＿＿＿＿＿＿＿。

4) 美洲大陆<u>以</u>巴拿马运河(*Bānámǎ Yùnhé*, Panama Canal)<u>为界</u>分为南北美洲。运河的北部<u>称为</u>北美洲，南部<u>则被称为</u>南美洲。

    ＿＿＿＿＿＿＿＿＿＿＿＿＿＿＿＿＿＿＿＿＿＿＿＿＿＿＿＿＿＿＿＿

    ＿＿＿＿＿＿＿＿＿＿＿＿＿＿＿＿＿＿＿＿＿＿＿＿＿＿＿＿＿＿＿＿。

5) <u>由于</u>成功的企业管理，<u>尤其</u>是成功的人力资源管理，"百度"公司迅速发展<u>成为</u>家喻户晓的中文搜索引擎。

    ＿＿＿＿＿＿＿＿＿＿＿＿＿＿＿＿＿＿＿＿＿＿＿＿＿＿＿＿＿＿＿＿

    ＿＿＿＿＿＿＿＿＿＿＿＿＿＿＿＿＿＿＿＿＿＿＿＿＿＿＿＿＿＿＿＿。

6 自行查找参考资料，解释与本课话题有关的词语。Using available resources as a reference, explain the following terms, which are related to this lesson's topic.

1) 管理决策　　　4) 企业文化

2) 业务流程　　　5) 企业竞争力

3) 目标与绩效管理　6) 企业并购和重组

7 阅读理解与讨论。Reading comprehension and discussion.

摩托罗拉的绩效管理

　　摩托罗拉公司(Motorola, Inc.)是全球芯片制造和电子通信的领导者，世界财富百强企业之一。该公司认为"创新、利润、人才是公司生存的保障，"为了实现其人才战略，必须加强绩效管理。他们的指导思想是："企业 = 产品 + 服务；企业管理 = 人力资源管理；人力资源管理 = 绩效管理。"正是这样的重视程度，使得摩托罗拉的绩效管理成为了业界的楷模。

　　摩托罗拉的绩效管理是一个完整的系统，由五个部分组成：一、绩效计划：强调员工和主管是合作伙伴关系，双方共同决定员工全年的绩效目标，包括业务目标和行为标准。二、持续不断的绩效沟通：在整个过程中强调全年的沟通和全渠道的沟通。三、事实的收集、观察和记录：主管通过平时的努力为年终考核做准备。四、绩效评估会议：定期召开会议，不仅评估员工，而且解决问题。五、绩效的诊断和改进：不断提高绩效管理水平。至于绩效结果的运用，摩托罗拉的做法是论功行赏。

绩效	jìxiào	performance and results	主管	zhǔguǎn	chief; director
芯片	xīnpiàn	(electronic) chip	包括	bāokuò	include; embrace
制造	zhìzào	make; manufacture	标准	biāozhǔn	standard; criterion
电子	diànzǐ	electron; electronic	持续不断	chíxù bùduàn	continue; continuous
通信	tōngxìn	communication	事实	shìshí	fact
领导	lǐngdǎo	lead; leading	收集	shōují	collect; gather
财富	cáifù	wealth; fortune	观察	guānchá	observe; observation
百强	bǎiqiáng	top hundred	记录	jìlù	note-taking; record
创新	chuàngxīn	innovate; innovation	年终	niánzhōng	end of the year
生存	shēngcún	exist; survive	考核	kǎohé	check; review; assessment
保障	bǎozhàng	ensure; guarantee	评估	pínggū	assess; evaluate
战略	zhànlüè	strategy	召开	zhàokāi	hold (a meeting)
加强	jiāqiáng	strengthen; enhance	解决	jiějué	settle; solve
指导	zhǐdǎo	guide; direct	诊断	zhěnduàn	diagnosis
业界	yèjiè	business circle	改进	gǎijìn	improve
楷模	kǎimó	model	提高	tígāo	raise
完整	wánzhěng	complete; full	至于	zhìyú	as for; as to
系统	xìtǒng	system	论功行赏	lùn gōng xíng shǎng	award people according to their contribution
强调	qiángdiào	emphasize			

选择填空 Select the correct answer for each blank.

1) 摩托罗拉认为 _____ 是公司生存的保障。

   a) 产品＋服务

   b) 创新、利润、人才

   c) 人力资源管理

2) 摩托罗拉员工的绩效目标 _____。

   a) 是由员工自己决定的

   b) 是由主管决定的

   c) 是由员工和主管共同决定的

3) 绩效评估会议的目的是 _____。

   a) 评估员工

   b) 评估主管

   c) 评估员工而且解决问题

4) 对于绩效结果的运用，摩托罗拉的做法是 _____。

   a) 论功行赏

   b) 奖罚分明

   c) 不予考虑

讨论 Discussion.

　　摩托罗拉的绩效管理为什么能够成为业界的楷模？ 根据你了解的情况或所查的资料，请你谈谈摩托罗拉（中国）公司的管理情况。Why has Motorola's performance management become a model in business circles? Can you remark upon the administration of Motorola (China) based on what you know or what you have found via research?

8 实践活动。Tasks.

1) 用中文和英文写出企业常用的 12–15 个职务名称。Make a list of 12–15 commonly used administrative titles in the business world. Each title should be provided in Chinese and English.

2) 做一个10分钟的口头报告，介绍一个成功的企业或失败的企业。可以谈该企业某一个方面的管理（如人力资源管理、财务管理、生产管理、采购管理、营销管理等），也可以对该企业进行全面介绍，目的是说明它为什么成功或失败。先查看最近六个月之内的资料，然后根据老师的要求为自己准备一个简单的提纲。Give a ten-minute oral report about a successful or unsuccessful company. As long as you show why it has succeeded or failed, you may choose to focus on one aspect of its administration (e.g. human resources management,

financial management, manufacturing management, purchasing management, marketing management) or present an overall picture. Ideally, you should base your report on information from within the past six months and prepare a brief outline for yourself as per your teacher's instructions.

3) 选一个你感兴趣的公司，写一篇400个字左右的报道，简单介绍该公司最近一年来的两个或三个主要的管理决策和变动，并加上你自己的看法。Pick a company you are interested in and write a short report of about 400 characters to introduce two or three of its major administrative decisions and changes from the past year. Be sure to include your own comments.

4) 如果你对一个不同的任务有兴趣，请结合本课的主题向老师提出建议，然后在老师的指导下完成这个任务。If you are interested in a different kind of task, you are encouraged to suggest your proposal and to complete it under your teacher's guidance.

学习指导 Learning guide

语序（二）Word order (2)

- Modifying + Modified

  As a "left-branching" language, Chinese typically places modifiers before the word they modify. The modifiers are all underlined in the following examples:

  企业 目标　　中国的 国情　　独立于联合国的 永久性 国际 组织
  更好地 提供　　多多 拜托　　从外部 对员工 进行控制

  Notes: 1) An exception is the order of a verb and its complement, which always occurs after the verb, such as in 发展 得很快. 2) Multiple modifiers may represent different modifying relationships in different cases. For example, in 实时通讯工具, 通讯 modifies 工具，while 实时 modifies 通讯工具, but in 知识经济 时期, 知识 modifies 经济, and 知识经济 as a special term modifies 时期.

- General + specific

  This order applies to units of time, addresses, etc.:

  2011 年 5 月 14 日 上午 9 时 30 分
  中国 上海市 浦东新区 申江路 1500号 上海通用汽车有限公司
  北京大学 社会科学部 经济学院 金融学系

- Inversion

  Inversion signifies a diversion from the typical SVO order in a sentence. A frequently observed inversion is OSV, which gives importance to the object and keeps the object as the topic in the context. An example from Lesson 3 is:

  方总的意思 我 懂。

PRACTICE: Form meaningful, grammatical, and natural sentences with the given words and phrases.

1　靠　基本上　规模小的　人治　企业

2　特别　到国外投资的　都　商人　小心

3　津津有味　两个人　得　谈　在咖啡店里

4　标识　10月　世贸组织　1997年　新的　启用　9日

5　外贸司　马可的　在　商务部　实习　女朋友　进口处　中国
(部 Ministry, 司 Department, 处 Division: PRC central government offices of varying levels)

6　说　同意　你　这样　很　我 (in OSV order)

词语搭配 Collocation

Just as you use "strong" but not "powerful" for "coffee" in English, you can only use a certain word to go with another word so as to sound natural in Chinese. If you use flash cards, do not discard them after using them for a single lesson. A good approach is to keep reorganizing and reusing them as you add new usage information, such as collocation, to them.

What follows are examples of collocation from previous lessons in this book.

- Verb and object
  改善-条件　实现-目标　获得-利润　存在-差异　导致-纠纷
  起-作用　留-面子　下-功夫　顶得住-压力　认识到-重要性

- Subject and predicate
  价格:上涨/下跌　货币:升值/贬值　实力:强/弱　汇率:高/低

- Modifier and modified
  丰富的-信息　更高的-权威性　充分-开发　进行-得很顺利

- Classifier and noun
  一门课　一套方案　一种方式　一番功夫　一家公司

With these examples, we mean to advise you to learn a word along with its collocating word. It is always better to remember a phrase than an isolated word. This principle applies to many other cases such as prepositional phrases:

对 ... 的看法　经 ... 的介绍　由于 ... 的不同　随着 ... 的发展
由 ... 决定　对 ... 特别佩服　向 ... 表示祝贺　跟 ... 学着点儿

PRACTICE: Start making lists of collocated words to use in reviewing previous lessons and learning new lessons.

REVIEW PRACTICE: Based on your knowledge of characters and character components, review or figure out the meanings of the following items, which will all occur in the following lesson: (Refer to L2's learning guide if necessary.)

1　销售; 共同

2　网点; 子公司; 对手; 卖场; 中期; 先机; 售后

3　扩大; 加强

4　合资; 分工

5　本土化

第六课 跨国经营

Lesson 6 *Transnational operations*

课文一 Text 1

　　跨国公司又称为国际公司或多国公司，由位于两个或两个以上国家的经济实体组成，从全球策略出发安排生产、销售和其他经营活动。跨国企业大多实力雄厚，具有信息、资金和技术方面的优势。部分跨国企业的某些产品在一些地区带有不同程度的垄断性。

　　跨国经营是指跨国企业通过对外直接投资，在国外建立子公司或分支机构，并以此为基础展开跨国界的、以赢利为目的的生产经营活动。企业跨国经营的性质多种多样，但大多是为了获得资源、劳动力、人才、技术、市场等生产要素的比较优势，在世界范围内建立最佳的生产地区、销售地区和原材料供应基地。

　　跨国经营的发展主要经历以下三个阶段。第一，建立国外营销网点，扩大国外销售。第二，在国外投资设厂，直接进行生产和销售。第三，在国外直接进行生产和销售的同时，实现企业内部的国际性分工，形成联合的整体优势，以达到共同占领国际市场的目的。

　　跨国公司的发展推动了生产要素在全球范围内的流动，促进了世界产业结构的调整，也促进了科学技术的不断创新和推广，从而加速了世界经济的发展。

　　跨國公司又稱為國際公司或多國公司，由位於兩個或兩個以上國家的經濟實體組成，從全球策略出發安排生產、銷售和其他經營活動。跨國企業大多實力雄厚，具有信息、資金和技術方面的優勢。部分跨國企業的某些產品在一些地區帶有不同程度的壟斷性。

跨國經營是指跨國企業通過對外直接投資，在國外建立子公司或分支機搆，並以此為基礎展開跨國界的、以贏利為目的的生產經營活動。企業跨國經營的性質多種多樣，但大多是為了獲得資源、勞動力、人才、技術、市場等生產要素的比較優勢，在世界範圍內建立最佳的生產地區、銷售地區和原材料供應基地。

跨國經營的發展主要經歷以下三個階段。第一，建立國外營銷網點，擴大國外銷售。第二，在國外投資設廠，直接進行生產和銷售。第三，在國外直接進行生產和銷售的同時，實現企業內部的國際性分工，形成聯合的整體優勢，以達到共同佔領國際市場的目的。

跨國公司的發展推動了生產要素在全球範圍內的流動，促進了世界產業結構的調整，也促進了科學技術的不斷創新和推廣，從而加速了世界經濟的發展。

词语表 Words and expressions

1	跨国	跨國	kuàguó	*transnational*
2	实体	實體	shítǐ	*entity*
3	安排		ānpái	*arrange*
4	销售	銷售	xiāoshòu	*sell; sale;* 卖
5	雄厚		xiónghòu	*solid; abundant*
6	垄断	壟斷	lǒngduàn	*monopolize; monopolization*
7	直接		zhíjiē	*direct; directly*
8	子公司		zǐgōngsī	*subsidiary company*
9	分支		fēnzhī	*branch; division*
10	展开	展開	zhǎnkāi	*unfold; carry out;* 开展
11	国界	國界	guójiè	*national boundary or border*
12	赢利	贏利	yínglì	*earn a profit;* 盈利; 赚钱
13	性质	性質	xìngzhì	*nature; character*
14	比较	比較	bǐjiào	*relative; relatively*
15	佳		jiā	*good; superior;* 好

16	原材料		yuáncáiliào	*raw material*
17	基地		jīdì	*base of operations*
18	网点	網點	wǎngdiǎn	*network point*
19	扩大	擴大	kuòdà	*expand; broaden the scope*
20	设	設	shè	*establish; set up;* 办
21	厂	廠	chǎng	*factory*
22	分工		fēngōng	*division of work*
23	联合	聯合	liánhé	*unite; ally*
24	整体	整體	zhěngtǐ	*overall; whole; entirety*
25	共同		gòngtóng	*together;* 一起
26	占领	佔領	zhànlǐng	*occupy*
27	推动	推動	tuīdòng	*push forward*
28	结构	結構	jiégòu	*structure*
29	调整	調整	tiáozhěng	*adjust; regulate*
30	不断	不斷	bùduàn	*continuously*
31	创新	創新	chuàngxīn	*innovate; innovation*
32	推广	推廣	tuīguǎng	*popularize; expand the use of*
33	加速		jiāsù	*speed up; accelerate*

理解考核 Comprehension check

对错选择 True or false

		True	False
1	跨国公司必须由位于两个或两个以上国家的经济实体组成。	☐	☐
2	跨国经营是一种跨国界的，以营利为目的的生产经营活动。	☐	☐
3	企业跨国经营只有一种性质，就是为了获得某些生产要素的比较优势。	☐	☐
4	实现企业内部的国际分工，是跨国经营发展的第二个阶段。	☐	☐
5	跨国公司的发展加速了世界经济的发展。	☐	☐

语言提示 Language tips

1 从 . . . 出发: start from . . . in doing sth

   ■ 跨国公司 . . . <u>从</u>全球策略<u>出发</u>安排 . . . 经营活动。

   一个企业必须<u>从</u>实际情况<u>出发</u>确定目标市场。
   这门课要求学生<u>从</u>理论<u>出发</u>研究各种实际问题。

2 具有 . . . 的优势: have advantage in

   ■ 跨国企业大多实力雄厚，<u>具有</u>信息、资金和技术方面<u>的优势</u>。

   跟中小城市相比，大城市<u>具有</u>科技和人才方面<u>的优势</u>。
   有些企业在资金和技术等方面<u>具有</u>明显<u>的优势</u>，却在市场竞争中失
   败了。

3 以 V: so as to; in order to

   ■ 跨国公司 . . . 实现企业内部的国际性分工，. . . <u>以</u>达到共同占领国际
   市场的目的。

   他们努力把西方的管理模式中国化，<u>以</u>适合中国的国情。
   各大公司都努力吸引创新型人才，<u>以</u>推动新技术的研究和开发。

4 达到 . . . 的目的: attain the goal of

   ■ 跨国公司 . . . 实现企业内部的国际性分工，. . . 以<u>达到</u>共同占领国际
   市场<u>的目的</u>。

   新的房地产政策基本上<u>达到</u>了改善居民居住条件<u>的目的</u>。
   这次促销<u>达到</u>了在本校师生中推广这种产品<u>的目的</u>。

5 从而: thus; therefore; hence; a conjunction connecting reasons, methods, etc. with
   results, purposes, etc.

   ■ 跨国公司推动了生产要素 . . . 的流动，促进了世界产业结构的调
   整，. . . <u>从而</u>加速了经济的发展。

   改革开放以后很多外企来华投资，<u>从而</u>增加了各地的就业机会。
   这次市场调查做得非常充分，<u>从而</u>使我们公司增加了大量的业务。

课文二 Text 2

　　这一天，马可和钱亮一起去一家广告公司联系业务。谈完之后，两个人从办公楼出来，走进附近的一家肯德基快餐店。他们各自买了午餐，好不容易在窗口找到一张桌子坐了下来。

钱　亮：马可，你这个美国人来这儿吃饭，该是"宾至如归"吧？

马　可：怎么说呢？刚才看菜单，什么老北京鸡肉卷啊，川香辣子鸡啊，香菇鸡肉粥啊，这都不像是肯德基了。

钱　亮：可是你想，要是不搞产品本土化，能有这么多中国人上这儿来吃饭吗？要知道，现在在中国肯德基是最受欢迎的外国品牌了。就因为它的本土化比较彻底，才把老对手麦当劳抛在了后边。

马　可：真有意思。跨国公司到了一个国家，产品啊，人才啊，管理啊，都还要面临本土化的竞争。

钱　亮：那是肯定的。你看马路对面是一个家乐福的大卖场。虽然全世界零售业的"老大"是沃尔玛，可是在中国却是家乐福第一。这又是一个本土化竞争的例子。

马　可：听说这两家公司都是在90年代中期进入中国的。当时家乐福进了上海，可是沃尔玛进不了，只好去了深圳。

钱　亮：对，沃尔玛完全自营，所以受到当时中国政策的限制。它没能最先进入上海这一点直接影响了它在全国市场的布局。而家乐福却巧妙地采取合资的方式，避开了政策上的障碍。这就是说，家乐福从一开始就在本土化方面走在了前面，所以它的发展要快得多。

马　可：你这是说，沃尔玛失去了先机。可是现在好像沃尔玛跟中国政府的关系比较好，是吧？

钱　亮：没错。这些年沃尔玛的政府公关确实做得很好。另外，沃尔玛在卖场布置、商品价格、购物享受、售后服务这些环节也都加强了本土化。许多人认为，它的经营模式和赢利模式代表了未来的发展趋势。

马　可：看来沃尔玛的厉害在后头呢。

這一天，馬可和錢亮一起去一家廣告公司聯繫業務。談完之後，兩個人從辦公樓出來，走進附近的一家肯德基快餐店。他們各自買了午餐，好不容易在窗口找到一張桌子坐了下來。

錢　亮：馬可，你這個美國人來這兒吃飯，該是"賓至如歸"吧？

馬　可：怎麼說呢？剛才看菜單，什麼老北京雞肉卷啊，川香辣子雞啊，香菇雞肉粥啊，這都不像是肯德基了。

錢　亮：可是你想，要是不搞產品本土化，能有這麼多中國人上這兒來吃飯嗎？要知道，現在在中國肯德基是最受歡迎的外國品牌了。就因為它的本土化比較徹底，才把老對手麥當勞拋在了後邊。

馬　可：真有意思。跨國公司到了一個國家，產品啊，人才啊，管理啊，都還要面臨本土化的競爭。

錢　亮：那是肯定的。你看馬路對面是一個家樂福的大賣場。雖然全世界零售業的"老大"是沃爾瑪，可是在中國卻是家樂福第一。這又是一個本土化競爭的例子。

馬　可：聽說這兩家公司都是在90年代中期進入中國的。當時家樂福進了上海，可是沃爾瑪進不了，只好去了深圳。

錢　亮：對，沃爾瑪完全自營，所以受到當時中國政策的限制。
　　　　它沒能最先進入上海這一點直接影響了它在全國市場的
　　　　佈局。而家樂福卻巧妙地採取合資的方式，避開了政策
　　　　上的障礙。這就是說，家樂福從一開始就在本土化方面
　　　　走在了前面，所以它的發展要快得多。

馬　可：你這是說，沃爾瑪失去了先機。可是現在好像沃爾瑪跟
　　　　中國政府的關係比較好，是吧？

錢　亮：沒錯。這些年沃爾瑪的政府公關確實做得很好。另外，
　　　　沃爾瑪在賣場佈置、商品價格、購物享受、售後服務這
　　　　些環節也都加強了本土化。許多人認為，它的經營模式
　　　　和贏利模式代表了未來的發展趨勢。

馬　可：看來沃爾瑪的厲害在後頭呢。

词语表 Words and expressions

(* Refer to notes or language tips following the word list.)

1	广告	廣告	guǎnggào	*advertisement; commercial*
2	联系	聯繫	liánxì	*establish contact*
3	附近		fùjìn	*vicinity; nearby*
4	各自		gèzì	*respective; respectively*
5	宾至如归	賓至如歸	bīn zhì rú guī	*Guests arrive as if they had returned home.*
6	菜单	菜單	càidān	*menu*
7	搞		gǎo	*do; carry on;* 做
8	本土		běntǔ	*local;* 本地
9	彻底	徹底	chèdǐ	*thoroughgoing; thorough*
10	对手	對手	duìshǒu	*opponent; competitor*
11	抛		pāo	*throw; fling*
12	面临	面臨	miànlín	*face;* 面对
13	马路	馬路	mǎlù	*street; road*
14	卖场	賣場	màichǎng	*marketplace*

15	零售		língshòu	retail sale
16	业	業	yè	business; industry; often as a suffix
17	自营	自營	zìyíng	self-run
18	限制		xiànzhì	limit; restriction
19	布局	佈局	bùjú	overall arrangement; layout
20	巧妙		qiǎomiào	ingenious; clever
21	采取	採取	cǎiqǔ	select and adopt (a measure, plan, etc.)
22	合资	合資	hézī	joint venture
23	避开	避開	bìkāi	avoid
24	障碍	障礙	zhàng'ài	obstacle
25	公关	公關	gōngguān	public relations
26	布置	佈置	bùzhì	arrangement and decoration
27	享受		xiǎngshòu	enjoy
28	售后	售後	shòuhòu	after-sale
29	加强	加強	jiāqiáng	strengthen; enhance
30	厉害	厲害	lìhai	power to develop; momentum

专有名词 Proper nouns

1	肯德基*		Kěndéjī	KFC
2	老北京鸡肉卷	老北京雞肉卷	Lǎo Běijīng jīròu juǎn	authentic Beijing chicken roll
3	川香辣子鸡	川香辣子雞	Chuān xiāng làzi jī	Sichuan spicy chicken
4	香菇鸡肉粥	香菇雞肉粥	Xiānggū jīròu zhōu	Mushroom chicken porridge
5	麦当劳	麥當勞	Màidāngláo	McDonald's
6	家乐福	家樂福	Jiālèfú	Carrefour
7	沃尔玛	沃爾瑪	Wòěrmǎ	Walmart

理解考核 Comprehension check

回答问题 Answer the following questions

1 马可到肯德基吃饭有没有"宾至如归"的感觉，为什么？

2 为什么现在在中国肯德基是最受欢迎的外国品牌？

3 跨国公司到了一个国家要面临哪些本土化的竞争？

4 为什么全世界零售业的"老大"是沃尔玛，在中国却是家乐福第一？

5 为什么说沃尔玛的厉害在后头呢？

注释 Notes

1 肯德基快餐店

KFC was founded as Kentucky Fried Chicken by Harland David Saunders in 1952. It is now an operating segment of the restaurant company Yum! Brands, Inc. As a popular fast food brand, KFC does not have as much market share in the United States as its competitor McDonald's. In China, however, it is the largest and fastest-growing chain of fast food restaurants. Many people attribute KFC's success in China to its early entry into China's market—its China business started in Beijing in 1987, years earlier than McDonald's, which opened its first restaurant in Shenzhen in 1990. Another important factor that has contributed to its booming China business is its successful localization.

语言提示 Language tips

1 好不容易/好容易: Both mean "not at all easy."

- 他们各自买了午餐，<u>好不容易</u>在窗口找到一张桌子坐了下来。

  洽谈的双方一直在讨价还价，今天<u>好不容易</u>签约了。
  这套房子真不便宜，他们花了10年时间才<u>好容易</u>把房款付清。

2 ...这一点: This expression anchors a topic for the sentence, to be followed by a comment.

- 它没能最先进入上海<u>这一点</u>直接影响了它在全国市场的布局。

  马可实习经验丰富<u>这一点</u>会让他在找工作时具有很大的优势。
  北京工作机会多，<u>这一点</u>吸引了不少大学毕业生。

3 这就是说: this means; this is to say

■ 家乐福却巧妙地采取合资的方式 . . . 。这就是说，家乐福 . . . 走在了前面。

中国人都比较重面子，这就是说，我们在跟中国人洽谈时得注意给对方留面子。

最近人民币又升值了，这就是说，在中国买进口商品价格更便宜了。

练习 Exercises

1 将左栏的主语部分和右栏的谓语部分配对，每个词语只能用一次。
Match each topic in the left column with an appropriate comment in the right column. Each item can be used only once.

1)	历史 _____	a)	先进
2)	速度 _____	b)	便宜
3)	汇率 _____	c)	长
4)	国情 _____	d)	快
5)	竞争力 _____	e)	高
6)	风险 _____	f)	强
7)	商品 _____	g)	多
8)	管理 _____	h)	不同
9)	好处 _____	i)	满意
10)	客户 _____	j)	大

2 听写并用汉语解释下列词组。Complete a dictation of the following phrases and explain them in Chinese.

1)	全球策略	7)	本土化
2)	子公司	8)	失去先机
3)	比较优势	9)	政府公关
4)	国际性分工	10)	购物享受
5)	产业结构	11)	售后服务
6)	宾至如归	12)	赢利模式

3　选词填空。 Fill in the blanks with the provided words and expressions.

1) 具有，出发，从而，达到，以

跨国公司 ＿＿＿＿ 多方面的优势，从全球策略 ＿＿＿＿ 安排经营活动，＿＿＿＿ ＿＿＿＿ 占领国际市场的目的。跨国公司的发展促进了世界产业结构的调整，＿＿＿＿ 加速了世界经济的发展。

2) 竞争，布局，障碍，先机，公关，本土化

跨国公司进入一个国家都会面临激烈的 ＿＿＿＿。只有在各个环节实现 ＿＿＿＿，做好 ＿＿＿＿，避开政策的 ＿＿＿＿，在全国市场巧妙 ＿＿＿＿，才能抢到 ＿＿＿＿，把对手抛在后面。

4　用指定的表达方式完成句子或对话。 Complete the following sentences and dialogues with the designated words or expressions.

1) 从...出发
   a) ＿＿＿＿＿＿＿＿＿＿＿＿＿，肯德基在中国推出了有中国特色的菜单。
   b) 成功的市场营销应该 ＿＿＿＿＿＿＿＿＿＿，比竞争者更好地提供消费者所需要的产品和服务。

2) 具有...的优势
   a) A: 为什么这些年来中国的外贸出口企业发展较快？
      B: ＿＿＿＿＿＿＿＿＿＿＿＿＿＿＿。
   b) A: 为什么许多跨国公司都进入了中国市场？
      B: ＿＿＿＿＿＿＿＿＿＿＿＿＿＿＿。

3) 达到...的目的
   a) 这家公司降低了产品的价格，＿＿＿＿＿＿＿＿＿＿＿＿。
   b) 这家美国公司跟一家中国公司合作，＿＿＿＿＿＿＿＿＿＿＿。

4) 从而
   a) 1979年中国实行了改革开放政策，＿＿＿＿＿＿＿＿＿＿＿＿。
   b) "百度"在不同阶段采用不同的人力资源管理方法，＿＿＿＿＿＿＿＿＿＿＿＿＿＿＿＿。

5) 好不容易/好容易

    a) 每天中午到肯德基吃午饭的人都特别多，＿＿＿＿＿＿＿＿＿＿＿＿＿＿。

    b) 沃尔玛在刚进入中国市场时遇到了很多困难，＿＿＿＿＿＿＿＿＿＿＿＿＿

        ＿＿＿＿＿＿＿＿＿＿＿＿＿＿。

6) ...这一点

    a) 中国政府对房地产市场进行调控，＿＿＿＿＿＿＿＿＿＿＿＿＿＿＿＿。

    b) 摩托罗拉公司重视员工的绩效管理，＿＿＿＿＿＿＿＿＿＿＿＿＿＿＿。

7) 这就是说

    a) 中国股票在香港市场上所占的份额越来越大，＿＿＿＿＿＿＿＿＿＿＿＿＿

        ＿＿＿＿＿＿＿＿＿＿＿＿＿＿。

    b) 世界贸易组织被称为"经济联合国"，＿＿＿＿＿＿＿＿＿＿＿＿＿＿＿。

5 把下面的句子改成不太正式的语体。Paraphrase the following sentences in a less formal style, paying special attention to the underlined words and phrases.

1) 跨国公司由位于两个或两个以上国家的经济实体组成，故亦被称为多国公司。其经营活动多从全球策略出发进行安排。

    ＿＿＿＿＿＿＿＿＿＿＿＿＿＿＿＿＿＿＿＿＿＿＿＿＿＿＿＿＿＿＿＿＿

    ＿＿＿＿＿＿＿＿＿＿＿＿＿＿＿＿＿＿＿＿＿＿＿＿＿＿＿＿＿＿＿。

2) 由于跨国企业大多实力雄厚，具有信息、资源及技术等方面的优势，使得部分跨国企业的某些产品在一些地区带有不同程度的垄断性。

    ＿＿＿＿＿＿＿＿＿＿＿＿＿＿＿＿＿＿＿＿＿＿＿＿＿＿＿＿＿＿＿＿＿

    ＿＿＿＿＿＿＿＿＿＿＿＿＿＿＿＿＿＿＿＿＿＿＿＿＿＿＿＿＿＿＿。

3) 跨国企业对外直接投资，并以此为基础展开跨国界的、以赢利为目的的生产经营活动，从而在世界范围内建立最佳的生产、销售地区及原材料供应基地。

    ＿＿＿＿＿＿＿＿＿＿＿＿＿＿＿＿＿＿＿＿＿＿＿＿＿＿＿＿＿＿＿＿＿

    ＿＿＿＿＿＿＿＿＿＿＿＿＿＿＿＿＿＿＿＿＿＿＿＿＿＿＿＿＿＿＿。

4) 某些跨国企业在国外直接进行生产和销售的同时，亦积极实现企业内部的国际性分工，以达到共同占领国际市场的目的。

    ＿＿＿＿＿＿＿＿＿＿＿＿＿＿＿＿＿＿＿＿＿＿＿＿＿＿＿＿＿＿＿＿＿

    ＿＿＿＿＿＿＿＿＿＿＿＿＿＿＿＿＿＿＿＿＿＿＿＿＿＿＿＿＿＿＿。

6　自行查找参考资料，解释与本课话题有关的词语。 Using available resources as a reference, explain the following terms, which are related to this lesson's topic.

1) 全球经营意识

2) 全球产业链

3) 国际品牌

4) 人才国际化

5) 本土差异化经营

6) 跨文化管理

7　阅读理解与讨论。 Reading comprehension and discussion.

中国企业的国际化之路

随着产业全球化的加深，中国企业也开始进入国际市场。目前，中国企业的国际化走的是两条路径：一条是"中国制造"之路，即为国外企业代工生产制造，没有自己的品牌；二是"中国创造"之路，形成自有品牌。至于实现"中国创造"的方式，主要有两种：一是"内部成长"，即自己投资新建海外企业；二是"跨国并购"。

早在20世纪90年代，联想(Lenovo)就在为自己的国际化战略作准备。经过长期思考和多方论证，联想得出结论：要想在强手如林的欧美市场树立自己的品牌，成本极高，时间太长，自建销售渠道也相当困难。只有收购强势品牌才是走国际化道路的捷径。2004年12月8日，联想在北京正式宣布，以总价12.5亿美元收购IBM的全球PC业务。

为了成功实现跨国并购，联想在事前进行了充分的准备，尤其是对并购后战略、制度、品牌、业务、组织人事、文化等方面的整合工作做了全面细致的考虑。目前看来，联想并购IBM PC业务可以说是实现了"双赢"。

但是，跨国并购是一把"双刃剑"，并购成功的中国企业案例少之又少。由此可见，中国企业的国际化之路任重道远。

路径	lùjìng	route; way		自建	zìjiàn	build by oneself
制造	zhìzào	make; manufacture		收购	shōugòu	purchase; buy
代工	dàigōng	manufacture for another (factory)		强势	qiángshì	with a great momentum
				捷径	jiéjìng	short cut
创造	chuàngzào	create; initiate		宣布	xuānbù	announce; declare
至于	zhìyú	as for; as to		事前	shìqián	in advance
并购	bìnggòu	mergers and acquisitions		人事	rénshì	personnel matters
战略	zhànlüè	strategy		细致	xìzhì	detailed; meticulous
思考	sīkǎo	think over; ponder on		双赢	shuāngyíng	win-win
多方	duōfāng	in many ways		案例	ànlì	case
论证	lùnzhèng	expound and prove		少之又少	shǎo zhī yòu shǎo	very few
结论	jiélùn	conclusion; verdict				
强手如林	qiángshǒu rú lín	capable opponents abound		由此可见	yóu cǐ kě jiàn	can be seen from this; this shows
树立	shùlì	establish; erect		任重道远	rèn zhòng dào yuǎn	The burden is heavy and the road is long—shoulder heavy responsibilities
成本	chéngběn	cost				
极	jí	extremely				

选择填空 Select the correct answer for each blank.

1) "中国制造"是指 _____。

    a) 生产中国自己设计的产品

    b) 为国外企业代工生产制造，没有自己的品牌

    c) 为国外企业代工生产制造，标明中国自己的品牌

2) "中国创造" _____。

    a) 是"中国制造"的第二个阶段

    b) 可以通过"内部成长"和"跨国并购"两种方式实现

    c) 还没有成功的例子

3) 关于跨国并购<u>不正确</u>的是 _____。

    a) 需要在事前做充分的准备

    b) 是一把"双刃剑"，可能成功也可能失败

    c) 不适合中国企业

4) 联想的国际化之路 _____。

    a) 实现了双赢

    b) 靠的是自己投资新建海外企业

    c) 还在思考和论证中

讨论 Discussion.

    中国企业的国际化有哪些路径？根据你了解的情况或所查的资料，谈谈为什么中国企业的国际化之路任重道远？联想在实现跨国并购后出现过问题吗？它现在的情况怎么样？What routes are available for a Chinese company to become internationalized? According to what you know or what you have found in research, why do Chinese companies still have a long way to go to reach internationalization? Did Lenovo experience any problems after its transnational acquisition? How is the company now?

8　实践活动。Tasks.

1) 了解和对比肯德基及麦当劳在过去5年中在中国的经营情况，列出当前各自的店面数和营业额。Research and compare KFC's and McDonald's operations in China over the past five years, in terms of number of restaurants and annual business volume.

2) 做一个10分钟的口头报告，介绍一个在国际市场上本土化成功的跨国企业的案例。在报告中请介绍这家企业的具体做法，并发表自己的意见。先查看最近六个月之内的资料，然后根据老师的要求为自己准备一个简单的提纲。Give a ten-minute case report about a transnational company with successful localization in the international market. You should introduce the company's practice

and provide your own comments. Ideally, you should base your report on information from within the past six months and prepare a brief outline for yourself according to your teacher's instructions.

3) 假定现在你和一位同学在上海的一家营销策划公司实习，公司让你们写一份去年中国手机市场海外品牌市场份额的调查报告。这份报告可以附带图表，但是不能超过一页。Suppose you and another student are doing an internship at a marketing company in Shanghai. The company would like you to write a report about respective market shares of overseas-brand cell phones in China from the previous year. You can include a chart in the report, but should limit the report to one page.

4) 如果你对一个不同的任务有兴趣，请结合本课的主题向老师提出建议，然后在老师的指导下完成这个任务。If you are interested in a different kind of task, you are encouraged to suggest your proposal and to complete it under your teacher's guidance.

学习指导 Learning guide

简单句和主谓结构 Simple sentences and "subject + predicate" structures

A simple sentence is a sentence with only one "subject + predicate" structure. All the example sentences provided in the learning guides so far have been simple sentences. A simple sentence may or may not have an object, depending on the nature of the predicate. Moreover, the subject, predicate, and object (if any) can all carry modifiers, so a simple sentence is merely grammatically simple—not necessarily short.

When we say "one 'subject + predicate' structure," it does not mean that in a simple sentence there can be only one word as the subject and one word as the predicate. As a matter of fact, juxtaposed subjects or predicates are very common. Consider the following examples:

产品、价格、渠道和促销是市场营销的四个要素。(juxtaposed subjects)
该种股票以外币认购和交易。(juxtaposed predicates)

These sentences are still "simple" because there is only one "subject + predicate" structure in them. However, subject and predicate are often much more complicated. The subject can be a nominal phrase including modifiers, or any structure which is in the position of being connected upon.

生产要素在世界范围内的充分利用具有重要意义。(nominal phrase)
在国外建立子公司是跨国经营的一种方式。(verbal phrase)
企业掌握目标市场的信息是走向成功的第一步。(SVO)

On the other hand, the predicate can be even more complicated. For example, it may include two or more verbs, all saying something about the subject:

两个人一起<u>去</u>一家广告公司<u>联系</u>业务。

他们好不容易<u>找</u>到一张桌子<u>坐</u>下来 <u>吃</u>饭。

In some other cases, the predicate is a pivotal structure, in which the object of the main verb serves as the subject of another verb or the subject of an adjective (as in the third example):

企业<u>喜欢</u>员工积极<u>向上</u>。

汇率下降<u>要</u>引起进口商品的价格<u>上涨</u>。

李总就<u>怕</u>我们在什么环节上<u>大意</u>。

Since the grammatical relationship between subject and predicate in Chinese is based more on meaning than on form, the grammatical meanings of subject and predicate in Chinese are sometimes referred to as "topic" and "comment." For your purpose and at your current level of study, you do not need to worry about how the "comment" is formed as long as you can recognize the "topic" and understand the "comment."

PRACTICE: Locate the "topic" and parse the "comment" in each sentence. Place a slash between them.

1 家乐福和沃尔玛都是在90年代中期进入中国的。

2 中国消费者需要什么外国企业必须了解。

3 王静文的舅舅和舅妈请马可周末去吃饭。

4 满满一屋子的人都等着方总下楼来给他们出点子。

5 我家对面那个大卖场商品很多，生意很好，利润很高。

6 汇率是以一种货币表示另一种货币的价格。

REVIEW PRACTICE: Find likenesses in each group and reason out the undefined item by analogy. (Refer to L2's learning guide if necessary.)

1 增加; 增强; 增长   增多 _____

2 引起; 引入; 引进   引导 _____

3 实力; 实体; 实时   实物 _____

4 创立; 创新; 创业   创造 _____

5 基本; 基础; 基地   基金 _____

6 人力; 财力; 物力; 竞争力; 劳动力   权力 _____

7 地点; 网点; 热点; 重点; 出发点   特点 _____

8 营销; 经营; 自营   国营 _____

REVIEW PRACTICE: Find words in the designated lessons that are antonyms to the given words. (Refer to L3's learning guide if necessary.)

1 宏观 grand view, macro-   ＿＿＿＿ tiny view, micro- (L3)

2 逆差 deficit (in foreign trade) ＿＿＿＿ surplus (in foreign trade) (L4)

3 询价 inquiry (in trade)   ＿＿＿＿ offer (in trade) (L4)

4 惩罚 punishment   ＿＿＿＿ award (L5)

5 生人 stranger   ＿＿＿＿ familiar person (L5)

6 独资 wholly owned   ＿＿＿＿ jointly owned (L6)

REVIEW PRACTICE: Write out the short forms of the following phrases. (Refer to L3's learning guide if necessary.)

1 外国资本 ＿＿＿＿ (L1)

2 国有企业 ＿＿＿＿ (L2)

3 供给和需求 ＿＿＿＿ (L5)

4 国家的情况 ＿＿＿＿ (L1)

5 研究和开发 ＿＿＿＿ (L5)

6 公共关系 ＿＿＿＿ (L6)

第七课 所有制与经营方式

Lesson 7 *Ownership and modes of operation*

课文一 Text 1

1978年以前，中国的生产资料实行"社会主义公有制"，主要表现为全民所有制和集体所有制。当时，组织生产、分配资源及安排产品消费等，都由政府事先进行计划。

计划经济的出发点是避免市场自由发展的盲目性和不确定性。然而，在计划经济的实践过程中，生产与需求脱节，劳动者动力不足，生产效率低下，市场缺乏活力，严重制约了经济的发展。

1978年，中国开始改革开放，确定了公有制为主体、多种所有制经济共同发展的基本方针。公有资产（即国有经济、集体经济及混合所有制经济中的国有成分和集体成分）在社会总资产中占优势，对经济发展起主导作用。国家运用多种手段进行宏观调控，引导个体经济、私营经济和外资经济共同发展。与此同时，计划经济向市场经济转变，产品和服务的生产及销售开始由自由市场的价格机制引导。

中国的全民所有制企业在改革开放以前由国家直接经营，故称为国营企业；改革开放后由企业自主经营，经营权与所有权分离，故改称国有企业。目前，中国的国有企业、民营企业和外资企业正在共同推动中国经济的发展。

1978年以前，中國的生產資料實行"社會主義公有制"，主要表現為全民所有制和集體所有制。當時，組織生產、分配資源及安排產品消費等，都由政府事先進行計劃。

　　計劃經濟的出發點是避免市場自由發展的盲目性和不確定性。然而，在計劃經濟的實踐過程中，生產與需求脫節，勞動者動力不足，生產效率低下，市場缺乏活力，嚴重制約了經濟的發展。

　　1978年，中國開始改革開放，確定了公有制為主體、多種所有制經濟共同發展的基本方針。公有資產（即國有經濟、集體經濟及混合所有制經濟中的國有成分和集體成分）在社會總資產中佔優勢，對經濟發展起主導作用。國家運用多種手段進行宏觀調控，引導個體經濟、私營經濟和外資經濟共同發展。與此同時，計劃經濟向市場經濟轉變，產品和服務的生產及銷售開始由自由市場的價格機制引導。

　　中國的全民所有制企業在改革開放以前由國家直接經營，故稱為國營企業；改革開放後由企業自主經營，經營權與所有權分離，故改稱國有企業。目前，中國的國有企業、民營企業和外資企業正在共同推動中國經濟的發展。

词语表 Words and expressions

(* Refer to notes or language tips following the word list.)

1	所有		suǒyǒu	*ownership*
2	制		zhì	*system;* 制度; *often as a suffix*
3	社会	社會	shèhuì	*society*
4	主义	主義	zhǔyì	*-ism; doctrine*
5	公有		gōngyǒu	*publicly owned;* 公共所有
6	全民*		quánmín	*all the people (within a country)*
7	集体	集體	jítǐ	*collective*
8	分配		fēnpèi	*allot; distribute*
9	事先		shìxiān	*in advance; beforehand*
10	避免		bìmiǎn	*avoid*
11	盲目		mángmù	*blind*

12	实践	實踐	shíjiàn	*practice; put into practice*
13	脱节	脫節	tuōjié	*be disconnected*
14	劳动	勞動	láodòng	*labor*
15	动力	動力	dònglì	*motivational power; driving force*
16	足		zú	*sufficient; plentiful*
17	效率		xiàolǜ	*efficiency; effectiveness*
18	缺乏		quēfá	*lack; be short of;* 缺少
19	严重	嚴重	yánzhòng	*serious; seriously*
20	制约	制約	zhìyuē	*restrict*
21	改革		gǎigé	*reform*
22	主体	主體	zhǔtǐ	*main body*
23	方针*	方針	fāngzhēn	*guiding principle*
24	资产	資產	zīchǎn	*assets; property*
25	国有	國有	guóyǒu	*state-owned;* 国家所有
26	混合		hùnhé	*mix; mingle*
27	成分		chéngfèn	*element*
28	占		zhàn	*hold (a certain status)*
29	主导	主導	zhǔdǎo	*leading; predominant*
30	运用	運用	yùnyòng	*make use of;* 使用
31	手段		shǒuduàn	*means; measure;* 方法; 办法
32	引导	引導	yǐndǎo	*guide; lead*
33	个体	個體	gètǐ	*individual; individuality*
34	私营	私營	sīyíng	*privately operated; private*
35	转变	轉變	zhuǎnbiàn	*change; transform*
36	机制	機制	jīzhì	*mechanism*
37	自主		zìzhǔ	*autonomy; act on one's own*
38	权	權	quán	*right;* 权利; *power;* 权力
39	分离	分離	fēnlí	*separate; segregate;* 分开
40	改称	改稱	gǎichēng	*be renamed as*
41	民营	民營	mínyíng	*privately operated; private;* 私营

理解考核 Comprehension check

对错选择 True or false

		True	False
1	在1978年以前，中国的生产组织、资源分配及产品消费都由政府事先计划。	☐	☐
2	计划经济在实践过程中严重制约了经济的发展。	☐	☐
3	中国改革开放以后，多种所有制经济共同发展，公有制不再占主导地位。	☐	☐
4	在市场经济条件下，产品和服务的生产及销售是由自由市场的价格机制引导的。	☐	☐
5	国有企业是指国家所有、自主经营的企业。	☐	☐

注释 Notes

1 全民所有制/集体所有制

"Ownership by the whole people" is a social system according to which all means of production and all products are owned by the people as a whole. An enterprise "owned by the whole people" is an independent entity with its own commodity production and business operations. It acts on its own according to law and assumes sole responsibility for profits and losses. Such an enterprise is also known as a state-owned enterprise although state ownership has a broader definition. Collective ownership is a form of public ownership according to which the means of production in an enterprise is equally possessed by its workers. Its products are equally distributed among employees. In such a system significant differences will exist between and among enterprises.

语言提示 Language tips

1 A表现为B: A is displayed or manifested as B.

- 1978年以前，中国的...“社会主义公有制”...主要表现为全民所有制和集体所有制。

  一个国家的经济实力主要表现为GDP的高低。
  跨国企业的竞争优势大多表现为信息、资金和技术方面的优势。

2 进行: carry out; execute; conduct. Note that this word is used especially to describe ongoing formal and serious actions, not short-term or everyday actions. One is not supposed to say, for example, 进行上课。

- 〔计划经济时期，〕组织生产 ... 等，都由政府事先<u>进行</u>计划。
- 国家运用多种手段<u>进行</u>宏观调控，引导个体 ...、私营 ... 和外资经济共同发展。
- 企业的具体业务活动，如 ... 等，通常由专门的职能部门来<u>进行</u>。

(L5-1)

企业在进入一个市场以前要对目标市场<u>进行</u>调查。
关于这项业务，我们希望尽快跟贵公司<u>进行</u>洽谈。

3　A 的出发点是 B: A has B as a starting point. A starts from B.

- 计划经济<u>的出发点是</u>避免市场自由发展的盲目性和不确定性。

这项政策<u>的出发点是</u>改善老百姓的居住条件。
肯德基开发本土化产品<u>的出发点是</u>吸引本地顾客。

4　确定 ... 的方针: determine the guiding principle of

- 1978 年，中国 ... <u>确定</u>了公有制为主体、多种所有制经济共同发展<u>的</u>基本<u>方针</u>。

两国领导人<u>确定</u>了"面向未来、全面合作"<u>的方针</u>。
<u>确定</u>本土化<u>的方针</u>是跨国经营的一项重要任务。

5　对 ... 起 ... 作用/在 ... 中起 ... 作用: play a ... role in

- 公有资产 ... 在社会总资产中占优势，<u>对</u>经济发展<u>起</u>主导<u>作用</u>。

市场营销<u>对</u>企业经营<u>起</u>关键<u>作用</u>。
"以人为本"的理念<u>在</u>现代企业管理<u>中起</u>着重要的<u>作用</u>。

6　与此同时: at the same time; meanwhile

- 国家运用多种手段进行宏观调控 ...。<u>与此同时</u>，计划经济也向市场经济转变。

这些年来，中国经济发展迅速。<u>与此同时</u>，也出现了不少社会问题。
人民币升值会使进口的商品降价，但<u>与此同时</u>，出口会变得困难，就业也会受到影响。

7　由 ... V: (an action taken) by

- 组织生产、分配资源及安排产品消费等，都<u>由</u>政府事先<u>进行</u>计划。
- 中国的全民所有制企业在改革开放以前<u>由</u>国家直接<u>经营</u>，故称为国营企业。
- 在计划经济下什么都<u>由</u>政府<u>决定</u>，政府的权力太大，民主太少。(L7-2)

国际贸易主要<u>由</u>进口贸易和出口贸易<u>组成</u>，故亦称"进出口贸易"。
　　(L4-1)
A 股<u>由</u>大陆公司<u>发行</u>。(L1-1)
汇率的高低与变化归根到底是<u>由</u>供求关系<u>决定</u>的。(L2-1)

课文二 Text 2

马可选修的经济课这个星期正在讨论经济体制的问题。因为他对计划经济不太理解，所以在答疑时间去找老师。林汉华教授见到他很高兴。两个人面对面坐下来，谈得很热烈。

马　可：林老师，很多人把计划经济说得一无是处，可是您好像在课上说了一些计划经济的好话，我不知道是不是听错了。

林汉华：噢，我的意思是，计划经济也有过重大的成功。比如中国和前苏联都在历史上靠计划经济实现过高速发展。有些数据，我已经放到网上了。

马　可：您好像还谈到了计划经济的一些别的好处，比如所有的人都有工作啊，节省自然资源啊，贫富差距小啊，等等。这些都是我原来不了解的。

林汉华：我们可以这样来看问题：为什么在二十世纪会出现计划经济呢？就是因为人们看到了市场经济的弊病，这在当时是一种进步。在经济还不发达的情况下，计划经济能把人力、物力和财力集中起来用到最重要的地方，而且保障人民生活中最基本的需要。可是我在课上也介绍了计划经济的缺点，是吧？

马　可：我想您说了，在现代的经济生活中，人们的需求比较复杂，变化也快，很难让计划符合实际。

林汉华：是啊。正因为这样，计划经济反而容易造成供不应求或供过于求。再说，在计划经济下什么都由政府决定，政府的权力太大，民主太少。同时，又因为没有竞争，大家不容易有积极性和创造性。这些问题在讲义里都提到了。

马　可：所以您的结论是，计划经济不适合搞现代化？

林汉华：没错。这就是为什么中国需要改革开放，需要市场经济。

马　可：可是为什么有些人还觉得计划经济可能有前途呢？

林汉华：那是因为科学技术的发展使得信息的收集和处理变得方便了。这些人认为，也许计算机能帮助我们再把计划经济搞起来。

马　可：这个想法挺有意思。谢谢您，林老师。

馬可選修的經濟課這個星期正在討論經濟體制的問題。因為他對計劃經濟不太理解，所以在答疑時間去找老師。林漢華教授見到他很高興。兩個人面對面坐下來，談得很熱烈。

馬　可：林老師，很多人把計劃經濟說得一無是處，可是您好像在課上說了一些計劃經濟的好話，我不知道是不是聽錯了。

林漢華：噢，我的意思是，計劃經濟也有過重大的成功。比如中國和前蘇聯都在歷史上靠計劃經濟實現過高速發展。有些數據，我已經放到網上了。

馬　可：您好像還談到了計劃經濟的一些別的好處，比如所有的人都有工作啊，節省自然資源啊，貧富差距小啊，等等。這些都是我原來不瞭解的。

林漢華：我們可以這樣來看問題：為什麼在二十世紀會出現計劃經濟呢？就是因為人們看到了市場經濟的弊病，這在當時是一種進步。在經濟還不發達的情況下，計劃經濟能把人力、物力和財力集中起來用到最重要的地方，而且保障人民生活中最基本的需要。可是我在課上也介紹了計劃經濟的缺點，是吧？

馬　可：我想您說了，在現代的經濟生活中，人們的需求比較複雜，變化也快，很難讓計劃符合實際。

林漢華：是啊。正因為這樣，計劃經濟反而容易造成供不應求或供過於求。再說，在計劃經濟下什麼都由政府決定，政府的權力太大，民主太少。同時，又因為沒有競爭，大家不容易有積極性和創造性。這些問題在講義裡都提到了。

馬　可：所以您的結論是，計劃經濟不適合搞現代化？

林漢華：沒錯。這就是為什麼中國需要改革開放，需要市場經濟。

馬　可：可是為什麼有些人還覺得計劃經濟可能有前途呢？

林漢華：那是因為科學技術的發展使得信息的收集和處理變得方便了。這些人認為，也許計算機能幫助我們再把計劃經濟搞起來。

馬　可：這個想法挺有意思。謝謝您，林老師。

词语表 Words and expressions

(* Refer to notes or language tips following the word list.)

1	讨论	討論	tǎolùn	*discuss*
2	理解		lǐjiě	*understand; comprehend;* 懂
3	答疑		dáyí	*answer questions;* 回答疑问
4	热烈	熱烈	rèliè	*enthusiastic; ardent*
5	一无是处	一無是處	yī wú shì chù	*without a single redeeming feature*
6	重大		zhòngdà	*great; significant;* 重要
7	高速		gāosù	*high speed*
8	数据	數據	shùjù	*data*
9	节省	節省	jiéshěng	*save*
10	贫富	貧富	pínfù	*the poor and the rich*
11	差距		chājù	*gap*

12	弊病		bìbìng	defect
13	发达	發達	fādá	developed
14	物力		wùlì	material resources
15	财力	財力	cáilì	financial capability; financial resources
16	集中		jízhōng	centralize; gather up
17	保障		bǎozhàng	ensure; protect
18	缺点	缺點	quēdiǎn	shortcoming; defect; weakness
19	符合		fúhé	conform to; tally with
20	实际	實際	shíjì	reality
21	供不应求	供不應求	gōng bù yìng qiú	supply falls short of demand
22	供过于求	供過於求	gōng guò yú qiú	supply exceeds demand
23	权力	權力	quánlì	power; authority
24	民主		mínzhǔ	democracy
25	创造	創造	chuàngzào	create; initiate
26	讲义	講義	jiǎngyì	lecture handout; teaching material
27	提到		tídào	mention; 说到
28	结论	結論	jiélùn	conclusion
29	适合	適合	shìhé	be fit for; suit
30	前途		qiántú	future; prospect
31	收集		shōují	collect; gather
32	处理	處理	chǔlǐ	process; deal with; handle
33	计算机	計算機	jìsuànjī	computer; calculating machine; 电脑
34	挺		tǐng	quite; very; 非常

专有名词 Proper nouns

前苏联*	前蘇聯	qián Sūlián	the former Soviet Union

理解考核 Comprehension check

回答问题 Answer the following questions

1　马可为什么要去找林汉华教授？

2　林教授谈到了计划经济的哪些好处？

3　为什么在二十世纪会出现计划经济？

4　林教授也谈到了计划经济的哪些缺点？

5　为什么有些人还觉得计划经济可能有前途？

注释 Notes

1 前苏联

The Union of Soviet Socialist Republics (USSR), abbreviated as CCCP in Russian, was founded on December 30, 1922 and dissolved on December 26, 1991. It was the first unitary communist state in the world to implement a socialist system, a planned economy, and one-party rule.

语言提示 Language tips

1　在 ... （的）情况下: under ... circumstances

- 在经济还不发达的情况下，计划经济能把人力、物力和财力集中 ... 用到最重要的地方。

  在一般情况下，贸易顺差能推进经济增长，增加就业。
  在经济高速发展的情况下尤其要重视教育、环境等社会问题。

2　反而: on the contrary; instead

- 在现代的经济生活中，人们的需求比较复杂，...，计划经济反而容易造成 ... 问题。

  要是不尊重人性，规章制度反而会在企业管理中造成问题。
  肯德基的本土化不但没有让它失去自己的特色，反而吸引了更多的本地顾客。

练习 Exercises

1 将左栏的动词和右栏的宾语配对，每个词语只能用一次。Match each verb in the left column with an appropriate object in the right column. Each item can be used only once.

1)	避免 _____	a)	员工
2)	运用 _____	b)	信息
3)	缺乏 _____	c)	实际情况
4)	制约 _____	d)	多种手段
5)	布置 _____	e)	盲目性
6)	符合 _____	f)	国际市场
7)	收集 _____	g)	经济发展
8)	奖励 _____	h)	活力
9)	占领 _____	i)	资源
10)	分配 _____	j)	卖场

2 听写并用汉语解释下列词组。Complete a dictation of the following phrases and explain them in Chinese.

1)	社会主义公有制	7)	个体经济
2)	全民所有制	8)	私营经济
3)	集体所有制	9)	价格机制
4)	混合所有制	10)	经营权与所有权分离
5)	计划经济	11)	一无是处
6)	市场经济	12)	贫富差距

3 选词填空。Fill in the blanks with the provided words and expressions.

1) 表现为，主导作用，基本方针，宏观调控，占优势

   中国改革开放以后，确立了以公有制为主体，多种所有制经济共同发展的 _____，_____：公有资产在社会总资产中 _____，对经济发展起 _____。国家运用多种手段进行 _____，引导个体、私营、外资经济共同发展。

2) 供不应求，与此同时，一无是处，贫富差距

   计划经济并不是 _____。节省自然资源，缩小 _____ 等都是计划经济的好处。但 _____，由于计划很难符合实际，计划经济也会造成 _____ 或供过于求的问题。

4 用指定的表达方式完成句子或对话。Complete the following sentences and dialogues with the designated words or expressions.

1) A 表现为 B

   a) 肯德基在中国的本土化 _____。

   b) 一家公司的经营状况 _____。

2) A 的出发点是 B

   a) A: 跨国公司是怎么组织和安排生产经营活动的？

      B: _____。

   b) A: 中国政府为什么要对房市进行调控？

      B: _____。

3) 确定 ... 的方针

   a) 为了进入国际市场，联想公司早就 _____。

   b) 二十世纪七十年代末，中国政府制定了独生子女政策，_____

      _____。

4) 对 ... 起 ... 作用

   a) 市场调查帮助企业知己知彼，_____。

   b) 人力资源管理是企业管理的重要部分，_____。

5) 与此同时

   a) 跨国并购是一把"双刃剑"，它可以帮助中国企业实现国际化，_____

      _____。

   b) 人民币升值使进口高档商品更便宜了，_____。

6) 在 ... 的情况下

   a) _____，计划经济也带来了许多好处。

   b) _____，政府应该对经济进行宏观调控。

7) 反而

   a) 在激烈的竞争中许多中小企业破产了，但这家公司 _____。

   b) 有专家认为，人民币的币值不但没有被低估，_____。

5 把下面的句子改成不太正式的语体。 Paraphrase the following sentences in a less formal style, paying special attention to the underlined words and phrases.

1) 1978年以前，中国的生产资料实行"社会主义公有制"。<u>当时</u>，组织生产、分配资源<u>及</u>安排产品消费<u>等</u>，都<u>由</u>政府<u>事先进行</u>计划。

_____

_____。

2) 公有资产（<u>即</u>国有经济、集体经济<u>以及</u>混合所有制经济中的国有成分和集体成分）<u>在</u>社会<u>总</u>资产<u>中占优势</u>，对经济发展起<u>主导</u>作用。

_____

_____。

3) 计划经济向市场经济<u>转变</u>，产品和服务的生产<u>及</u>销售开始<u>由</u>自由市场的价格机制<u>引导</u>。

_____

_____。

4) 改革开放前，中国的全民所有制企业<u>由</u>国家直接经营，<u>故称为</u>国营企业；改革开放后，<u>则由</u>企业<u>自主经营</u>，<u>故改称</u>国有企业。

_____

_____。

6 自行查找参考资料，解释与本课话题有关的词语。 Using available resources as a reference, explain the following terms, which are related to this lesson's topic.

1) 政企合一   4) 大锅饭
2) 财政补贴   5) "猫论"
3) 定量配给

7 阅读理解与讨论。 Reading comprehension and discussion.

中国市场经济地位的确认问题

市场经济地位是反倾销调查中的一个重要概念。反倾销案发起国如果认定被调查商品的出口国为"市场经济"国家，那么在进行反倾销调查时，就必须根据该产品在生产国的实际成本和价格来计算其正常价格；如果认定被调查商品的出口国为"非市场经济"国家，则不再使用该国的原始数据，而是找出一个与该国经济发展水平大致相当的市场经济国家，然后引用这一国家的成本数据来计算所谓的正常价格，并进而确定倾销幅度。如20世纪90年代，欧盟对中国的彩电反倾销，就是将新加坡作为替代国来计算中国彩电的生产成本的。当时，新加坡劳动力成本高出中国20多倍，中国的产品自然被计算成倾销，这对中国十分不利。

自加入世贸组织以来，中国政府一直在努力争取国际贸易各国承认中国的完全市场经济地位。但由于其他世贸成员不承认中国的市场经济地位，中国企业在应诉国外反倾销调查时，不但败诉率高，而且被裁定的倾销税率也往往难以承受。同时，这也间接导致了针对中国的反倾销案件的增加。

地位	dìwèi	position; status	幅度	fúdù	range
确认	quèrèn	affirm; confirm	欧盟	Ōuméng	European Union
反	fǎn	anti-	彩电	cǎidiàn	color TV
倾销	qīngxiāo	dumping	替代	tìdài	substitute for
概念	gàiniàn	general idea; concept	争取	zhēngqǔ	strive for; fight for
案	àn	case (in legal or police matters)	承认	chéngrèn	admit; confess
发起	fāqǐ	originate; initiate	应诉	yìngsù	respond to a lawsuit
认定	rèndìng	firmly believe	败诉	bàisù	lose a lawsuit
计算	jìsuàn	calculate	率	lǜ	rate
正常	zhèngcháng	normal	裁定	cáidìng	decide or declare judicially
非	fēi	not; non-	税	shuì	tax
原始	yuánshǐ	firsthand; original	承受	chéngshòu	bear; endure
大致	dàzhì	approximately; roughly	间接	jiànjiē	indirect
引用	yǐnyòng	quote; cite	针对	zhēnduì	be aimed at
所谓	suǒwèi	so-called	案件	ànjiàn	legal case
进而	jìn'ér	proceed to the next step			

选择填空 Select the correct answer for each blank.

1) 反倾销案的发起国如果认定被调查商品的出口国为"市场经济国家"，则_____。

   a) 对反倾销案的发起国不利
   b) 根据这种产品在生产国的实际成本和价格来计算正常价格
   c) 根据这种产品在进口国的实际成本和价格来计算正常价格

2) 反倾销案的发起国如果认定被调查商品的出口国为"非市场经济国家"，则_____。

   a) 根据这种产品在生产国的实际成本和价格来计算正常价格
   b) 根据这种产品在进口国的实际成本和价格来计算正常价格
   c) 根据与出口国经济发展水平大致相当的市场经济国家的情况来计算正常价格

3) 在20世纪90年代欧盟对中国的彩电反倾销案中，中国处于不利地位是因为_____。

   a) 中国当时被认定为非市场经济国家
   b) 新加坡的彩电比中国彩电更有竞争力
   c) 中国的劳动力成本太低

4) 有些世贸成员不承认中国的市场经济地位，由此造成的对中国的不利影响<u>不包括</u> _____。

    a) 中国企业在反倾销案中败诉率高

    b) 中国企业被裁定的倾向税率难以承受

    c) 外国企业向中国倾销商品

<u>讨论</u> Discussion.

为什么说市场经济地位是反倾销调查中的一个重要概念？根据你了解的情况或所查的资料，请你谈谈中国政府为争取国际贸易各国承认中国的完全市场经济地位做出了哪些努力。Why is market economy status an important concept in anti-dumping investigations? According to what you know or what you have found in research, please talk about the Chinese government's efforts in winning international recognition for China's complete market economy status.

8 实践活动。Tasks.

1) 查阅资料，找出在一百年以内实行过"生产资料公有制"和"计划经济"的国家。其中尚在继续实行的，请加以注明。Use research to make a list of countries that have practiced public ownership of production means and a planned economy during the past century. Mark those that still continue this practice (if any) with an asterisk.

2) 做一个10分钟的口头报告，介绍中国国有企业改革的现状。报告中可以集中举一个国企的例子，也可以全面谈国企改革的概况和问题。先上网查看一条最近六个月之内与国企改革有关的新闻，然后根据老师的要求为自己准备一个简单的提纲。在报告时要尽可能提供事实和例子。Give a ten-minute oral report about the current situation of the reform of China's state-owned enterprises. The report can either focus on one enterprise or briefly state the overall status of this issue along with existing problems. You should search for a relevant news article from within the past six months and prepare a brief outline for yourself as per your teacher's instructions. Please make an effort to include facts and examples.

3) 采访一位经历过中国计划经济时期的长辈、老师、邻居或朋友，把他（她）的介绍中给你留下最深刻印象的一件事情记下来（不要超过一页）。Interview someone who experienced China's period of planned economy and write a short article (limited to one page) about an event or an anecdote that impressed you the most.

4) 如果你对一个不同的任务有兴趣，请结合本课的主题向老师提出建议，然后在老师的指导下完成这个任务。If you are interested in a different kind of task, you are encouraged to suggest your proposal and to complete it under your teacher's guidance.

学习指导 Learning guide

复合句和关联词 Composite sentences and connectives

While a simple sentence is formed by words and phrases, a composite sentence is formed by two or more clauses (i.e. simple sentences) which are related in meaning. Relationships between or among clauses are specified by the order of clauses and, more importantly, by the use of connectives (i.e. certain conjunctions and adverbs). It is often the connective or connectives that clarify the logic in a composite sentence. See how the following sentences differ in logic and how the differences are directly due to the connectives used.

是A公司同意合资，还是B公司同意合资？	(whether . . . or)
A公司同意合资，B公司也同意合资。	(also)
不但A公司同意合资，而且B公司也同意合资。	(not only . . . but also)
因为A公司同意合资，所以B公司也同意合资。	(because)
A公司同意合资，以致B公司同意合资。	(so that)
A公司同意合资，于是B公司同意合资。	(so)
A公司同意合资，甚至B公司也同意合资。	(even)
不论A公司同意不同意合资，B公司都同意合资。	(no matter whether)
A公司什么时候同意合资，B公司就什么时候同意合资。	(whenever)
如果A公司同意合资，那么B公司就同意合资。	(if)
只有A公司同意合资，B公司才同意合资。	(if only)
除非A公司同意合资，否则B公司不会同意合资。	(unless)
虽然A公司同意合资，但是B公司还是不同意合资。	(although)
就是A公司同意合资，B公司也不会同意合资。	(even if)

You should be familiar with all the connectives in these sentences, but the list of connectives can be much longer as there are different ways to express the same kind of logic. Now that you are using a formal language style, you will come across more composite sentences in your readings, so you cannot afford not to pay special attention to them. You may want to make a list of Chinese connectives for yourself based on the logical relationships in English.

When you compare composite sentences in Chinese with complex sentences in English, you should keep the following in mind:

- In English the main clause usually comes up first, followed by the subordinate clause. In Chinese, however, a composite sentence typically starts with the subordinate clause. The main clause occurs at the start only when it receives a special emphasis.

- Unlike in English, connectives are often used in pairs in Chinese. Do not neglect the second one (i.e. the one in the main clause); this connective is often indispensable. It is more likely that the first one (i.e. the one in the subordinate clause) can be dropped. This is not a rule of thumb, however.

- In Chinese, if the subordinate clause and the main clause share the same subject, usually the second subject is omitted. When this happens, the one that is retained (usually the one in the first clause or subordinate clause) may be placed after the connective.

PRACTICE: Mark the connectives in the following composite sentences.

1 他因为对计划经济不太理解，所以去找林老师。

2 以前这些企业由国家直接经营，故称为国营企业。

3 计划经济能把人、财、物用到最重要的地方，而且保障生活中最基本的需要。

4 因为科学技术发展了，所以有些人觉得计划经济可能有前途。

5 跨国经营多种多样，但大多是为了获得生产要素的比较优势。

6 企业内部实现国际性分工，以达到共同占领国际市场的目的。

7 要是不搞本土化，就不会有这么多人上这儿来吃饭。

8 就因为肯德基本土化比较彻底，才把麦当劳抛在了后边。

9 沃尔玛虽然在中国失去了先机，可是现在跟中国政府的关系比较好。

10 若出口额和进口额相当，即为"贸易平衡"。

REVIEW PRACTICE: Categorize the two-character compounds according to their internal structures. (Refer to Lɪ's learning guide if necessary.)

人性, 扩大, 热烈, 答疑, 学术, 贫富, 公有, 分工, 先机, 提到, 增长, 创业

1 Synonyms or antonyms

2 Modifying + modified

3 Verb + complement

4 Verb + object

REVIEW PRACTICE: Categorize the three-character compounds according to their internal structures.

三位数, 联合国, 出洋相, 计算机, 打招呼, 下功夫, 所有制, 娶媳妇

1　X + XX　　_____　_____　_____　_____

2　XX + X　　_____　_____　_____　_____

第八课 经济衰退与通货膨胀

Lesson 8 *Economic recession and inflation*

课文一 Text 1

　　由于市场对商品总需求减少，经济连续两个季度以上停滞或负增长，便被认为进入经济衰退。经济衰退与消费量下降，商品存货过量有关，也与缺乏技术创新和新资本积累以及股市的随机性有关。经济衰退时，经济活力下降，失业率上升。严重的经济衰退被定义为经济萧条，毁灭性的经济衰退则被称为经济崩溃。

　　通货膨胀，简称"通胀"，指社会总需求大于社会总供给时整体物价水平上升，货币购买力下降的现象。一般来说，经济的持续增长会带动需求，使物价上升，客观上造成通货膨胀。低度的通货膨胀能对经济起"润滑"作用，因为物价的提高及利润的增加能刺激厂商投资的积极性。但持续的通胀又将使消费下降，以至进入经济衰退。通胀率达两位数时，人们对货币的信心产生动摇，经济和社会将发生动荡。一旦通胀率达到三位数，物价飞涨，货币大幅贬值，社会金融体系和经济关系受到破坏，最终将导致社会崩溃和政府垮台。

　　通货膨胀的反义为通货紧缩，系指市场上流通的货币不足，购买力下降，进而造成物价下跌。长期的货币紧缩会抑制投资与生产，导致失业率升高与经济衰退。

　　由於市場對商品總需求減少，經濟連續兩個季度以上停滯或負增長，便被認為進入經濟衰退。經濟衰退與消費量下降，商品存貨過量有關，也與缺乏技術創新和新資本積累以及股市的隨機性有關。經濟衰退時，經濟活力下降，失業率上升。嚴重的經濟衰退被定義為經濟蕭條，毀滅性的經濟衰退則被稱為經濟崩潰。

通貨膨脹，簡稱"通脹"，指社會總需求大於社會總供給時整體物價水平上升，貨幣購買力下降的現象。一般來說，經濟的持續增長會帶動需求，使物價上升，客觀上造成通貨膨脹。低度的通貨膨脹能對經濟起"潤滑"作用，因為物價的提高及利潤的增加能刺激廠商投資的積極性。但持續的通脹又將使消費下降，以至進入經濟衰退。通脹率達兩位數時，人們對貨幣的信心產生動搖，經濟和社會將發生動盪。一旦通脹率達到三位數，物價飛漲，貨幣大幅貶值，社會金融體系和經濟關係受到破壞，最終將導致社會崩潰和政府垮臺。

通貨膨脹的反義為通貨緊縮，系指市場上流通的貨幣不足，購買力下降，進而造成物價下跌。長期的貨幣緊縮會抑制投資與生產，導致失業率升高與經濟衰退。

词语表 Words and expressions

(* Refer to notes or language tips following the word list.)

1	通货	通貨	tōnghuò	*currency*
2	膨胀	膨脹	péngzhàng	*inflate; inflation*
3	减少	減少	jiǎnshǎo	*reduce; decrease*
4	连续	連續	liánxù	*continuously; successively*
5	季度		jìdù	*quarter of a year*
6	停滞		tíngzhì	*cease moving or making progress*
7	负	負	fù	*minus; negative*
8	便*		biàn	*thereupon;* 就
9	存货	存貨	cúnhuò	*goods in stock*
10	过量	過量	guòliàng	*excess; excessive;* 太多
11	有关*	有關	yǒuguān	*be related to*
12	积累	積累	jīlěi	*accumulate; accumulation*
13	随机	隨機	suíjī	*random*
14	失业	失業	shīyè	*unemployment*
15	率		lǜ	*rate; often as a suffix*

16	定义	定義	dìngyì	*define*
17	萧条	蕭條	xiāotiáo	*depression*
18	毁灭	毀滅	huǐmiè	*destructive*
19	崩溃	崩潰	bēngkuì	*collapse*
20	供给	供給	gōngjǐ	*supply*
21	购买力	購買力	gòumǎilì	*purchasing power*
22	现象	現象	xiànxiàng	*phenomenon*
23	持续	持續	chíxù	*continuous*
24	带动	帶動	dàidòng	*bring along*
25	客观	客觀	kèguān	*objective*
26	低度		dīdù	*low grade*
27	润滑	潤滑	rùnhuá	*lubricate*
28	刺激		cìjī	*stimulate*
29	以至*		yǐzhì	*to such an extent as to*
30	达	達	dá	*reach (a place or a figure)*; 达到
31	两位数	兩位數	liǎngwèishù	*double-digit*
32	动摇	動搖	dòngyáo	*waver; fluctuate*
33	发生	發生	fāshēng	*occur; take place*
34	动荡	動盪	dòngdàng	*turbulence; upheaval*
35	一旦*		yīdàn	*once; in case*
36	大幅		dàfú	*substantially*
37	体系	體系	tǐxì	*system*
38	破坏	破壞	pòhuài	*destroy*
39	最终*	最終	zuìzhōng	*finally; eventually*; 最后
40	垮台	垮臺	kuǎtái	*collapse; fall from power*
41	反义	反義	fǎnyì	*antonym*
42	紧缩	緊縮	jǐnsuō	*retrench*
43	系*		xì	*be*; 是
44	流通		liútōng	*circulate; flow*
45	进而*	進而	jìn'ér	*and then; after that*
46	抑制		yìzhì	*restrain; control*

理解考核 Comprehension check

对错选择 True or false

		True	False
1	经济持续三个月以上停滞或负增长，便被认为进入经济萧条。	☐	☐
2	消费量下降、商品存货过量、缺乏技术创新和新资本积累以及股市的随机性都可能导致经济衰退。	☐	☐
3	整体物价水平下跌，货币购买力上升，都是通货膨胀的表现。	☐	☐
4	一般来说，经济的持续增长会造成通货膨胀，低度的通货膨胀对经济有利。	☐	☐
5	长期的通货膨胀和通货紧缩都会导致经济衰退。	☐	☐

语言提示 Language tips

1　便: same as 就, but formal

- 经济连续两个季度以上停滞或负增长，便被认为进入经济衰退。
- 两个人都想谈谈，便在草地上坐了下来。(L8-2)

  大家对这份合同还有一些问题，便讨论了起来。
  股市最近很火，不少人便开始投资股市。

2　被 V 为: be … as

- 严重的经济衰退被定义为经济萧条，毁灭性的经济衰退则被称为经济崩溃。

  奥巴马于2008年被选为美国的第44任总统。
  中国发行的股票被分为A股、B股、H股、N股和S股等。

3　与 … 有关: relate to; have something to do with

- 经济衰退与消费量下降、商品存货过量有关，也与 … 股市的随机性有关。

  股价的变化与市场的需求有关。
  市场营销策略与很多因素有关，如企业内部的管理、中间商、竞争者等。

4 以至: same as 以至于; to such an extent that. It is used at the beginning of the second half of a sentence to indicate the result of the situation or action expressed in the first half of the sentence.

- 持续的通胀又将使消费下降，<u>以至</u>进入经济衰退。

  这个公司不注重新产品的研发，<u>以至</u>在市场上的竞争力明显下降。
  该国货币的升值引起了劳动力成本上升，<u>以至</u>不少外资转移到其他国家。

5 一旦: referring to an indefinite time in the future

- <u>一旦</u>通胀率达到三位数，物价飞涨，货币大幅贬值，...。

  <u>一旦</u>这次的营销计划成功，我们便可抢得先机。
  <u>一旦</u>洽谈中出现问题，我们就需要随机应变。

6 最终: finally; ultimately; same as 最后, but formal

- ...社会金融体系和经济关系受到破坏，<u>最终</u>将导致社会崩溃和政府垮台。

  如果房价上涨得不到控制，<u>最终</u>会引起严重的社会问题。
  虽然目前的贫富差距难以避免，但<u>最终</u>一定会实现共同富裕 (*fùyù*, well off)。

7 系: same as 是, but formal

- 通货膨胀的反义为通货紧缩，<u>系</u>指市场上流通的货币不足，购买力下降，...。

  汇率<u>系</u>一国货币兑换另一国货币的比率，是以一种货币表示另一种货币的价格。
  国际贸易<u>系</u>指不同国家或地区之间的商品、服务和生产要素的交换活动。

8 进而: and then; after that

- 市场上流通的货币不足，购买力下降，<u>进而</u>造成物价下跌。

  跨国公司在国外直接进行生产和销售，并<u>进而</u>实现企业内部的国际性分工。
  美国总统的这次访问加深了相互了解，<u>进而</u>扩大了两国的合作 (*hézuò*, cooperation)。

课文二 Text 2

　　马可前几天在电话上听王静文的舅舅说，这一阵子物价涨得厉害。他的经济课正好也在讨论通货膨胀的问题。今天下课以后，他和李瑛瑛一起走出教学楼。两个人都想谈谈，便在草地上坐了下来。

李瑛瑛：你这个老外不知道吧？最近我们这儿食品和日用品的价格涨得可快了。

马　可：我看到过一些报道，好像不少人在担心通胀失控。

李瑛瑛：没错。特别是低收入的家庭叫苦连天。他们只好从嘴里省钱，从身上省钱。

马　可：在美国，通胀也在抬头。能源和原料涨价提高了成本，这几个月的食品价格一直在上升。

李瑛瑛：美国人的收入比较高，社会福利又比较好，不至于人心惶惶吧？

马　可：那也不一定。至少现在失业率高，大家花钱都比较谨慎。不过，美国人习惯靠债务生活，通胀也把欠银行的钱打了折扣，这就是说，我们的债务也缩了水。

李瑛瑛：而中国人是把钱存在银行里，什么时候物价指数上升得快，存款实际上就是负利率，所以我们面对的可是财富的缩水啊。哎，我来考你一下，林老师说了通胀的两个原因，你都听明白了吗？

马　可：当然听明白了。一个是全球新兴市场的需求增加，造成了物资短缺；另一个是国家发行了过量的货币。要是市场上钱太多而商品没那么多，物价就会上涨，货币就会贬值。林老师认为，中国的这次通胀，就是政府发放了过多的人民币引起的。

李瑛瑛：对，他是这么说的。他还说，低通胀有利于推动经济增长，中国政府本来是想通过发放货币来刺激消费的，但结果货币的发行过了头。

马　可：我想美国也有这样的问题。在美国决定货币政策的是美联储，它也常常得选择通胀来刺激经济。到了需要宏观调控的时候，它就调整利率。

李瑛瑛：（看手机）"说曹操，曹操到。"你看这条短信，我们的央行今天加息了！

马可前几天在电话上听王静文的舅舅说，这一阵子物价涨得厉害。他的经济课正好也在讨论通货膨胀的问题。今天下课以后，他和李瑛瑛一起走出教学楼。两个人都想谈谈，便在草地上坐了下来。

李瑛瑛：你这个老外不知道吧？最近我们这儿食品和日用品的价格涨得可快了。

马　可：我看到过一些报导，好像不少人在担心通胀失控。

李瑛瑛：没错。特别是低收入的家庭叫苦连天。他们只好从嘴里省钱，从身上省钱。

马　可：在美国，通胀也在抬头。能源和原料涨价提高了成本，这几个月的食品价格一直在上升。

李瑛瑛：美国人的收入比较高，社会福利又比较好，不至于人心惶惶吧？

马　可：那也不一定。至少现在失业率高，大家花钱都比较谨慎。不过，美国人习惯靠债务生活，通胀也把欠银行的钱打了折扣，这就是说，我们的债务也缩了水。

李瑛瑛： 而中國人是把錢存在銀行裡，什麼時候物價指數上升得快，存款實際上就是負利率，所以我們面對的可是財富的縮水啊。哎，我來考你一下，林老師說了通脹的兩個原因，你都聽明白了嗎？

馬　可： 當然聽明白了。一個是全球新興市場的需求增加，造成了物資短缺；另一個是國家發行了過量的貨幣。要是市場上錢太多而商品沒那麼多，物價就會上漲，貨幣就會貶值。林老師認為，中國的這次通脹，就是政府發放了過多的人民幣引起的。

李瑛瑛： 對，他是這麼說的。他還說，低通脹有利於推動經濟增長，中國政府本來是想通過發放貨幣來刺激消費的，但結果貨幣的發行過了頭。

馬　可： 我想美國也有這樣的問題。在美國決定貨幣政策的是美聯儲，它也常常得選擇通脹來刺激經濟。到了需要宏觀調控的時候，它就調整利率。

李瑛瑛： （看手機）"說曹操，曹操到。"你看這條短信，我們的央行今天加息了！

词语表 Words and expressions

(* Refer to notes or language tips following the word list.)

1	食品		shípǐn	*food*
2	日用品		rìyòngpīn	*daily commodities*
3	报道	報道	bàodào	*report*
4	失控		shīkòng	*out of control;* 失去控制
5	收入		shōurù	*income; revenue*
6	叫苦连天	叫苦連天	jiào kǔ lián tiān	*complain incessantly and bitterly*
7	抬头	抬頭	táitóu	*raise one's head*
8	能源		néngyuán	*energy resources*
9	原料		yuánliào	*raw materials*
10	福利		fúlì	*welfare*

11	不至于*	不至於	bùzhìyú	*cannot go so far; be unlikely*
12	人心惶惶		rénxīn huánghuáng	*public disquiet*
13	至少		zhìshǎo	*at least*
14	谨慎	謹慎	jǐnshèn	*prudent; careful; cautious;* 小心
15	债务	債務	zhàiwù	*debt*
16	欠		qiàn	*owe*
17	折扣		zhékòu	*discount*
18	缩水	縮水	suōshuǐ	*shrink;* 变少
19	存		cún	*deposit*
20	指数*	指數	zhǐshù	*index*
21	存款		cúnkuǎn	*savings deposits*
22	利率		lìlǜ	*interest rate*
23	财富	財富	cáifù	*wealth; fortune*
24	新兴	新興	xīnxīng	*burgeoning; newly risen*
25	物资	物資	wùzī	*goods and materials*
26	短缺		duǎnquē	*shortage;* 缺少; 缺乏
27	发放	發放	fāfàng	*(of a government or organization) distribute (money or goods)*
28	过头	過頭	guòtóu	*go beyond the limit*
29	选择	選擇	xuǎnzé	*choose; select*
30	短信		duǎnxìn	*short message*
31	央行*		yāngháng	*central bank;* 中央银行
32	加息		jiāxī	*raise interest rates*

专有名词 Proper nouns

	美联储*	美聯儲	Měiliánchǔ	*US Federal Reserve Board*

俗语 Common sayings

	说曹操，曹操到*	說曹操，曹操到	Shuō Cáo Cāo, Cáo Cāo dào	*Talk of a person and he will appear.*

理解考核 Comprehension check

回答问题 Answer the following questions

1 通货膨胀给中国人民的生活带来了哪些影响？

2 通货膨胀给美国人民的生活带来了哪些影响？

3 林教授说了通货膨胀的哪两个原因？

4 林教授认为中国的这次通货膨胀是怎么引起的？

5 中国和美国的货币政策是由什么部门决定的？他们对通货膨胀的做法一样吗？

注释 Notes

1 物价指数 (CPI)

The Consumer Price Index is a statistical estimate based on the prices of a sample of representative consumer goods and services whose prices are collected periodically. China's CPI is calculated and published by its National Bureau of Statistics (国家统计局).

2 美联储 (US Federal Reserve Board)

美联储 is the short form of 美国联邦储备委员会 (The Board of Governors of The Federal Reserve System). The Federal Reserve System, also known as the Federal Reserve and informally as the Fed, is the central banking system of the United States. In its role as the central bank (see Note 4) of the United States, the Federal Reserve serves as a banker's bank as well as the government's fiscal agent. Unlike the government-controlled Central People's Bank of China 中央人民银行, which is China's central bank, the Federal Reserve is a private central bank in which the government holds zero share of stock but keeps a checking account. 美联储 (the seven-member Board of Governors), however, is a federal agency with its chairman and vice chairman appointed by the US president.

3 说曹操，曹操到

The original meaning of this popular saying was that *Cáo Cāo*, a shrewd statesman and warlord during the Three Kingdoms period who was well informed and quick in taking actions, would appear before you the moment you said his name. Because his name had negative connotations, one had to be on guard against him all the time. The saying's current meaning is "Talk of a person and he will appear."

4 央行

央行 is short for 中央银行. A central bank is a public institution that provides the nation's money supply. It also controls interest rates and acts as the lender of last resort during times of financial crisis. With its supervisory powers, it works to prevent financial institutions from reckless or fraudulent behavior. Central banks in most developed nations are free from political interference because they operate under rules.

语言提示 Language tips

1 不至于: This is always followed by a situation that is unlikely to happen due to the reason mentioned in a previous statement.

- 美国人的收入比较高，社会福利又比较好，<u>不至于</u>人心惶惶吧？

  他有这么多实习经验，<u>不至于</u>找不到工作的。

  别担心，这次讲座虽然都用中文，但是你的中文也不错，<u>不至于</u>听不懂。

练习 Exercises

1 将左栏的主语部分和右栏的谓语部分配对，每个词语只能用一次。
Match each subject in the left column with an appropriate predicate in the right column. Each item can be used only once.

1)	货币 _____	a)	产生动摇
2)	能源和原材料 _____	b)	带动需求
3)	社会 _____	c)	贬值
4)	政府 _____	d)	涨价
5)	财富 _____	e)	抑制投资与生产
6)	人们对货币的信心 _____	f)	发生动荡
7)	经济的持续增长 _____	g)	过量
8)	商品存货 _____	h)	垮台
9)	失业率 _____	i)	升高
10)	长期的货币紧缩 _____	j)	缩水

2 听写并用汉语解释下列词组。Complete a dictation of the following phrases and explain them in Chinese.

1) 经济衰退 　　7) 通胀失控

2) 股市的随机性 　8) 叫苦连天

3) 社会总需求 　　9) 人心惶惶

4) 货币购买力 　　10) 负利率

5) 经济崩溃 　　　11) 物资短缺

6) 货币紧缩 　　　12) 说曹操，曹操到

3 选词填空。Fill in the blanks with the provided words and expressions.

1) 便，与，被，以至，一旦，最终，系

通货膨胀_____指整体物价水平上升，货币购买力下降的现象，_____社会总需求大于社会总供给有关。一般来说，低度的通货膨胀 _____ 认为能对经济起"润滑"作用，_____ 通胀持续发生 _____ 会使消费下降，_____进入经济衰退。当通货膨胀率达到三位数时，物价飞涨，货币贬值，社会金融体系和经济关系受到破坏，_____导致社会崩溃。

2) 叫苦连天，财富缩水，物价飞涨，人心惶惶

通货膨胀使得_____，_____。低收入家庭只好从嘴里省钱，从身上省钱。通货膨胀也使得物价指数上升得快，对把钱存在银行的人来说，存款就成了负利率，造成了_____。再加上失业率高，通货膨胀让很多人_____。

4 用指定的表达方式完成句子或对话。Complete the following sentences and dialogues with the designated words or expressions.

1) 便

a) 马可对中国的房地产市场很感兴趣，_____。

b) 李瑛瑛打算毕业以后到一家跨国公司工作，_____。

2) 与 ... 有关

a) 股票价格的涨跌_____。

b) 一个国家的汇率水平_____。

3) 以至

a) 人民币不断升值，_____。

b) 近来物价持续上涨，_____。

4) 一旦

    a) ＿＿＿＿＿＿＿＿＿＿＿＿＿＿＿＿，这家公司便只能宣布破产。

    b) ＿＿＿＿＿＿＿＿＿＿＿＿＿＿＿＿，企业就能在市场竞争中占有优势。

5) 最终

    a) 这次贸易洽谈进行了三天，＿＿＿＿＿＿＿＿＿＿＿＿＿＿＿＿＿。

    b) "联想"为进入国际市场进行了长期的准备，＿＿＿＿＿＿＿＿＿＿＿。

6) 进而

    a) 这次市场调查充分了解了消费者的需求，并＿＿＿＿＿＿＿＿＿＿。

    b) 股票成功上市提高了这家公司的知名度，＿＿＿＿＿＿＿＿＿＿＿。

7) 不至于

    a) A：这次经济危机这么厉害，咱们不会失业吧。

        B：别担心，＿＿＿＿＿＿＿＿＿＿＿＿＿＿＿＿＿＿。

    b) A：听说中国大城市的房价高得可怕，老百姓会不会没有房子住啊？

        B：没那么严重，＿＿＿＿＿＿＿＿＿＿＿＿＿＿＿＿。

5 把下面的句子改成不太正式的语体。Paraphrase the following sentences in a less formal style, paying special attention to the underlined words and phrases.

1) 经济连续两个季度或以上停滞或负增长，便被认为进入经济衰退。该现象与消费量下降，商品存货过量有关。

    ＿＿＿＿＿＿＿＿＿＿＿＿＿＿＿＿＿＿＿＿＿＿＿＿＿＿＿

    ＿＿＿＿＿＿＿＿＿＿＿＿＿＿＿＿＿＿＿＿＿＿＿＿＿＿＿。

2) "通胀"亦被称为"通膨"，系指社会总需求大于社会总供给时整体物价水平上升，货币购买力下降的现象。

    ＿＿＿＿＿＿＿＿＿＿＿＿＿＿＿＿＿＿＿＿＿＿＿＿＿＿＿

    ＿＿＿＿＿＿＿＿＿＿＿＿＿＿＿＿＿＿＿＿＿＿＿＿＿＿＿。

3) 流通中的货币过多被称为"通货膨胀"，反之则为"通货紧缩"。后者系指市场上流通的货币不足，购买力下降，进而造成物价下跌。

    ＿＿＿＿＿＿＿＿＿＿＿＿＿＿＿＿＿＿＿＿＿＿＿＿＿＿＿

    ＿＿＿＿＿＿＿＿＿＿＿＿＿＿＿＿＿＿＿＿＿＿＿＿＿＿＿。

4) 持续的通胀将使消费下降，以至进入经济衰退。一旦通胀率达到三位数，物价飞涨，货币大幅贬值，最终将导致社会崩溃和政府垮台。

    ＿＿＿＿＿＿＿＿＿＿＿＿＿＿＿＿＿＿＿＿＿＿＿＿＿＿＿

    ＿＿＿＿＿＿＿＿＿＿＿＿＿＿＿＿＿＿＿＿＿＿＿＿＿＿＿。

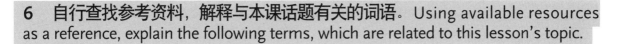

6 自行查找参考资料，解释与本课话题有关的词语。Using available resources as a reference, explain the following terms, which are related to this lesson's topic.

1) 滞胀 5) 凯恩斯主义

2) 泡沫经济 6) CCI 指数（消费者信心指数）

3) 次贷危机 7) CSI 指数（消费者情绪指数）

4) 货币危机 8) 痛苦指数

7 阅读理解与讨论。Reading comprehension and discussion.

经济衰退也有好处

面对衰退，人们关注的往往是资金、金融和经济。然而长期而言，衰退对工作和工作习惯的影响可能是正面的。

1981 年至 1982 年的衰退预示了"终身工作"的终结。工作和职业不再是一回事。在那次衰退过后，越来越多的人成了"自由职业者"，弹性工作也渐渐变成一种可行的选择。1990 年至 1991 年的衰退不但加速了这些变化，还带来了一个更加重要的影响——全球化。通过把工作从发达国家转移到印度和东欧等新兴国家的劳动力市场，成本下降了。

那么，2007 年 12 月开始的这次衰退会给未来10年造成什么样的影响呢？首先，领导和决策将会得到改善。目前，大公司的首席执行官可以单方面做出有关整个公司的决定。未来几年，人们将会把决策权和领导权分配给更广泛的不同人群，从而产生更好的效果。其次，一些不太被看好的做法可能会在衰退后加速发展，就好像外包在上世纪90年代的衰退后不断得到扩大和深化，最终变成了一种标准一样。最后，衰退也可能会改变人们看待职业的方式。上世纪90年代的衰退放慢了人们涌向科技和初创企业的步伐。当前的危机很可能对银行业产生同样的影响，最优秀的人才可能不会再把事业目标仅仅放在投资银行。

关注	guānzhù	follow with interest	广泛	guǎngfàn	extensive; widespread
长期而言	chángqī ér yán	in the long run	人群	rénqún	crowd
正面	zhèngmiàn	positive	效果	xiàoguǒ	effect
预示	yùshì	indicate	其次	qícì	secondly
终身	zhōngshēn	lifelong; lifetime	外包	wàibāo	outsourcing
终结	zhōngjié	end; terminate	深化	shēnhuà	deepen
弹性	tánxìng	elasticity; resilience	标准	biāozhǔn	standard; criterion
可行	kěxíng	feasible; practicable	看待	kàndài	treat; regard
发达	fādá	developed	涌向	yǒngxiàng	flock to
转移	zhuǎnyí	shift; transfer	科技	kējì	science and technology
印度	Yìndù	India	初创	chūchuàng	newly established
东欧	Dōng'ōu	Eastern Europe	步伐	bùfá	steps
决策	juécè	make a strategic decision	危机	wēijī	crisis; crunch
首席	shǒuxí	chief	优秀	yōuxiù	excellent; outstanding
执行官	zhíxíngguān	executive officer	事业	shìyè	career; undertaking
单方面	dānfāngmiàn	one-sided	仅仅	jǐnjǐn	only; barely

选择填空 Select the correct answer for each blank.

1) 经济衰退 _____。

    a) 仅仅影响到资金、金融和经济

    b) 的长期影响肯定是正面的

    c) 对工作和工作习惯的影响可能是正面的

2) 1981 至 1982 年的经济衰退以后 _____。

    a) 越来越多的人成为自由职业者

    b) 人们更希望找到"终身工作"

    c) 人们觉得职业不再重要

3) 关于 1990 至 1991 年的衰退，下面<u>不正确</u>的说法是 _____。

    a) 加速了人们成为自由职业者

    b) 降低了新兴国家的劳动力成本

    c) 引起了全球化

4) 关于"外包"，下面<u>不正确</u>的说法是 _____。

    a) 在20世纪90年代以前不被看好

    b) 在20世纪90年代的衰退后不断发展，最终成为了一种标准

    c) 是2007年开始的这次衰退带来的最大的影响

讨论 Discussion.

    文章指出2007年12月开始的这次衰退会给未来10年造成什么样的影响？根据你了解的情况或所查的资料，请你谈谈自己的看法。This article talks about the current economic recession, which started in December of 2007. According to the author, what kind of impact will this recession have on the ten years that follow? Please add your own comments based on what you know or what you have found in research.

8 实践活动。Tasks.

1) 查出20世纪以来一次影响较大的经济危机，简要列出它发生和持续的时间，所涉及的国家及基本情况。Find an influential economic crisis from the twentieth century or thereafter and make a brief list of its basic information, such as when it started, how long it lasted, what countries were affected, and what happened.

2) 选择中国、美国或任何一个别的国家，做一个10分钟的口头报告，介绍该国刺激经济的某项措施，说明这项措施的具体做法及效果，并提出你自己的看法。先查看最近六个月之内的资料，然后根据老师的要求为自己准备一个简单的提纲。在报告时要尽可能提供事实和例子。Pick China, the United States, or another country to be the subject of a ten-minute oral report, in which you

introduce and provide your own comments about a stimulatory measure for that country's economy. Ideally, you should base your report on information from within the past six months and prepare a brief outline for yourself as per your teacher's instructions. Make an effort to include facts and examples.

3) 写一个简单的调查报告（不要超过一页），列出中国和美国六个月来的 CPI 和 ICS 指数，并据此对两国的经济情况加以分析和对比。In a brief written report (limited to one page), compare the economic situations of China and the United States by listing their CPI and ICS indexes from the past six months and summarizing your analysis.

4) 如果你对一个不同的任务有兴趣，请结合本课的主题向老师提出建议，然后在老师的指导下完成这个任务。If you are interested in a different kind of task, you are encouraged to suggest your proposal and to complete it under your teacher's guidance.

学习指导 Learning guide

句子中的"短缺""Missing" elements in sentences

As English speakers, you might sometimes feel that Chinese grammar is not as rigid as English. Occasionally, you will find an element missing from a Chinese sentence, which would not have been allowed in English. For example, you may suspect that a pronoun is missing from the following sentences:

该种股票以人民币标明ˇ面值。(它的)
他们只好从ˇ嘴里省钱。(他们的)

But this is the way Chinese is: An attributive pronoun is dropped more often than not when the simplification does not cause misunderstanding.

The omission of subjects is more complicated. A subject is usually dropped when it occurs the second time:

因为<u>他</u>对计划经济不太理解，所以ˇ去找林老师。(他)
<u>两个人</u>都想谈谈，ˇ便在草地上坐了下来。(他们)
<u>一个企业</u>只有掌握了市场信息ˇ才能组织各项经营活动。(它)

A missing subject, however, is not necessarily the same subject in the preceding clause:

企业跨国经营的<u>性质</u>多种多样，但ˇ大多是为了获得比较优势，在世界范围内建立最佳的基地。(The subject in the first clause is 性质, but the subject in the second clause cannot be 性质. It has to be 企业跨国经营 to make sense. 企业跨国经营 is dropped because a direct reference exists in the context.)

In the following examples, the missing subject is not the same subject as in the preceding clause. The subject is implied, and you have to figure it out based on the context.

他们买了一套二手房，^V一直在装修。(这套二手房)

他想买一套大一点儿的房子，^V既能改善生活条件，又是一项投资。(这样做)

市场上流通的货币不足，购买力下降，^V进而造成物价下跌。（这些现象）

These examples would be regarded as ungrammatical in English. However, in Chinese, they are not only accepted in casual situations, they also appear frequently in formal speeches and writings.

Now let's move on to another issue by revisiting a sentence from Lesson 1:

它们^V简称为"上交所"和"深交所"，通常也被称为"沪市"和"深市"。

You must have noticed the obvious looseness in the usage of 被, the passive preposition. Generally speaking, it sounds a little more formal without 被 than with 被 in a context like this. 被 is grammatically desirable where it is marked with ^V, but you can also drop the underlined 被 to sound more formal. Native Chinese speakers may not feel too strongly about the difference.

You should not be surprised by "missing" elements in a Chinese sentence that you would have had to keep in English. It is typical Chinese practice to drop one element or another as long as the meaning is clear from the context. Remember, however, that you cannot always drop elements. As a language learner, you must follow native speakers to sound idiomatic.

PRACTICE: Figure out what is "missing" in each sentence. Familiarize yourself with the omission by reading the sentence aloud a few times.

1 他们这个计划并不符合^V需要。

2 一个国家要把人力、物力、财力用到^V最重要的地方。

3 你比较有经验，^V有什么要提醒我的吗？

4 这些方面我们已经了解得差不多了，下个星期^V就要准备洽谈方案了。

5 中国还有很多新的市场，^V只要能抢得先机就可以大有作为。

6 因为肯德基的本土化比较彻底，^V才把老对手麦当劳抛在了后边。

7 在计划经济的实践过程中，生产与需求脱节，劳动者动力不足，生产效率低下，市场缺乏活力，^V严重制约了经济的发展。

REVIEW PRACTICE: Based on your knowledge of characters and character components, match the following items with their definitions. (Refer to L2's learning guide if necessary.)

a 文件 b 国债 c 税款 d 住宅 e 财政 f 方法
g 私人 h 发言 i 实物 j 相关 k 期间 l 拥有

1 private _____   5 residence _____   9 document _____

2 possess _____   6 finance _____   10 tax money _____

3 time period _____   7 method _____   11 related _____

4 state debt _____   8 real object _____   12 speech _____

第九课 税收

Lesson 9 *Taxation*

课文一 Text 1

国家凭借政治上的权力，按照法律规定的标准，对组织或个人无偿征收实物或货币,即为"征税"。所征得的实物或货币为"税"，也称"税收"。

财政收入的种类很多，如税收、货币、国债、收费、罚没等。税收作为国家取得财政收入的手段之一，具有以下特征：第一，无偿性。国家对课税对象无偿征收，不付报酬。第二，强制性。税收是以法律形式规定的，纳税人必须依照国家的税收法令缴纳税款。第三，固定性。与税收有关的一切方面都有税收法令的预先规定，并有相对稳定的适用期间。当然，由于中国地域广阔，不同地区和时期的税收制度是有可能存在差异的。

税收不但在组织财政收入中具有举足轻重的地位，而且在调节社会经济，监管社会经济活动，保持经济稳定，体现产业政策等方面发挥重要作用。改革开放以后，中国通过在多个相关行业提供税收优惠，吸引了大量外资。但随着经济的持续发展，为了让中国企业与外资企业在同一个高度上进行竞争，这种对于外资的优惠税收政策已于2010年12月1日正式全部取消。

國家憑藉政治上的權力，按照法律規定的標準，對組織或個人無償徵收實物或貨幣,即為"徵稅"。所征得的實物或貨幣為"稅"，也稱"稅收"。

財政收入的種類很多，如稅收、貨幣、國債、收費、罰沒等。稅收作為國家取得財政收入的手段之一，具有以下特徵：第一，無償性。國家對課稅對象無償徵收，不付報酬。第二，強制性。稅收是以法律形式規定的，納稅人必須依照國家的稅收法令繳納稅款。第三，固定性。與稅收有關的一切方面都有稅收法令的預先規定，並有相對穩定的適用期間。當然，由於中國地域廣闊，不同地區和時期的稅收制度是有可能存在差異的。

稅收不但在組織財政收入中具有舉足輕重的地位，而且在調節社會經濟，監管社會經濟活動，保持經濟穩定，體現產業政策等方面發揮重要作用。改革開放以後，中國通過在多個相關行業提供稅收優惠，吸引了大量外資。但隨著經濟的持續發展，為了讓中國企業與外資企業在同一個高度上進行競爭，這種對於外資的優惠稅收政策已於2010年12月1日正式全部取消。

词语表 Words and expressions

(* Refer to notes or language tips following the word list.)

1	税收*		shuìshōu	*taxation; tax revenue*
2	凭借	憑藉	píngjiè	*rely on; depend on;* 靠; 依靠
3	按照*		ànzhào	*according to;* 根据
4	规定	規定	guīdìng	*regulate; regulation*
5	无偿	無償	wúcháng	*gratuitously; free; gratis*
6	征收	徵收	zhēngshōu	*levy; collect*
7	实物	實物	shíwù	*material object*
8	财政	財政	cáizhèng	*finance*
9	种类	種類	zhǒnglèi	*kind; type*
10	国债	國債	guózhài	*national debt*
11	罚没	罰沒	fámò	*confiscate; confiscation*
12	特征	特徵	tèzhēng	*characteristic; feature; trait*
13	课税	課稅	kèshuì	*levy a tax;* 征税
14	对象	對象	duìxiàng	*object; target; subject*

15	报酬	報酬	bàochóu	*pay; remuneration; rewards*
16	强制	強制	qiǎngzhì	*force; compel*
17	形式		xíngshì	*form; style*
18	纳税	納稅	nàshuì	*pay tax;* 交税
19	依照*		yīzhào	*according to; in light of;* 按照
20	法令		fǎlìng	*laws and decrees*
21	缴纳	繳納	jiǎonà	*pay*
22	税款		shuìkuǎn	*tax payment; taxation*
23	固定		gùdìng	*fixed; immobile*
24	预先	預先	yùxiān	*in advance; beforehand;* 事先
25	相对	相對	xiāngduì	*relatively; comparatively*
26	稳定	穩定	wěndìng	*stable; steady*
27	适用	適用	shìyòng	*applicable*
28	期间	期間	qījiān	*time; period*
29	地域		dìyù	*region; area*
30	广阔	廣闊	guǎngkuò	*vast; wide*
31	举足轻重	舉足輕重	jǔ zú qīng zhòng	*play a decisive role*
32	监管	監管	jiānguǎn	*supervision and control;* 监督和管理
33	体现	體現	tǐxiàn	*embody; incarnate*
34	发挥*	發揮	fāhuī	*bring (skill, talent, etc.) into play*
35	相关	相關	xiāngguān	*related;* 有关
36	行业	行業	hángyè	*industry; trade*
37	优惠*	優惠	yōuhuì	*benefits; favorable treatment*
38	高度		gāodù	*elevation above a specified level*
39	取消		qǔxiāo	*cancel*

理解考核 Comprehension check

对错选择 True or false

		True	False
1	税收是国家财政收入的重要来源，国家也会付给纳税人相应的报酬。	☐	☐
2	税收是以法律形式规定的，纳税人必须依法纳税。	☐	☐
3	与税收有关的方面都有法律预先规定，并有相当稳定的适用期间。	☐	☐
4	中国各个地方的税收制度都是完全一样的。	☐	☐
5	2010年12月1日后外资企业在中国不再享受税收优惠政策。	☐	☐

注释 Notes

1 税收优惠

A tax credit is a sum deducted from the total amount a taxpayer owes to the state. Tax credits may be granted to businesses or individuals for various types of taxes in recognition of taxes already paid or to encourage investment or other behaviors. Although tax credits reduce a government's fiscal revenue, they help it realize certain goals.

语言提示 Language tips

1 按照/依照: according to

- 国家 ... 按照法律规定的标准，对组织或个人无偿征收实物或货币，即为"征税"。
- 税收是以法律形式规定的，纳税人必须依照国家的税收法令缴纳税款。

我们已经按照王总的要求，把计划书准备好了。
科学管理依照规章制度对员工进行惩罚和奖励。

2 ... 之一: one of

- 税收作为国家取得财政收入的手段之一，具有以下特征。

摩托罗拉公司（Motorola, Inc.）是世界财富百强企业之一。
通货紧缩会产生不少影响，失业率上升就是其中之一。

3 如...等: such as; for instance; (refer to L3-1, LT6)

- 财政收入的种类很多，<u>如</u>税收、货币、国债、收费、罚没<u>等</u>。

  个人投资的渠道很多，<u>如</u>股市、汇市、房市、保险<u>等</u>。
  目前中国还有很多市场没有充分开发，<u>如</u>农村市场、老年市场、旅游市场<u>等</u>。

4 具有...的地位: have a ... status or position. The verb 具有 is typically used for something immaterial.

- 税收...在组织财政收入中<u>具有</u>举足轻重<u>的地位</u>。

  宜家家居（IKEA）一直在中国家居市场的竞争中<u>具有</u>领先<u>地位</u>。
  中国经济在世界经济中<u>具有</u>重要<u>的地位</u>。

5 （在...方面）发挥...作用: play a ... role (in)
  （对...）具有...作用: have a ... impact (on)
  （对...）起...作用: affect (...) in the capacity of

- 税收...<u>在</u>调节社会经济、监管社会经济活动...等<u>方面发挥</u>重要<u>作用</u>。

  世贸组织将<u>在</u>持久和有序地扩大世界贸易<u>方面发挥</u>关键<u>作用</u>。
    (L4, Ex7)
  国际贸易...<u>对</u>参与贸易的国家及世界经济的发展都<u>具有</u>重要<u>作用</u>。(L4-1)
  公有资产...在社会总资产中占优势，<u>对</u>经济发展<u>起</u>主导<u>作用</u>。
    (L7-1)
  低度的通货膨胀能<u>对</u>经济<u>起</u>"润滑"<u>作用</u>。(L8-1)

6 随着: 随 means "to follow," so 随着 carries the meaning of "along with."

- <u>随着</u>经济的持续发展，...对于外资的优惠税收政策已...正式全部取消。

  <u>随着</u>外资企业的增加，进出口贸易也得到了很大的发展。
  <u>随着</u>研究的深入，我们对中国的计算机市场有了更多的了解。

课文二 Text 2

　　马可的经济课开始学习"税收"这一章，学生们对房地产税特别有兴趣，因为它一直是社会关注的焦点。林教授已经让马可准备在课上介绍一下美国的房地产税。这一天，马可来找林教授谈一谈。

林汉华：　发言准备得怎么样了？有困难吗？

马　可：　林老师，我在做一个 PowerPoint 文件，打算从三个方面来介绍：第一，美国房地产税的性质；第二，美国房地产税的用途；第三，美国房地产税的征收方法。您看可以吗？

林汉华：　我看很好。就是同学们到时候还会问一些问题。

马　可：　这倒没关系，我最喜欢跟大家讨论了。就是我对中国的房地产税知道得太少了。

林汉华：　中国的税收制度还不完善，政府一直在研究和推进房地产税的改革。你有什么问题吗？

马　可：　在美国，房地产税是地方政府按照房子的市值征收的，而且专款专用，用来改善当地的教育、治安和环境。在中国也是这样吗？

林汉华：　中国也是按照评估值来计征城镇房地产税的，但目前有一个确保自住需求的免征面积，首先只对高档房、大户型和非自住的住宅征税。另外，因为房地产税的评估和征收都比较复杂，所以只能由各地从实际出发来制定制度，收入也归地方财政所有。至于它的用途，今后会慢慢明确的。

马　可：　听您这么说，好像房地产税的问题现在还有很多东西不清楚。

林汉华：　是这样的。中国经济市场化的历史毕竟太短了，税收制度的建立和完善是需要一个过程的。

马　可：　还有一个问题。美国的土地是私人拥有的，所以房产和地产是连在一起的。可是在中国，土地是国有的，人们买房时只是买了几十年的土地使用权，并没有买地，所以并没有地产，为什么也要叫"房地产税"呢？

林汉华： 这个问题有意思。中国的国情不一样，我想你就叫它
　　　　 "房产税"好了。

马　可： 那，老师，您是让我"入乡"不"随俗"呀！

　　馬可的經濟課開始學習"稅收"這一章，學生們對房地產稅特別有興趣，因為它一直是社會關注的焦點。林教授已經讓馬可準備在課上介紹一下美國的房地產稅。這一天，馬可來找林教授談一談。

林漢華： 發言準備得怎麼樣了？有困難嗎？

馬　可： 林老師，我在做一個 PowerPoint 文件，打算從三個方面來介紹：第一，美國房地產稅的性質；第二，美國房地產稅的用途；第三，美國房地產稅的徵收方法。您看可以嗎？

林漢華： 我看很好。就是同學們到時候還會問一些問題。

馬　可： 這倒沒關係，我最喜歡跟大家討論了。就是我對中國的房地產稅知道得太少了。

林漢華： 中國的稅收制度還不完善，政府一直在研究和推進房地產稅的改革。你有什麼問題嗎？

馬　可： 在美國，房地產稅是地方政府按照房子的市值徵收的，而且專款專用，用來改善當地的教育、治安和環境。在中國也是這樣嗎？

林漢華： 中國也是按照評估值來計徵城鎮房地產稅的，但目前有一個確保自住需求的免徵面積，首先只對高檔房、大戶型和非自住的住宅徵稅。另外，因為房地產稅的評估和徵收都比較複雜，所以只能由各地從實際出發來制定制度，收入也歸地方財政所有。至於它的用途，今後會慢慢明確的。

馬　可： 聽您這麼說，好像房地產稅的問題現在還有很多東西不清楚。

林漢華： 是這樣的。中國經濟市場化的歷史畢竟太短了，稅收制度的建立和完善是需要一個過程的。

馬　可： 還有一個問題。美國的土地是私人擁有的，所以房產和地產是連在一起的。可是在中國，土地是國有的，人們買房時只是買了幾十年的土地使用權，並沒有買地，所以並沒有地產，為什麼也要叫"房地產稅"呢？

林漢華： 這個問題有意思。中國的國情不一樣，我想你就叫它"房產稅"好了。

馬　可： 那，老師，您是讓我"入鄉"不"隨俗"呀！

词语表 Words and expressions

(* Refer to notes or language tips following the word list.)

1	章		zhāng	*chapter*
2	关注	關注	guānzhù	*pay close attention to*
3	焦点	焦點	jiāodiǎn	*focal point; focus*
4	发言	發言	fāyán	*make a statement or speech*
5	文件		wénjiàn	*document; paper*
6	用途		yòngtú	*use; application;* 用处

7	方法		fāngfǎ	*method; way;* 做法
8	完善		wánshàn	*perfect; flawless;* 完美
9	专款专用	專款專用	zhuānkuǎn zhuānyòng	*earmark a fund for a specified purpose*
10	治安		zhì'ān	*public security; public order*
11	评估	評估	pínggū	*assessment; evaluation*
12	值		zhí	*value; often as a suffix*
13	计征	計征	jìzhēng	*calculation and levy*
14	城镇	城鎮	chéngzhèn	*cities and towns*
15	免征		miǎnzhēng	*exemption*
16	面积	面積	miànjī	*measure of area; square measure*
17	大户型		dàhùxíng	*large dwelling-size (house; apartment)*
18	非		fēi	*not-, un-; non-; often as a prefix*
19	住宅		zhùzhái	*residence*
20	制定		zhìdìng	*set up; institute*
21	归	歸	guī	*belong to; be attributed to*
22	至于*	至於	zhìyú	*as for; as to*
23	明确	明確	míngquè	*clear and definite;* 清楚
24	毕竟	畢竟	bìjìng	*after all*
25	私人		sīrén	*private*
26	拥有	擁有	yōngyǒu	*possess; have;* 有
27	连	連	lián	*linked; connected*
28	使用		shǐyòng	*use;* 用

俗语 Common sayings

入乡随俗	入鄉隨俗	rù xiāng suí sú	*Wherever you are, follow local customs.*

理解考核 Comprehension check

回答问题 Answer the following questions

1 马可打算怎么介绍美国的房地产税？

2 美国的房地产税是按什么征收的？用来做什么？

3 中国的房地产税是按什么征收的？目前只对哪些房子征收房地产税？

4 马可为什么说中国的房地产税还有很多东西不清楚？

5 为什么马可觉得在中国不应该叫"房地产税"而应该叫"房产税"？

注释 Notes

1 土地使用权

Under the 1982 Constitution, urban land in China is owned by the State and rural land by the collectives. Since the rural collectives are administered by the local and central governments, all land ownership is actually under the control of the State. However, an Amendment Act of 1988 states that a land-use right may be transferred in accordance to law. Based on this statement, a land-use right becomes divisible from land ownership and, therefore, privatized. Nowadays, real estate sales in China take place in the form of the transfer of land-use rights. The land user signs a land-grant contract with the local land authority and pays a land-grant fee up front. The grantee will enjoy a fixed land-grant term and must use the land for the specified purpose. The maximum term of a land grant ranges from 40 years for commercial usage, 50 years for industrial purposes, to 70 years for residential use. In fact, the transfer of land-use rights has accounted for most of the business activity in China's present primary real estate market. The rumors in January 2011 that land-use rights will be recovered by the State without compensation after their terms expire caused great concern.

语言提示 Language tips

1 就是: Among various usages of 就是, this one introduces an afterthought that is usually incongruous with the previous statement.

- 我看〔从三个方面来介绍这个问题〕很好，就是同学们到时候还会问一些问题。

  这份工作各方面都不错，就是工资低了点儿。
  这次讲座让我深受启发，就是有一两个细节 (xìjié, details) 我没听明白。

2 非: This prefix means 不是, just like non-, in-, and un- in English.

- 中国 ... 房地产税 ... 只对高档房、大户型和非自住的住宅征税。

  不少世贸成员国至今认为中国是"非市场经济国家"。
  非正式员工不用参加今天下午的会议。

3 至于: as to; as for; used typically to change the topic

- 房地产税的评估和征收都比较复杂 .... 至于它的用途,今后会慢慢明确的。

  今天我们主要讨论税收的种类,至于税收的作用,我们下节课再学习。
  很多人都认为人民币应该继续升值,至于该升多快,各有各的说法。

练习 Exercises

1 将左栏的定语和右栏的名词或名词短语配对,每个词语只能用一次。
Match each attributive modifier in the left column with an appropriate noun or noun phrase in the right column. Each item can be used only once.

1)	过硬的 ___	a)	经济衰退
2)	不正当的 ___	b)	公司
3)	假冒伪劣的 ___	c)	地位
4)	优秀的 ___	d)	技术
5)	本土化的 ___	e)	经营模式
6)	实力雄厚的 ___	f)	手段
7)	举足轻重的 ___	g)	规定
8)	严重的 ___	h)	成功
9)	重大的 ___	i)	社会公民
10)	预先的 ___	j)	商品

2 听写并用汉语解释下列词组。 Complete a dictation of the following phrases and explain them in Chinese.

1)	无偿征收	5)	举足轻重
2)	国债	6)	税收优惠
3)	地域广阔	7)	房地产税
4)	课税对象	8)	免征面积

154

9) 专款专用　　11) 土地使用权

10) 地方财政　　12) 入乡随俗

3 选词填空。 Fill in the blanks with the provided words and expressions.

1) 按照，之一，如，具有，随着，非法

　　税收是国家财政收入的重要来源 _____，具有许多特征，_____ 无偿性、强制性、固定性等。纳税人必须 _____ 法律缴纳税款，不得 _____ 逃税。_____ 经济的发展，税收在国家经济生活中 _____ 越来越重要的地位。

2) 地域广阔，专款专用，举足轻重，入乡随俗，高度关注

　　税收是国家财政收入的重要来源，具有 _____ 的地位，其中的"房地产税"更是让人 _____。美国的"房地产税"按房子的市值征收，_____。中国由于 _____，情况比较复杂，房地产税的问题还有很多东西不清楚，外国人到了中国就得 _____。

4 用指定的表达方式完成句子或对话。 Complete the following sentences and dialogues with the designated words or expressions.

1) 按照

   a) _____，高档房、大户型和非自住的住宅必须缴纳房地产税。

   b) _____，这家公司成功地制定了市场营销方案。

2) 如...等

   a) 影响市场营销的因素很多，_____。

   b) 企业管理包括很多方面，_____。

3) 具有...的地位

   a) 世界贸易组织 _____。

   b) 美国的科学技术 _____。

4) 在...方面发挥...作用

   a) 摩托罗拉的人力资源管理 _____。

   b) 政府的宏观调控 _____。

5) 随着

    a) _____，中国的房地产市场日益完善。

    b) 随着越来越多的中国企业进入国际市场，_____。

6) 就是

    a) A：静文，你实习的那家公司怎么样？

        B：还不错，学到了不少东西，_____。

    b) A：我毕业以后打算考研 (kǎoyán, apply to graduate school)，你觉得怎么样？

        B：能读硕 (shuò, master's degree)、读博 (bó, doctorate degree) 当然好，

        _____。

7) 至于

    a) 中国人和美国人的理财观念不一样。美国人习惯靠债务生活，_____

        _____。

    b) 沃尔玛和家乐福都是零售业的"老大"。家乐福刚进入中国市场的时候抢得了先机，_____

        _____。

5 把下面的句子改成不太正式的语体。 Paraphrase the following sentences in a less formal style, paying special attention to the underlined words and phrases.

1) 税收作为国家取得财政收入的<u>手段之一</u>，<u>具有以下</u>特征：无偿性，强制性，固定性。

    _____

    _____。

2) 国家<u>凭借</u>政治上的权力，<u>依照</u>法律规定的标准，对组织<u>或</u>个人<u>无偿</u>征收实物<u>或</u>货币，<u>即为</u>"征税"。

    _____

    _____。

3) 财政收入种类很多，<u>如</u>税收、货币、国债、收费、罚没<u>等</u>。税收在组织财政收入中<u>具有举足轻重</u>的地位。

    _____

    _____。

4) 税收是<u>以</u>法律形式规定的，纳税人必须<u>依照</u>国家的税收法令<u>缴纳税款</u>，<u>否则将被视为非法</u>。

    _____

    _____。

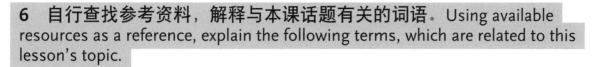

6 自行查找参考资料，解释与本课话题有关的词语。Using available resources as a reference, explain the following terms, which are related to this lesson's topic.

1) 征税项目
2) 个人所得税
3) 税率
4) 个税起征点
5) 超额累进税率
6) 合理避税

7 阅读理解与讨论。Reading comprehension and discussion.

关税与国民生活高度相关

关税是国际通行税种，每个国家都会对进出口的商品根据其种类和价值征收一定的税款。关税的作用在于抬高进口商品的价格，降低其市场竞争力，从而减少在市场上对本国产品的不良影响。

2010年8月，中国海关总署发布公告，个人境外购买 iPad 入境时需缴进口税1,000元。这一做法引起了广泛争议。

这件事之所以引起社会关注，与中国国门日益开放有关。以前，中国普通居民出国的机会很少，因此关税话题并没有进入公共关注层面。现在，随着国家的开放以及国际经济贸易的广泛联系，中国人不但能够很方便地在商场、超市买到进口商品，而且已经开始把出国购物或者从国外邮购、托购物品作为自己的选择。在这种情况下，关税不仅与国家的政治、经济高度关联，也直接影响到了国民的日常生活。

在开放的前提下，国与国的联系是经济上的，也是国民生活上的。国家可以从国际市场中获得利益，国民也应当分享到国家开放与国际交流的好处。从iPad征税争议中可以看出，关税影响民众生活的一面确实在显现出来。对于这一点，政府有必要正视并加以回应。

关税	guānshuì	customs duty	层面	céngmiàn	level
通行	tōngxíng	in common practice; current	超市	chāoshì	supermarket
税种	shuìzhǒng	tax category	邮购	yóugòu	mail order
抬高	táigāo	raise; elevate	托购	tuōgòu	entrust sb. to purchase
不良	bùliáng	harmful; unhealthy	物品	wùpǐn	article; thing
总署	zǒngshǔ	head office	关联	guānlián	connect
发布	fābù	issue; publish	前提	qiántí	premise; prerequisite
公告	gōnggào	announcement	利益	lìyì	benefit; interest
入境	rùjìng	enter a country	分享	fēnxiǎng	share
缴	jiǎo	pay; hand in	交流	jiāoliú	exchange; interchange
广泛	guǎngfàn	extensive	民众	mínzhòng	masses; common people
争议	zhēngyì	dispute	显现	xiǎnxiàn	appear; show
日益	rìyì	increasingly; day by day	正视	zhèngshì	face squarely; face up to
普通	pǔtōng	ordinary; common	加以	jiāyǐ	(before a verb) deal with
公共	gōnggòng	public	回应	huíyìng	respond; response

选择填空 Select the correct answer for each blank.

1) 关税的作用<u>不包括</u> ＿＿＿＿。

    a) 降低进口商品的市场竞争力

    b) 减少进口商品对本国商品的不良影响

    c) 限制本国人民从国外购买商品

2) 按照2010年8月中国海关总署的公告 ＿＿＿＿。

    a) 中国人在国外购买的 iPad 在回到中国时要缴进口税1,000元

    b) 中国人在国外购买 iPad 时要缴进口税1,000元

    c) 美国人在国外购买的 iPad 在进入中国时要缴进口税1,000元

3) 从 iPad 征税引起关注可以看出 ＿＿＿＿。

    a) 中国老百姓反对征税

    b) 关税直接影响到了国民的日常生活

    c) 中国人喜欢买进口商品

4) 中国人购买进口商品的方式<u>不包括</u> ＿＿＿＿。

    a) 出国直接购买

    b) 托人从国外购买

    c) 从邮局购买

讨论 Discussion.

作者对 iPad 入境时需缴关税有什么看法？根据你了解的情况或所查的资料，谈谈你对这种情况的看法。What is the author's opinion regarding the tariff on iPads purchased overseas? According to what you know from research, what are your opinions about this issue?

8 实践活动。Tasks.

1) 查阅中国个人所得税的最新规定，找出目前中国对工资和薪金征收个税时的起征点和超额累进税率。Search for China's most recent regulations on individual income tax, and find out the current collecting point and excess progressive rates for wages and salaries.

2) 做一个10分钟的口头报告，介绍当前中国某个城市对居民征收"房产税"的做法及其存在的问题。在报告中要提供事实和例子，并加上自己的看法。先查看最近六个月之内的资料，然后根据老师的要求为自己准备一个简单的提纲。Give a ten-minute oral report about the residential house tax in a city in China, including how it is implemented and any existing problems. You should provide your own opinions as well as facts and examples in the report. Ideally, you should base your report on information from within the past six months and prepare a brief outline for yourself as per your teacher's instructions.

3) 根据第7题中的阅读短文，写一封给中国海关总署的信，告诉他们你对这件事情的看法和建议。写信时要注意按照中文书信的格式，不要超过一页。Based on the reading article in Exercise 7, write a letter to the PRC's General Administration of Customs with your comments and suggestions. Follow the Chinese conventions for letter writing and limit the length to one page.

4) 如果你对一个别的任务有兴趣，请结合本课的主题向老师提出建议，然后在老师的指导下完成这个任务。If you are interested in a different kind of task, you are encouraged to suggest your proposal and to complete it under your teacher's guidance.

学习指导 Learning guide

长句分析（一）Analysis of long sentences (1)

Long sentences are one of the characteristics of formal language, especially in writing. Since Chinese for business purposes tends to be formal, a great number of sentences in this textbook may be longer than those you have experienced before.

It is true that many long sentences are composite sentences with a relatively complex makeup, but a long sentence can also be a simple sentence with just one "subject + predicate" structure. A simple sentence will be long if its basic elements carry more modifiers or if a basic element is complex in structure. Comprehension of such a sentence relies first of all on successful identification of its basic elements—the subject, the predicate, and the object (if any), and then on correct analyses of their modifiers. Let's go over a few examples, starting with the simplest. (Refer to L4's learning guide if necessary.)

- 这些年中国的<u>房价</u> // <u>上涨</u>得很厉害。
  房价 // 上涨 (S + VP)
  Here, the verbal predicate 上涨 is modified by both 这些年 (an adverbial) and 得很厉害 (a complement). 这些年 may appear after the subject too.

- 随着经济的持续发展，为了让中国企业与外资企业在同一个高度上进行竞争，这种对于外资的优惠税收<u>政策</u> // 已于2010年12月1日<u>被</u>正式全部<u>取消</u>。
  政策 // 被取消 (S + VP)
  The main verb 被取消 is modified by a 随着 prepositional phrase, a 为了 prepositional phrase, and some other adverbials directly before it.

- 马可的<u>老师</u> // 在课上也<u>介绍</u>了计划经济的<u>缺点</u>。
  老师 // 介绍缺点 (S + VP + O)

- <u>提供</u>税收<u>优惠</u> // <u>吸引</u>了大量外资。
  提供优惠 // 吸引外资 (S + VP + O)
  Here the subject 提供优惠 is not a single word but a verbal phrase.

159

- 在中国越来越多的<u>人</u> // <u>认为</u>沃尔玛的政府公关做得很好。
  人 // 认为 . . . (S + VP + O)
  The object in this simple sentence 沃尔玛的政府公关做得很好 is itself a sentence structure.

- <u>国际贸易</u> // <u>调节</u>各国市场的供求<u>关系</u>，<u>促进</u>劳动力、资本、土地、技术等生产要素在世界范围内的充分<u>利用</u>，对参与贸易的国家及世界经济的发展都具有重要<u>作用</u>。
  贸易 // 调节关系, 促进利用, 具有作用 (S + <<VP + O>>, <<VP + O>>, <<VP + O>>)

- 马可正在实习的那家公司的<u>客户</u> // 对这份营销计划非常<u>满意</u>。
  客户 // 满意 (S + AP)

- <u>企业管理</u> // <u>是</u>企业对生产经营活动进行组织、计划、指挥、监督和调节的<u>总称</u>。
  管理 // 是总称 (S + 是 + NP)

- <u>国家</u>凭借政治上的权力，按照法律规定的标准，对组织或个人无偿<u>征收实物或货币</u>, // 即<u>为</u>"<u>征税</u>"。
  国家征收实物或货币 // 为"征税" (S + 为 + NP)
  The subject 国家征收实物或货币 is itself a sentence structure, in which the verbal predicate 征收 has a number of adverbial modifiers in the form of prepositional phrases, which are 凭借 . . . , 按照 . . . , and 对 . . . .

We hope that the analysis of these examples has helped you better understand simple sentences in Chinese. This issue, however, can be much more complex than what is presented here. It is helpful if you are able to decode the structure of a long sentence, especially when you have to provide accurate translation of the Chinese original, but we do not mean to ask you to analyze every sentence you come across. In most cases, you will be fine if you recognize the "topic" and the "comment," and make sense of the content by following the gist.

PRACTICE: Following the above examples, reduce each sentence to its basic elements, separate the "topic" and the "comment" with a double slash, and specify the sentence's structure, such as (S + VP + O) or (S + AP).

1 汇率对短期资本流动有很大的影响。

2 目前，中国的国有企业、民营企业和外资企业正在共同推动中国经济的发展。

3 跨国公司的发展推动了生产要素在全球范围内的流动，促进了世界产业结构的调整，也促进了科学技术的不断创新和推广。

4 特别是上市以后，公司对人才的需求就很不一样了。

5 计划经济的出发点是避免市场自由发展的盲目性和不确定性。

REVIEW PRACTICE: Find likenesses in each group and reason out the undefined item by analogy. (Refer to L2's learning guide if necessary.)

1　商品; 商场; 商业; 商人　　　　商标 _____

2　发展; 发行; 发放; 发挥　　　　发生 _____

3　增加; 增强; 增长　　　　　　　增进 _____

4　同事; 同时; 同行　　　　　　　同路 _____

5　汇率; 利率; 税率; 通胀率; 失业率　成功率 _____

6　面值; 市值; 价值; 评估值　　　　币值 _____

7　商务; 财务; 业务; 债务　　　　　公务 _____

8　速度; 角度; 满意度; 高度　　　　难度 _____

第十课 个人理财与保险

Lesson 10 *Personal finance management and insurance*

课文一 Text 1

随着经济的发展，投资活动在个人理财方面所占的比例与日俱增，个人理财也呈现出多元化的趋势。一般来说，个人理财的形式主要有对黄金、基金、股票、国债、债券等的投资。而保险作为一种个人理财的手段也越来越受到人们的关注。

保险是指投保人根据合同约定向保险人支付保险费，而保险人对于合同约定的可能发生的事故及财产损失承担赔偿保险金的责任，或者在被保险人死亡、伤残、患病或达到合同约定的年龄、期限时承担给付保险金的责任。

保险可分为社会保险和商业保险两种。社会保险由政府承担，具有强制性，是为丧失劳动能力、暂时失去劳动岗位或因健康原因造成损失的人口提供收入或补偿的保险，包括养老社会保险、医疗社会保险等。商业保险由专门的保险企业经营，以营利为目的，是通过当事人双方自愿订立保险合同来运营的保险，包括财产保险、责任保险等。

保险的主要功能是：增强社会和个人抵御风险的能力，有利于企业加强危险管理，有利于民事赔偿责任的履行，从宏观上保证国家财政和信贷收支平衡的顺利实现。

隨著經濟的發展，投資活動在個人理財方面所占的比例與日俱增，個人理財也呈現出多元化的趨勢。一般來說，個人理財的形式主要有對黃金、基金、股票、國債、債券等的投資。而保險作為一種個人理財的手段也越來越受到人們的關注。

保險是指投保人根據合同約定向保險人支付保險費，而保險人對於合同約定的可能發生的事故及財產損失承擔賠償保險金的責任，或者在被保險人死亡、傷殘、患病或達到合同約定的年齡、期限時承擔給付保險金的責任。

保險可分為社會保險和商業保險兩種。社會保險由政府承擔，具有強制性，是為喪失勞動能力、暫時失去勞動崗位或因健康原因造成損失的人口提供收入或補償的保險，包括養老社會保險、醫療社會保險等。商業保險由專門的保險企業經營，以營利為目的，是通過當事人雙方自願訂立保險合同來運營的保險，包括財產保險、責任保險等。

保險的主要功能是：增強社會和個人抵禦風險的能力，有利於企業加強危險管理，有利於民事賠償責任的履行，從宏觀上保證國家財政和信貸收支平衡的順利實現。

词语表 Words and expressions

(* Refer to notes or language tips following the word list.)

1	理财	理財	lǐcái	*manage financial affairs*
2	比例*		bǐlì	*ratio; proportion*
3	与日俱增	與日俱增	yǔ rì jù zēng	*grow with each passing day*
4	俱		jù	*all; complete*
5	呈现*	呈現	chéngxiàn	*show; display;* 表现
6	多元		duōyuán	*multi-element; multi-variant*
7	黄金		huángjīn	*gold*
8	基金		jījīn	*fund; treasury*
9	债券	債券	zhàiquàn	*bond; debenture*
10	投保		tóubǎo	*buy insurance;* 购买保险
11	约定	約定	yuēdìng	*agree on*
12	支付		zhīfù	*pay (money);* 付
13	事故		shìgù	*accident*

14	财产	財產	cáichǎn	property; fortune
15	损失	損失	sǔnshī	loss
16	承担*	承擔	chéngdān	bear; undertake; assume
17	赔偿	賠償	péicháng	compensate
18	保险金	保險金	bǎoxiǎnjīn	insured amount
19	责任*	責任	zérèn	duty; responsibility
20	伤残	傷殘	shāngcán	wounded and disabled
21	患病		huànbìng	fall ill; 生病
22	年龄	年齡	niánlíng	age
23	期限		qīxiàn	deadline
24	给付	給付	jǐfù	give; pay; 支付
25	丧失	喪失	sàngshī	lose; 失去
26	暂时	暫時	zànshí	temporary; for the moment
27	岗位	崗位	gǎngwèi	post; position
28	补偿	補償	bǔcháng	compensate; make up for
29	包括*		bāokuò	include
30	养老	養老	yǎnglǎo	live out one's life in retirement
31	医疗	醫療	yīliáo	medical treatment
32	营利	營利	yínglì	seek profits
33	当事人	當事人	dāngshìrén	person or party concerned; litigant
34	自愿	自願	zìyuàn	voluntarily; willingly; 自己愿意
35	订立	訂立	dìnglì	conclude or make (a treaty, agreement, etc.)
36	运营	運營	yùnyíng	operate
37	功能		gōngnéng	function
38	抵御	抵禦	dǐyù	resist; withstand
39	民事		mínshì	civil; relating to civil law
40	履行		lǚxíng	perform; fulfill
41	信贷	信貸	xìndài	financial credit; usu. bank loans
42	收支		shōuzhī	income and expense; 收入和支出

理解考核 Comprehension check

对错选择 True or false

		True	False
1	和投资黄金、基金、股票一样，买保险也可以作为一种个人理财手段。	☐	☐
2	投保人支付保险费及保险人赔偿或给付保险金都必须按照合同的约定进行。	☐	☐
3	社会保险包括养老社会保险和医疗社会保险，是以营利为目的的。	☐	☐
4	商业保险包括财产保险、责任保险等，不具有强制性。	☐	☐
5	保险的主要功能之一是增加国家财政收入。	☐	☐

语言提示 Language tips

1 在...（中/方面）所占的比例: the proportion of a subcategory (in a category)

- 随着经济的发展，投资活动在个人理财方面所占的比例与日俱增。

  税收在国家财政收入中所占的比例很大。
  跨国企业的高科技产品在科技创新方面所占的比例具有明显增加的趋势。

2 呈现出...的趋势: show the tendency of

- 个人理财呈现出多元化的趋势。

  近年来，私有企业缴纳的税款呈现出明显上升的趋势。
  随着中国大陆劳动力成本的上升，外资呈现出向东南亚转移 (zhuǎnyí, transfer) 的趋势。

3 主要有...: there mainly exist (followed by a list of items)

- 一般来说，个人理财的形式主要有对黄金、基金...等的投资。

  在中国，进出口交易的常用外币主要有美元、港币、日元、欧元等。
  4P理论认为，影响营销的因素主要有产品、价格、渠道和促销。

4 作为: as; in the role and character of

- 保险作为一种个人理财的手段也越来越受到人们的关注。

  中国经济作为世界经济的重要组成部分，对世界的影响越来越大。
  公有资产作为中国经济的主导成分在社会总资产中占优势。

5 承担...的责任: bear the responsibility of

- 保险人...<u>承担</u>赔偿保险金<u>的责任</u>，或者...<u>承担</u>给付保险金<u>的责任</u>。

这个计划是我准备的，如果有什么问题，我愿意<u>承担</u>全部<u>的责任</u>。
不按规定缴税的企业必须<u>承担</u>相应的法律<u>责任</u>。

6 分为 A 和 B 两种: be divided into two types such as A and B, 分为 being the same as 分成.

- 保险可<u>分为</u>社会保险和商业保险<u>两种</u>。

国际贸易主要<u>分为</u>进口贸易<u>和</u>出口贸易<u>两种</u>。
该国的高等院校<u>分为</u>公立和私立<u>两种</u>。

7 包括...等: include (Refer to L3-1, LT6 for the usage of 等.)
包括...这许多方面: include the many aspects of (followed by a list)

- 社会保险...<u>包括</u>养老社会保险、医疗社会保险<u>等</u>。
- 商业保险...<u>包括</u>财产保险、责任保险<u>等</u>。
- 理财的范围很广，<u>包括</u>赚钱、用钱、存钱...和护钱<u>这许多方面</u>。(L10-2)

影响市场营销的宏观因素<u>包括</u>人口、教育水平、收入水平<u>等等</u>。

课文二 Text 2

马可这个周末又来看望王静文的舅舅和舅妈。张永安一听到他进门就从电脑前站起来打招呼。马可走过去，看到了屏幕上的几个大字："理财入门ABC"。张永安请马可坐下，两个人谈了起来。

张永安： 马可，你来得正好。你从美国来，一定会理财。我这儿正有问题要问你呢。

马　可： 我可不是理财专家，只是听说过一些皮毛罢了。怎么，张老师对理财有兴趣了？

张永安： 兴趣倒是谈不上，就算是"临时抱佛脚"吧。我们一向缺少理财意识，只会把钱存在银行里，可是现在通货膨胀，都成了负利率了。再不学习就吃大亏了。

马　可： 这一点我很理解。我们在美国从小就知道，每个人都得理财，而且理财不只是为了解决眼前的问题，而是要理一生的财。

张永安：我一直以为理财就是投资，就是赚钱。最近才明白理财的范围很广，包括赚钱、用钱、存钱、借钱、省钱和护钱这许多方面。

马　可：是啊，我父母就跟我说过，理财关系到对现金流量的管理和对风险的管理。这里边我不懂的东西太多了。

张永安：我现在最关心的是将来的生活保障。到我们年纪大了不再有工作收入的时候，怎么才能安度晚年呢？

马　可：看来您的理财目标是退休储蓄。等到不再有工作收入的时候，靠理财收入或变现资产来养老。

张永安：对，就是这么回事儿。那么你父母说的风险管理是什么意思呢？

马　可：他们说的风险是投资的风险，意思是只有先弄清自己能承受多大的风险才能合理地选择投资品种，像储蓄啊，股票啊，债券啊，基金啊，保险啊，不动产啊，等等。当然，选择投资的时间也很关键。

张永安： 我也听同事说起过，可以通过买保险来投资。这又是怎么一回事儿？

马　可： 哦，他们说的应该是收益类险种，那就是除了提供保障以外还能带来收入的保险，这好像也是投资理财的一个热点。

———————

马可这个週末又来看望王静文的舅舅和舅妈。张永安一听到他进门就从电脑前站起来打招呼。马可走过去，看到了屏幕上的几个大字："理财入门ABC"。张永安请马可坐下，两个人谈了起来。

张永安： 马可，你来得正好。你从美国来，一定会理财。我这儿正有问题要问你呢。

马　可： 我可不是理财专家，只是听说过一些皮毛罢了。怎么，张老师对理财有兴趣了？

张永安： 兴趣倒是谈不上，就算是"临时抱佛脚"吧。我们一向缺少理财意识，只会把钱存在银行里，可是现在通货膨胀，都成了负利率了。再不学习就吃大亏了。

马　可： 这一点我很理解。我们在美国从小就知道，每个人都得理财，而且理财不只是为了解决眼前的问题，而是要理一生的财。

张永安： 我一直以为理财就是投资，就是赚钱。最近才明白理财的范围很广，包括赚钱、用钱、存钱、借钱、省钱和护钱这许多方面。

马　可： 是啊，我父母就跟我说过，理财关系到对现金流量的管理和对风险的管理。这里边我不懂的东西太多了。

张永安： 我现在最关心的是将来的生活保障。到我们年纪大了不再有工作收入的时候，怎么才能安度晚年呢？

马　可： 看来您的理财目标是退休储蓄。等到不再有工作收入的时候，靠理财收入或变现资产来养老。

张永安： 对，就是这么回事儿。那么你父母说的风险管理是什么意思呢？

马　可： 他们说的风险是投资的风险，意思是只有先弄清自己能承受多大的风险才能合理地选择投资品种，像储蓄啊，股票啊，债券啊，基金啊，保险啊，不动产啊，等等。当然，选择投资的时间也很关键。

張永安: 我也聽同事說起過，可以通過買保險來投資。這又是怎麼一回事兒？

馬　可: 哦，他們說的應該是收益類險種，那就是除了提供保障以外還能帶來收入的保險，這好像也是投資理財的一個熱點。

词语表 Words and expressions

(* Refer to notes or language tips following the word list.)

1	看望		kànwàng	*call on; visit*
2	招呼		zhāohu	*greet; say hello*
3	屏幕		píngmù	*computer, TV, or hanging screen*
4	入门	入門	rùmén	*introductory guide; introduction*
5	专家	專家	zhuānjiā	*expert*
6	皮毛		pímáo	*(fig.) superficial knowledge*
7	罢了*	罷了	bàle	*only; nothing else*
8	一向		yīxiàng	*always; all the time*
9	缺少		quēshǎo	*lack; be short of*
10	吃亏	吃虧	chīkuī	*suffer losses*
11	意识	意識	yìshí	*consciousness; awareness*
12	解决		jiějué	*settle; solve*
13	眼前		yǎnqián	*at present;* 当前; 现在
14	一生		yīshēng	*all one's life; a lifetime;* 一辈子
15	赚钱	賺錢	zhuànqián	*make a profit; earn money;* 挣钱
16	广	廣	guǎng	*extensive; wide*
17	护钱	護錢	hùqián	*protect (one's own) money*
18	现金	現金	xiànjīn	*cash*
19	流量	流量	liúliàng	*rate or volume of flow*
20	年纪	年紀	niánjì	*age;* 年龄

21	安度		āndù	*spend (time) in peace and safety*
22	晚年		wǎnnián	*old age; one's later years*
23	退休		tuìxiū	*retire; retirement*
24	储蓄	儲蓄	chǔxù	*save; savings deposit;* 存钱
25	变现	變現	biànxiàn	*cash (a check, etc.); turn sth into cash*
26	承受		chéngshòu	*bear; endure*
27	合理		hélǐ	*reasonable*
28	品种	品種	pǐnzhǒng	*variety; breed*
29	不动产	不動產	bùdòngchǎn	*immovable property; real estate*
30	收益		shōuyì	*income; profit; earnings;* 收入
31	险种	險種	xiǎnzhǒng	*insurance type;* 保险的种类

俗语 Common sayings

| 临时抱佛脚 | 臨時抱佛脚 | línshí bào fójiǎo | *embrace Buddha's feet in one's hour of need; seek help at the last minute* |

理解考核 Comprehension check

回答问题 Answer the following questions

1 张永安为什么开始对理财有兴趣了？

2 理财包括哪些方面？

3 张永安理财的目标是什么？

4 马可父母说的风险管理是什么意思？

5 通过买保险来投资是怎么一回事？

语言提示 Language tips

1　只是 . . .（罢了）: This expression is used to denote "merely" or "nothing else" in a declarative sentence.

- 我可不是理财专家，<u>只是</u>听说过一些皮毛<u>罢了</u>。

  税收<u>只是</u>财政收入的种类之一（<u>罢了</u>）。
  中国目前的私房土地使用权<u>只是</u>七十年（<u>罢了</u>）。

2　关系到: relate to; have a bearing on

- 理财<u>关系到</u>对现金流量的管理和对风险的管理。

  理财<u>关系到</u>一个人退休以后的生活质量(zhìliàng, quality)。
  物价的涨跌<u>关系到</u>人民的日常生活，也<u>关系到</u>国家的安定和发展。

练习 Exercises

1　将左栏的副词和右栏的动词短语配对，每个词语只能用一次。 Match each adverb in the left column with an appropriate verbal phrase in the right column. Each item can be used only once.

1)	（各家子公司）共同 _____	a)	本土化
2)	（政府）无偿 _____	b)	欢迎马可发言
3)	（计划经济）严重 _____	c)	占领市场
4)	（跨国企业）彻底 _____	d)	制约经济发展
5)	（双方）自愿 _____	e)	征收税款
6)	（货币）大幅 _____	f)	花钱
7)	（低收入家庭）谨慎 _____	g)	订立合同
8)	（全班）热烈 _____	h)	贬值

2　听写并用汉语解释下列词组。 Complete a dictation of the following phrases and explain them in Chinese.

1)	与日俱增	7)	理财专家
2)	多元化	8)	临时抱佛脚
3)	投保人	9)	现金流量
4)	社会保险	10)	风险管理
5)	商业保险	11)	不动产
6)	信贷收支平衡	12)	收益类险种

3 选词填空。 Fill in the blanks with the provided words and expressions.

1) 呈现，作为，承担，包括，关系

　　保险 _____ 社会保险和商业保险，_____ 到人民生活的方方面面。根据合同，投保人需支付保险费，保险人则 _____ 赔偿或给付保险金的责任。近年来，保险 _____ 一种个人理财的方式越来越受到关注，人们对收益类险种的投资 _____ 出上升的趋势。

2) 临时抱佛脚，与日俱增，安度晚年

　　随着经济的发展，投资理财在老百姓个人生活中的重要性 _____。为了退休以后能 _____，很多习惯把钱存在银行的中老年人也开始 _____，学习起投资理财来。

4 用指定的表达方式完成句子或对话。 Complete the following sentences and dialogues with the designated words or expressions.

1) 主要有

　　a) A: 国家有哪些种类的财政收入？

　　　　B: _____。

　　b) A: 企业的具体业务活动是什么？

　　　　B: _____。

2) 作为

　　a) _____，"百度"在中国家喻户晓。

　　b) _____，税收与国家经济生活密切相关。

3) 承担 ... 的责任

　　a) 作为公司的总经理，方总 _____。

　　b) 由于产品质量不合格，这家公司 _____。

4) 分为 A 和 B 两种

　　a) 贸易差额 _____。

　　b) 中国企业的国际化之路 _____。

5) 包括 ... 等

　　a) 企业管理 _____。

　　b) 汇率对经济的影响 _____。

6) 只是 ... 罢了

    a) 许多老外对中国其实并不了解，＿＿＿＿＿＿＿＿＿＿＿＿＿＿＿＿＿＿＿＿。

    b) 在中国买房时并没有买地，＿＿＿＿＿＿＿＿＿＿＿＿＿＿＿＿＿＿＿＿。

7) 关系到

    a) 成功的市场调查 ＿＿＿＿＿＿＿＿＿＿＿＿＿＿＿＿＿＿＿＿＿＿＿＿。

    b) 政府发行多少货币 ＿＿＿＿＿＿＿＿＿＿＿＿＿＿＿＿＿＿＿＿＿＿。

5　把下面的句子改成不太正式的语体。 Paraphrase the following sentences in a less formal style, paying special attention to the underlined words and phrases.

1) <u>随着</u>经济的发展，投资活动在个人理财方面<u>所占的比例</u><u>与日俱增</u>，个人理财也<u>呈现出</u><u>多元化的趋势</u>。

    ＿＿＿＿＿＿＿＿＿＿＿＿＿＿＿＿＿＿＿＿＿＿＿＿＿＿＿＿＿＿＿＿

    ＿＿＿＿＿＿＿＿＿＿＿＿＿＿＿＿＿＿＿＿＿＿＿＿＿＿＿＿＿＿＿＿。

2) 保险人在被保险人死亡、<u>伤残</u>、<u>患病</u><u>或</u>达到合同约定的年龄、<u>期限时</u><u>承担</u><u>给付</u>保险金的<u>责任</u>。

    ＿＿＿＿＿＿＿＿＿＿＿＿＿＿＿＿＿＿＿＿＿＿＿＿＿＿＿＿＿＿＿＿

    ＿＿＿＿＿＿＿＿＿＿＿＿＿＿＿＿＿＿＿＿＿＿＿＿＿＿＿＿＿＿＿＿。

3) 商业保险<u>由</u>专门的保险企业<u>经营</u>，<u>以营利为目的</u>，是通过<u>当事人双方</u>自愿<u>订立</u>保险合同来<u>运营</u>的保险。

    ＿＿＿＿＿＿＿＿＿＿＿＿＿＿＿＿＿＿＿＿＿＿＿＿＿＿＿＿＿＿＿＿

    ＿＿＿＿＿＿＿＿＿＿＿＿＿＿＿＿＿＿＿＿＿＿＿＿＿＿＿＿＿＿＿＿。

6　自行查找参考资料，解释与本课话题有关的词语。 Using available resources as a reference, explain the following terms, which are related to this lesson's topic.

1) 合同行为　　　4) 风险承受能力

2) 工伤保险　　　5) KISS 原则

3) 资产和负债　　6) 收益率

7 阅读理解与讨论。Reading comprehension and discussion.

从拒绝开始——友邦保险在中国

1992年美国友邦保险有限公司（简称"友邦保险"或"AIA"）成为第一家获许在中国经营保险业务的外资公司，它也是到目前为止中国唯一一家独资的外资寿险公司。从进入中国市场的第一天起，友邦就向中国同行展示了新的寿险理念和经营方式，特别是为中国市场引入了寿险代理人制度。

友邦公司给中国保险业带来的首先是观念上的冲击。友邦认为，寿险不同于储蓄和投资，它首先是一项充满爱心的事业。寿险是爱心的产品，寿险事业是爱心的延伸。友邦还认为，在中国推进寿险事业，需要把西方观念同中国文化结合起来。中国的传统文化忌讳谈自己的身后事，不愿意谈意外或伤残，这是导致中国人投保意识薄弱的主要原因；但另一方面，中国人家庭观念和家庭责任心很强，这是推广寿险的有利基础。

中国在对外资开放保险市场前，尚无保险代理人。友邦公司进入上海后雇佣了大量年轻人作为专业保险推销员。这些人走上街头，不厌其烦地向市民灌输保险思想，通过走街串巷、散发材料、打电话、发名片等方式推销保险产品。刚开始时保险推销的难度相当大，但推销员们不气馁，坚信"推销从拒绝开始"。

拒绝	jùjué	rejection	薄弱	bóruò	weak
有限	yǒuxiàn	limited	责任心	zérènxīn	sense of responsibility
获许	huòxǔ	get permission	推广	tuīguǎng	popularize; spread
唯一	wéiyī	one and only	尚	shàng	still; yet
独资	dúzī	exclusively owned	无	wú	no; nothing; without
寿险	shòuxiǎn	life insurance	雇佣	gùyōng	employ; hire
同行	tóngháng	people of the same trade	专业	zhuānyè	professional
展示	zhǎnshì	show; display	推销员	tuīxiāoyuán	salesman
理念	lǐniàn	concept; philosophy	街头	jiētóu	street; street corner
代理人	dàilǐrén	agent	不厌其烦	bù yàn qí fán	not mind taking the trouble
冲击	chōngjī	attack; strike	灌输	guànshū	instill into; imbue with
充满	chōngmǎn	be filled with	走街串巷	zǒu jiē chuàn xiàng	go from street to street
爱心	àixīn	love; compassion	散发	sànfā	distribute
事业	shìyè	cause; career	材料	cáiliào	materials
延伸	yánshēn	extension; stretch	难度	nándù	degree of difficulty
忌讳	jìhuì	avoid as taboo	气馁	qìněi	be discouraged
意外	yìwài	accident; unexpected	坚信	jiānxìn	firmly believe

<u>选择填空</u> Select the correct answer for each blank.

1) 友邦是 _____。

    a) 第一家获许在中国经营保险业务的外资公司

    b) 唯一一家获许在中国经营保险业务的外资公司

    c) 中国唯一一家独资的保险公司

2) 友邦认为 _____。

    a) 寿险跟投资和储蓄不一样，它不是一种理财方式

    b) 寿险是一项充满爱心的事业

    c) 由于中西方观念不同，中国不具备推广寿险的基础

3) 友邦给中国保险业带来的<u>不包括</u> _____。

    a) 新的寿险理念

    b) 保险代理人制度

    c) 西方的家庭观念

4) 在中国推广寿险 _____。

    a) 需要把西方观念同中国文化结合起来

    b) 会遭到拒绝，因为中国人不相信保险代理人

    c) 会遭到拒绝，因为中国人家庭观念强，更愿意把钱留在家里

讨论 Discussion.

    友邦的保险代理人是怎么在中国推销寿险的？根据你了解的情况或所查的资料，谈谈你对这种推销方式的看法。How do AIA agents sell life insurance in China? According to what you know or what you have found in research, tell your classmates what you think about this approach.

8　实践活动。Tasks.

1) 查阅资料，找出"五险一金"的定义。Conduct research to find out the definition of 五险一金。

2) 做一个10分钟的口头报告，介绍一种你最看好的个人投资方式。请通过事实和例子说明这种方式的优点、缺点、收益的机会及风险，并谈谈你看好这种方式的原因。先查看最近六个月之内的资料，然后根据老师的要求为自己准备一个简单的提纲。在报告时要尽可能提供事实和例子。Give a ten-minute oral report about a promising method of personal investment, including its merits, defects, chance of profits and risks, and the reason why you think it promising. You should search for a relevant news article from the past six months and, following your teacher's instructions, prepare a brief outline. Make an effort to include facts and examples.

3) 给友邦（中国）的人力资源部写一封求职申请信（不超过一页）。在信中说明为什么希望在中国做友邦的寿险代理人，并突出自己的有利条件。Write a one-page cover letter to the HR department of AIA (China), applying for a life insurance agent's position in China. In the letter you should explain why you are interested in such a position and what advantages you would bring to the job.

4) 如果你对一个不同的任务有兴趣，请结合本课的主题向老师提出建议，然后在老师的指导下完成这个任务。If you are interested in a different kind of task, you are encouraged to suggest your proposal and to complete it under your teacher's guidance.

学习指导 Learning guide

长句分析（二）Analysis of long sentences (2)

Many long sentences are composite sentences, which consist of two or more "subject + predicate" structures called clauses. Clauses, just like simple sentences, may have various kinds of structural patterns, such as in the following example:

在计划经济的实践过程中，生产与需求脱节，劳动者动力不足，生产效率低下，市场缺乏活力。(L7)

There are four juxtaposed clauses following the adverbial 在计划经济的实践过程中, which are (S + VP), (S + AP), (S + AP), and (S + VP + O) respectively.

It is mentioned in Lesson 8's learning guide that, if clauses share the same subject, the subject is not usually repeated. Sometimes, a missing subject may not be the same as the subject in the preceding context. At other times, if the sentence bears a general reference, there may be no subject at all. In these cases you have to use the context. The following examples will serve as a review of issues regarding composite sentences:

就因为它的本土化比较彻底，ᵛ才把老对手麦当劳抛在了后边。(L6)

它 is dropped in the second clause to avoid repetition.

中国人都比较重面子，所以ᵛ在洽谈的时候得注意给对方留面子，让人家也有成就感才好。(L4)

The missing subject in the second clause is not 中国人 but 你们. 你们 is dropped because it is apparent in the context.

中国股市的历史不长，但ᵛ发展的速度很快。(L1)

The missing subject in the second clause is not 历史, which is the subject in the first clause. It is 中国股市 that has been dropped.

ᵛ只有先弄清自己能承受多大的风险ᵛ才能合理地选择投资品种。(L10)

The subject 任何人 does not have to appear because the sentence bears a general reference.

It should be noted that clauses in a composite sentence do not always have a main-subordinate relationship. They can also be independent from each other in meaning, such as in the following examples:

中国的税收制度还不完善，政府一直在研究和推进房地产税的改革。(L9)

外汇交易市场是世界上最大的金融市场，...外汇交易的目的有投资和投机两类。(L2)

In order to help you to understand composite sentences in their great variety and complexity, let's go over more examples from the covered texts. This might be a little challenging, but it will be helpful to your further studies.

许多<u>中国企业</u>已经<u>认识到</u>，<u style="text-decoration-style:dotted">由于中国的国情不同，^V在学习西方现代管理科学时必须把西方的管理模式中国化</u>。(L5)

- The part underlined in dots is the object of 认识到 in the overriding simple sentence 中国企业认识到 . . . (S + VP + O).

- This long object, 由于中国的国情不同，^V在学习西方现代管理科学时必须把西方的管理模式中国化, is a composite sentence itself, in which the subject of the main clause 中国企业 is dropped to avoid repetition.

要是市场上<u>钱</u>太多而<u>商品</u>没那么多，<u>物价</u>就会上涨，<u>货币</u>就会贬值。(L8)

- Overall, this is a composite sentence with a subordinate clause 要是 . . . and a main clause 物价就会上涨，货币就会贬值.

- The subordinate clause has the structure of a composite sentence, in which 钱太多 (S + AP) and 商品没那么多 (S + AP) are juxtaposed clauses.

- The main clause is structured as a composite sentence too, in which 物价会上涨 (S + VP) and 货币会贬值 (S + VP) are juxtaposed clauses.

百度的<u>人力资源管理</u>以公司上市的时间为界，<u>分为</u>两个阶段，<u>这</u>是<u>很英明</u>的。(L5)

- The first "subject + predicate" structure 人力资源管理分为阶段 (S + VP + O) is represented by 这 in the second "subject + predicate" structure.

- Therefore, 这是很英明的 means precisely 人力资源管理分为阶段是很英明的 (S + AP).

- In this sense, 人力资源管理分为阶段 is simply the S in (S + AP).

<u>保险</u>是指投保人根据合同约定向保险人支付保险费，而保险人对于合同约定的可能发生的事故及财产损失承担赔偿保险金的责任，或者在被保险人死亡、伤残、患病或达到合同约定的年龄、期限时承担给付保险金的责任。(L10)

- The basic structure of this long sentence is "S 是指 NP," so overall it is a simple sentence.

- The long nominal predicate (NP) here, <u>投保人</u>根据合同约定向保险人支付保险费，而<u>保险人</u>对于合同约定的可能发生的事故及财产损失承担赔偿保险金的责任，或者在被保险人死亡、伤残、患病或达到合同约定的年龄、期限时承担给付保险金的责任, is actually itself a composite sentence with two juxtaposed clauses led by 投保人 and 保险人 respectively.

- The first clause in the NP, <u>投保人</u>根据合同约定向保险人<u>支付保险费</u>, has a clear structure of (S + VP + O).

- The second clause in the NP, <u>保险人</u>对于合同约定的可能发生的事故及财产损失<u>承担</u>赔偿保险金的<u>责任</u>，或者在被保险人死亡、伤残、患病或达到合同约定的年龄、期限时<u>承担</u>给付保险金的<u>责任</u>, carries two juxtaposed verbal predicates 承担, each followed by the object 责任. Its basic structure is 保险人承担责任或者承担责任 (S + <<VP + O>>, <<VP + O>>).

- The analysis of this long sentence can be summarized in the following list:

S <u>投保人</u>

    VP (根据合同约定) (向保险人) <u>支付</u>

        O 保险费

而

S <u>保险人</u>

    VP (对于合同约定的可能发生的事故及财产损失) <u>承担</u>

        O (赔偿保险金的) <u>责任</u>，

    或者

    VP (在被保险人死亡、... 或达到合同约定的年龄、期限时) <u>承担</u>

        O (给付保险金的) <u>责任</u>。

As demonstrated here and in Lesson 9, sentence analysis is a useful means to ensure accurate comprehension of long sentences. We do not mean to ask you to analyze every sentence you come across, though. In most cases, you will be fine as long as you can identify the "topic" and the "comment," and make sense of them.

PRACTICE: Following the example, reduce each sentence to its basic elements. Keep connectives if any.

Example: 低度的通货膨胀能对经济起"润滑"作用，因为物价的提高及利润的增加能刺激厂商投资的积极性。(L8)

→ 通货膨胀能起作用，因为提高及增加能刺激积极性。

1 一个企业只有掌握了丰富的信息，才能有计划地组织各项经营活动，获得最大利润。(L3)

2 税收不但在组织财政收入中具有举足轻重的地位，而且在调节社会经济、监管社会经济活动、保持经济稳定、体现产业政策等方面发挥重要作用。(L9)

3 由于中国地域广阔，不同地区和时期的税收制度是有可能存在差异的。(L9)

4 社会保险 ... 具有强制性，是为丧失劳动能力、暂时失去劳动岗位或因健康原因造成损失的人口提供收入或补偿的保险，...。(L10)

REVIEW PRACTICE: Find words in the designated lessons that are antonyms to the given words. (Refer to L3's learning guide if necessary.)

1 支出 expense   _____ income (L8)

2 增加 increase   _____ decrease (L8)

3 跌价 reduce price   _____ raise price (L8)

4 主观 subjective   _____ objective (L8)

5 私有 private ownership   _____ public ownership (L7)

6 独资 sole proprietorship   _____ joint venture (L6)

第十一课 知识产权

Lesson 11 *Intellectual property*

课文一 Text 1

知识产权是一种无形产权，指权利人对其所创作的智力劳动成果所享有的专有权利。各种智力创造，比如发明，文学和艺术作品，以及在商业中使用的标志、名称、图像和外观设计，都可被认为是某一个人或组织所拥有的知识产权。

知识产权具有专有性、地域性、时间性等特点。也就是说，在通常情况下，第一，权利人以外的任何人不得享有或使用该项权利。第二，经一国法律所保护的某项权利只在该国范围内发生法律效力。第三，法律对各项权利的保护一般都规定了一定的有效期。

为了保护智力劳动成果，促进发明创新，早在一百多年前，国际上就已开始建立保护知识产权的制度。20世纪80年代，中国开始逐步建立知识产权制度，颁布并实行了《商标法》、《专利法》、《著作权法》等保护知识产权的法律。中国在加入世界知识产权组织时作出了将严格遵守重要国际公约的承诺。

对知识产权进行保护调动了人们从事科学技术研究和文学艺术创作的积极性和创造性，有助于将智力成果推广和应用到实际的生产生活，促进国际经济技术贸易和文化艺术交流。

知識產權是一種無形產權，指權利人對其所創作的智力勞動成果所享有的專有權利。各種智力創造，比如發明，文學和藝術作品，以及在商業中使用的標誌、名稱、圖像和外觀設計，都可被認為是某一個人或組織所擁有的知識產權。

知識產權具有專有性、地域性、時間性等特點。也就是說，在通常情況下，第一，權利人以外的任何人不得享有或使用該項權利。第二，經一國法律所保護的某項權利只在該國範圍內發生法律效力。第三，法律對各項權利的保護一般都規定了一定的有效期。

　　為了保護智力勞動成果，促進發明創新，早在一百多年前，國際上就已開始建立保護知識產權的制度。20世紀80年代，中國開始逐步建立知識產權制度，頒佈並實行了《商標法》、《專利法》、《著作權法》等保護知識產權的法律。中國在加入世界知識產權組織時作出了將嚴格遵守重要國際公約的承諾。

　　對知識產權進行保護調動了人們從事科學技術研究和文學藝術創作的積極性和創造性，有助於將智力成果推廣和應用到實際的生產生活，促進國際經濟技術貿易和文化藝術交流。

词语表 Words and expressions

(* Refer to notes or language tips following the word list.)

1	产权	產權	chǎnquán	*property right; ownership of property*
2	无形	無形	wúxíng	*invisible; intangible*
3	权利	權利	quánlì	*right*
4	创作	創作	chuàngzuò	*create literary and art works*
5	智力		zhìlì	*intelligence*
6	成果		chéngguǒ	*achievement; positive result*
7	享有		xiǎngyǒu	*possess; enjoy (prestige, right, etc.)*
8	专有	專有	zhuānyǒu	*proprietary*
9	发明	發明	fāmíng	*invention*
10	艺术	藝術	yìshù	*art*
11	作品		zuòpǐn	*works (of literature and art)*
12	标志	標誌	biāozhì	*symbol; sign*
13	名称	名稱	míngchēng	*name of a thing or an organization*
14	图像	圖像	túxiàng	*picture; produced image*
15	外观	外觀	wàiguān	*appearance; exterior;* 外表
16	任何		rènhé	*any*
17	不得*		bùdé	*must not; not be allowed;* 不准; 不可以

18	经*	經	jīng	*as a result of; through*
19	保护	保護	bǎohù	*protect; guard*
20	效力		xiàolì	*effect; favorable function*
21	有效		yǒuxiào	*effective; valid*
22	颁布	頒佈	bānbù	*promulgate; issue*
23	商标	商標	shāngbiāo	*trademark*
24	专利	專利	zhuānlì	*patent;* 专有权利
25	著作		zhùzuò	*writing; work*
26	严格	嚴格	yángé	*strict; rigorous, rigid*
27	遵守		zūnshǒu	*abide by; comply with*
28	公约	公約	gōngyuē	*convention; pact*
29	承诺	承諾	chéngnuò	*promise;* 答应
30	调动	調動	diàodòng	*bring into play; arouse*
31	有助于*	有助於	yǒuzhùyú	*contribute to; be conducive to;* 有利于
32	应用	應用	yìngyòng	*apply; put in use*
33	交流		jiāoliú	*exchange*

理解考核 Comprehension check

对错选择 True or false

		True	False
1	企业的商标可被认为是一个企业所拥有的知识产权。	☐	☐
2	中国法律保护的知识产权在美国也一定会受到法律保护。	☐	☐
3	一个企业拥有了一项知识产权就会永久拥有它。	☐	☐
4	知识产权制度的目的是保护智力劳动成果，促进发明创新。	☐	☐
5	中国在80年代加入世界知识产权组织并开始逐步建立知识产权制度。	☐	☐

注释 Notes

1 世界知识产权组织

The World Intellectual Property Organization (WIPO), headquartered in Geneva, Switzerland, is one of the 16 specialized agencies of the United Nations. It was created in 1967 to encourage creative activity and promote the protection of intellectual property throughout the world through cooperation among states and in collaboration with other international organizations. It currently has 184 member states and administers 24 international treaties. China joined WIPO on June 3, 1980 to become its 90th member state.

语言提示 Language tips

1 以及: Just like 和, 以及 connects nouns or nominal phrases; but it is mostly used in written language and may be preceded by a pause.

- . . . 发明 . . . 以及在商业中使用的标志 . . . , 都可被认为是 . . . 知识产权。
- 各国的语言、法律、经济政策以及风俗习惯不同, . . . 。（L4-1）

  经济衰退与缺乏技术创新，缺乏新资本积累以及股市的随机性有关。
  随着国家的开放以及国际经济贸易的广泛联系，中国人已经开始出国购物。
  香港不能不考虑跟内地的政治关系以及内地在其进出口贸易中的重要性。

2 不得: This is used before a verb to mean that the action represented by the verb is prohibited. This usage is often seen in documents and stipulations. 不准 and 不可以 are its equivalents.

- 权利人以外的任何人不得享有或使用该项权利。

  根据法律，本州21岁以下的居民不得饮酒。
  在中国，土地属于国家所有，任何人不得私自买卖。

3 经: When used as a preposition with a "subject + predicate" structure as its object, what follows is the result of the action.

- 经一国法律所保护的某项权利只在该国范围内发生法律效力。

  经大家研究决定的事情任何人都得照办。
  经董事会多次讨论，你的计划书已经获得通过。

4 早在: as early as

- 早在一百多年前，国际上就已开始建立保护知识产权的制度。

  早在两年前，他们就已经还清了所有的贷款。
  早在高中时期，马可就开始去有名的大公司实习。

5 V1 并 V2: When used to connect disyllabic verbs or verbal predicates of the same subject, the connected segments usually suggest a progressive enhancement in meaning.

■ 20世纪80年代，中国 … 颁布<u>并</u>实行了 … 保护知识产权的法律。

研究<u>并</u>确定价格是市场营销的要素之一。
这次事故，我方将赔偿贵方的损失，<u>并</u>承担所有的法律责任。

6 有助于: contribute to; be conducive to; 有利于

■ 对知识产权进行保护 … <u>有助于</u>将智力成果推广和应用到实际的生产生活。

从小学习理财<u>有助于</u>一生的幸福生活。
合理的税收制度<u>有助于</u>缩小贫富差距。

课文二 Text 2

马可一直想了解中国在保护知识产权方面的情况，今天方总让钱亮陪他一起去参加了一个新闻发布会。在会上他听到了国家知识产权局一位副局长的讲话，还了解到了一些案情。现在，他和钱亮正在回公司的路上。

马　可：真感谢方总给我安排了这样一个机会。今天我算是明白了，中美两国之间的知识产权问题比人民币汇率的问题更大。

钱　亮：其实，中国加入 WTO 以后涉外知识产权纠纷案件就一直在增加。

马　可：我原来以为这类诉讼都是外国企业发起的。跨国公司要进入中国市场，当然得拿起知识产权保护的武器了。没想到现在中国企业起诉外国企业的侵权案件也在增加。像今天会上介绍的中国通领科技集团在美国胜诉的案例就很说明问题。

钱　亮：这说明中国企业保护自身知识产权的意识增强了。中国企业毕竟也有自身发展的需求啊！随着越来越多的中国企业走出去，今后发生在国际市场的诉讼还会更多呢。

马　可：中国企业也好，美国企业也好，关键是得有过硬的专利技术。通领集团在美国的竞争对手莱伏顿公司是世界500强企业，西西姆公司也很有实力。美国法院之所以判定通领集团不侵犯这些公司的美国专利，正是因为通领集团在漏电保护技术上走的是一条自主创新的路子。

钱　亮：你说得很对。要是没有自主知识产权，就算有最好的律师，也赢不了。特别有意思的是，通领集团在法院的胜诉，居然把美国国际贸易委员会的错误裁定推翻了。这就叫做"有理走遍天下"。哦，对了，马可，你过几天就要回美国了，需要我送你去机场吗？

马　可：谢谢，不用了。方总说她会送我。

钱　亮：是吗？方总对你真不错呀。

马　可：那还用说？谁让她是我爸爸的得意门生呢？

钱　亮：原来如此！

　　馬可一直想瞭解中國在保護知識產權方面的情況，今天方總讓錢亮陪他一起去參加了一個新聞發佈會。在會上他聽到了國家知識產權局一位副局長的講話，還瞭解到了一些案情。現在，他和錢亮正在回公司的路上。

馬　可：真感謝方總給我安排了這樣一個機會。今天我算是明白了，中美兩國之間的知識產權問題比人民幣匯率的問題更大。

錢　亮：其實，中國加入 WTO 以後涉外知識產權糾紛案件就一直在增加。

馬　可：我原來以為這類訴訟都是外國企業發起的。跨國公司要進入中國市場，當然得拿起知識產權保護的武器了。沒想到現在中國企業起訴外國企業的侵權案件也在增加。像今天會上介紹的中國通領科技集團在美國勝訴的案例就很說明問題。

錢　亮：這說明中國企業保護自身知識產權的意識增強了。中國企業畢竟也有自身發展的需求啊！隨著越來越多的中國企業走出去，今後發生在國際市場的訴訟還會更多呢。

馬　可：中國企業也好，美國企業也好，關鍵是得有過硬的專利技術。通領集團在美國的競爭對手萊伏頓公司是世界500強企業，西西姆公司也很有實力。美國法院之所以判定通領集團不侵犯這些公司的美國專利，正是因為通領集團在漏電保護技術上走的是一條自主創新的路子。

錢　亮：你說得很對。要是沒有自主知識產權，就算有最好的律師，也贏不了。特別有意思的是，通領集團在法院的勝訴，居然把美國國際貿易委員會的錯誤裁定推翻了。這就叫做"有理走遍天下"。哦，對了，馬可，你過幾天就要回美國了，需要我送你去機場嗎？

馬　可：謝謝，不用了。方總說她會送我。

錢　亮：是嗎？方總對你真不錯呀。

馬　可：那還用說？誰讓她是我爸爸的得意門生呢？

錢　亮：原來如此！

词语表 Words and expressions

(* Refer to notes or language tips following the word list.)

1	陪		péi	*accompany*
2	发布	發佈	fābù	*issue; release*
3	局		jú	*bureau; office*
4	副		fù	*vice; deputy; associate*
5	局长	局長	júzhǎng	*bureau chief*
6	案情		ànqíng	*details of a legal case*
7	算是		suànshì	*at last;* 总算
8	涉外		shèwài	*concerning foreign affairs;* 涉及外事
9	案件		ànjiàn	*legal case*
10	诉讼	訴訟	sùsòng	*litigation; lawsuit*
11	发起	發起	fāqǐ	*originate*
12	武器		wǔqì	*arms; weapon*
13	起诉	起訴	qǐsù	*sue; prosecute*
14	侵权	侵權	qīnquán	*tort; infringe upon others' rights;* 侵犯权利
15	科技		kējì	*science and technology;* 科学技术
16	集团	集團	jítuán	*group*
17	胜诉	勝訴	shèngsù	*win a lawsuit*
18	案例		ànlì	*case*
19	过硬	過硬	guòyìng	*be well up to standard*
20	法院		fǎyuàn	*court*
21	判定		pàndìng	*determine; judge*
22	侵犯		qīnfàn	*violate; infringe upon*
23	漏电	漏電	lòudiàn	*electric leakage*
24	路子*		lùzi	*way*
25	赢	贏	yíng	*win; gain*
26	居然		jūrán	*unexpectedly; to one's surprise*

27	委员会	委員會	wěiyuánhuì	committee; commission
28	错误	錯誤	cuòwù	mistake; error; erroneous
29	裁定		cáidìng	ruling
30	推翻		tuīfān	overthrow; overturn
31	得意门生	得意門生	déyì ménshēng	favorite pupil
32	原来如此	原來如此	yuánlái rúcǐ	so that's how it is

专有名词 Proper nouns

1	通领科技集团	通領科技集團	Tōnglǐng Kējì Jítuán	Tongling Science and Technology Group, a Chinese company
2	世界500强	世界500強	Shìjiè Wǔbǎi Qiáng	top 500 in the world
3	莱伏顿公司	萊伏頓公司	Láifúdùn Gōngsī	Leviton Inc., a US company
4	西西姆公司		Xīxīmǔ Gōngsī	Pass & Seymour Inc., a US company, now belonging to a French company, Legrand Group

俗语 Common sayings

| 有理走遍天下 | | yǒulǐ zǒu biàn tiānxià | With justice on your side, you can go anywhere. |

理解考核 Comprehension check

回答问题 Answer the following questions

1) 马可去参加新闻发布会听到了什么？了解到了什么？

2) 马可以为中外知识产权诉讼都是谁发起的？他为什么这样以为？

3) 为什么中国企业起诉外国企业的侵权案件在逐渐增加？

4) 通领集团这次为什么能够胜诉？

5) 方总为什么对马可特别关心和照顾？

注释 Notes

1 国家知识产权局

The State Intellectual Property Office (SIPO), originally established in 1980 as the China Patent Bureau, changed to its current name in 1998 when it became a central government office directly affiliated with the State Council. It is in charge of China's patents and coordinates affairs concerning foreign intellectual property rights.

2 美国国际贸易委员会

The United States International Trade Commission (USITC) is an independent quasi-judicial federal agency with broad investigative responsibilities on matters of trade. It facilitates a rules-based international trading system through determining import injury to US industries in antidumping, countervailing duty, and global and China safeguard investigations. At the same time it directs actions against unfair trade practices involving patent, trademark, and copyright infringement. The agency also serves as a federal resource. It gathers and analyzes trade data and other trade policy-related information to facilitate the development of sound and informed US trade policy.

语言提示 Language tips

1 原来以为 . . . , 没想到 . . . : This pattern is used to ascertain a present situation in a contrast to one's original thought, suggesting that the situation is unexpected.

- 我原来以为这类诉讼都是 . . . 。没想到现在 . . . 的侵权案件也在增加。

  我原来以为中国人不喜欢美国快餐，没想到美国快餐在中国这么受欢迎。
  他们原以为这次洽谈会很顺利，没想到遇到了这么多困难。

2 之所以 . . . , 正是因为 . . . : In this form the cause in a cause-result sentence gets emphasized.

- 美国法院之所以判定 . . . , 正是因为通领集团 . . . 走的是一条自主创新的路子。

  低度的通货膨胀之所以能对经济起"润滑"作用，正是因为物价的提高及利润的增加能刺激厂商投资的积极性。
  之所以在跟中国人洽谈的时候得让他们也有成就感，正是因为中国人比较重面子。

3 走 . . . 的路子: This expression usually means "to adopt a certain approach in doing something," but 路子 may now also suggest "social connections or pull."

- 通领集团 . . . 走的〔路子〕是一条自主创新的路子。

  中国企业在管理上必须走"西方管理模式中国化"的路子。
  前苏联走的（路子）是计划经济的路子。
  马可是走了方总的路子到上海去实习的。

练习 Exercises

1 将左栏的动词或形容词和右栏的补语配对，每个词语只能用一次。
Match each verb or adjective in the left column with an appropriate complement in the right column. Each item can be used only once.

1) （房价）上涨得 _____	a) 一无是处
2) （你）来得 _____	b) 不亦乐乎
3) （马可）忙得 _____	c) 很厉害
4) （两个人）谈得 _____	d) 正好
5) （发言）准备得 _____	e) 越来越方便
6) （收集信息）变得 _____	f) 很规范
7) （把公司）管理得 _____	g) 津津有味
8) （把竞争对手）说得 _____	h) 很充分

2 听写并用汉语解释下列词组。Complete a dictation of the following phrases and explain them in Chinese.

1)	无形产权	7)	涉外知识产权纠纷
2)	智力劳动成果	8)	侵权案件
3)	专有性	9)	专利技术
4)	地域性新闻发布会	10)	世界五百强企业
5)	法律效力	11)	自主创新
6)	国际公约	12)	有理走遍天下

3 选词填空 Fill in the blanks with the provided words and expressions.

1) 以及，不得，经，早在，并，有助于

为了保护智力劳动成果，_____ 一百多年前，国际上已经开始建立 _____ 实行知识产权保护制度。知识产权具有专有性、地域性 _____ 时间性等特点。它 _____ 促进发明和创新。_____ 法律保护的知识产权任何个人和组织都 _____ 侵犯。

2) 自主创新，涉外纠纷，技术过硬，有理走遍天下

中国加入 WTO 后，关于知识产权的 _____ 逐渐增加。其实，中国企业也好，外国企业也好，只要 _____，走 _____ 的路子，就会受到法律的保护，在纠纷中胜诉。这就叫做 _____。

4　用指定的表达方式完成句子或对话。Complete the following sentences with the designated words or expressions.

1)　原来以为 . . . 没想到 . . .

　　a)　马可原来以为中国的肯德基跟美国的肯德基一样，＿＿＿＿＿＿＿＿＿＿＿
　　　　＿＿＿＿＿＿＿＿＿＿＿＿＿＿＿＿＿＿＿＿＿＿＿。

　　b)　张永安 ＿＿＿＿＿＿＿＿＿＿＿＿＿＿＿＿＿＿，没想到理财是要理一生
　　　　的财。

2)　之所以 . . . 正是因为 . . .

　　a)　家乐福之所以能在中国市场抢得先机，＿＿＿＿＿＿＿＿＿＿＿＿＿＿＿。
　　b)　计划经济 ＿＿＿＿＿＿＿＿＿＿，正是因为国家对经济进行了宏观调控。

3)　走 . . . 路子

　　a)　改革开放以来，中国政府一直说要 ＿＿＿＿＿＿＿＿＿＿＿＿＿＿＿。
　　b)　马可以为李瑛瑛的叔叔是百度的老总，想 ＿＿＿＿＿＿＿去百度工作。

5　把下面的句子改成不太正式的语体。Paraphrase the following sentences in a less formal style, paying special attention to the underlined words or phrases.

1)　知识产权具有专有性、地域性以及时间性等特点。对知识产权进行保护有助于将智力成果推广并应用到实际的生产生活。

　　＿＿＿＿＿＿＿＿＿＿＿＿＿＿＿＿＿＿＿＿＿＿＿＿＿＿＿＿＿＿＿＿
　　＿＿＿＿＿＿＿＿＿＿＿＿＿＿＿＿＿＿＿＿＿＿＿＿＿＿＿＿＿＿＿。

2)　权利人以外的任何人不得享有或使用该项权利。

　　＿＿＿＿＿＿＿＿＿＿＿＿＿＿＿＿＿＿＿＿＿＿＿＿＿＿＿＿＿＿＿。

3)　合同一经签订，双方便不得随意更改。

　　＿＿＿＿＿＿＿＿＿＿＿＿＿＿＿＿＿＿＿＿＿＿＿＿＿＿＿＿＿＿＿。

4)　经一国法律所保护的某项权利只在该国范围内发生法律效力。

　　＿＿＿＿＿＿＿＿＿＿＿＿＿＿＿＿＿＿＿＿＿＿＿＿＿＿＿＿＿＿＿。

5)　早在1905年，中国的第一家证券交易所就已于上海成立。

　　＿＿＿＿＿＿＿＿＿＿＿＿＿＿＿＿＿＿＿＿＿＿＿＿＿＿＿＿＿＿＿。

6)　联想之所以能在2004年成功地实现跨国并购，正是因为该公司早在20世纪90年代即开始为其今后的国际化战略做准备。

　　＿＿＿＿＿＿＿＿＿＿＿＿＿＿＿＿＿＿＿＿＿＿＿＿＿＿＿＿＿＿＿＿
　　＿＿＿＿＿＿＿＿＿＿＿＿＿＿＿＿＿＿＿＿＿＿＿＿＿＿＿＿＿＿＿。

6 自行查找参考资料，解释与本课话题有关的词语。 Using available resources as a reference, explain the following terms, which are related to this lesson's topic.

1) 假冒伪劣商品
2) 山寨产品
3) 网络盗版
4) 涉案金额

5) 防伪打假
6) 跨国执法
7) 有法可依、有法必依、执法必严
8) 非物质文化遗产

7 阅读理解与讨论。 Reading comprehension and discussion.

美国Google告北京谷歌

"谷歌"的名称权之争终于告一段落。法院认定北京谷歌科技有限公司（简称"北京谷歌"）构成不正当竞争，被判变更企业名称，并赔偿谷歌信息技术（中国）有限公司（简称"谷歌中国"）共计10万元。

谷歌中国是由美国Google公司的一个子公司在中国投资设立的外商独资企业。谷歌中国表示，北京谷歌先是企图恶意注册以"Google"的非正式中文译名"古狗"为字号的企业名称，被企业登记机关拒绝。此后，在美国Google公司对外公布"谷歌"中文名称时，北京谷歌又企图恶意注册以"谷歌"为字号的企业名称。于是谷歌中国将北京谷歌告上法庭。

法院裁定，美国Google公司和谷歌中国对"Google"享有驰名商标权和翻译名称权，其中文翻译名称"谷歌"根据在先受理原则享有了企业字号的合法权利。北京谷歌在企业名称中使用"谷歌"，既存在主观上的故意，也造成了相关公众混淆误认的后果。该公司的行为侵犯了美国Google公司和谷歌中国对"Google"的商标意义上的翻译名称权，也侵犯了"谷歌"已被核准为企业字号的企业名称权，违反了公平、诚信原则和公认的商业道德，构成了不正当竞争。

告	gào	accuse; sue	驰名	chímíng	well-known; famous
谷歌	Gǔgē	Google	翻译	fānyì	translation
争	zhēng	dispute	受理	shòulǐ	accept and handle
告一段落	gào yī duànluò	come to an end	原则	yuánzé	principle
认定	rèndìng	firmly believe; hold	合法	héfǎ	legal; lawful
构成	gòuchéng	constitute	主观	zhǔguān	subjective
正当	zhèngdāng	proper; legitimate	故意	gùyì	deliberately; purposely
判	pàn	judge; sentence	公众	gōngzhòng	public
变更	biàngēng	change; alter	混淆	hùnxiáo	confuse; mix up
赔偿	péicháng	indemnify; compensate	误认	wùrèn	make a mistake in identifying sb or sth
共计	gòngjì	amount to; add up to			
设立	shèlì	establish; set up	后果	hòuguǒ	consequence
独资	dúzī	exclusively owned	核准	hézhǔn	examine and approve
企图	qǐtú	attempt	违反	wéifǎn	violate; transgress
恶意	èyì	evil intention; malice	公平	gōngpíng	fair; impartial
字号	zìhào	name of a shop; trade name	诚信	chéngxìn	honesty
法庭	fǎtíng	court; law court	公认	gōngrèn	generally acknowledge

选择填空 Select the correct answer for each blank.

1) 北京谷歌 _____。

    a) 被法院裁定必须赔偿美国 Google 公司10万元

    b) 被法院裁定必须退出中国市场

    c) 构成了不正当竞争

2) 谷歌中国 _____。

    a) 是美国 Google 公司的中文名字

    b) 在"谷歌"的名称权之争中胜诉

    c) 对"谷歌"和"古狗"都拥有合法权利

3) 关于北京谷歌，下面的说法不正确的是 _____。

    a) 先试图注册"古狗"，又试图注册"谷歌"

    b) 不是故意侵犯谷歌中国的权利

    c) 被谷歌中国告上法庭

4) 下面的说法不正确的是 _____。

    a) 北京谷歌申请以"古狗"注册被拒是因为当时谷歌中国已经注册了这个译名

    b) 北京谷歌后来又使用"谷歌"字号，造成了公众的混淆

    c) 美国Google公司和谷歌中国对"Google"的中文译名"谷歌"享有合法 ... 权利是因为他们申请在先，受理在先

讨论 Discussion.

为什么说北京谷歌构成了不正当竞争？根据你了解的情况或所查的资料，谈谈你对侵犯企业名称权和商标权的行为的看法。Why was *Beijing Guge* held responsible for unfair competition? According to what you know or what you have found in research, give your opinion of infringement upon corporate names and trademarks.

8 实践活动。Tasks.

1) 请查阅资料，找出中国保护涉外知识产权的一个重要案例，并列出它的基本情况。Through research find an important case in which foreign intellectual property got protected in China. Make a brief list of the basic facts.

2) 做一个10分钟的口头报告，介绍一起中美之间知识产权纠纷的案例。请说明这起案例的经过和结果，并谈谈你自己的看法。先查看最近六个月之内的资料，然后根据老师的要求为自己准备一个简单的提纲。Give a ten-minute oral report about a legal case of an intellectual property dispute between China and the United States, including your own comments as well as the case's process and result.

You should base your report on information from within the past six months and, following your teacher's instructions, prepare a brief outline.

3) 查看第3课、第4课、第5课、第6课、第9课和第11课课文二中的有关部分，为马可夏天在上海的学习活动写一份小结（不超过一页）。请记住给这份小结加一个标题。Check text 2 in Lessons 3, 4, 5, 6, 9, and 11, and write a summary of Mark's summer learning experiences in Shanghai (limited to one page). Be sure to give it a title.

4) 如果你对一个不同的任务有兴趣，请结合本课的主题向老师提出建议，然后在老师的指导下完成这个任务。If you are interested in a different kind of task, you are encouraged to suggest your proposal and to complete it under your teacher's guidance.

学习指导 Learning guide

功能和表达 Functions and expressions

As learners of Chinese, you have to pay attention to how thoughts are organized and expressed in the language. The way sentences are structured in Chinese, as discussed in previous lessons, is directly relevant because the sentence is the basic unit in communication. At the same time, you should collect functional words and expressions to serve your various communicative needs. From this textbook, you should have acquired at minimum the following functional abilities.

- Providing a definition 定义
  汇率<u>是</u>一国货币兑换另一国货币的比率。(L2-1)
  国际贸易<u>是指</u>不同国家或地区之间的商品、服务和生产要素的交换活动。(L4-1)
  通货 ... 紧缩，<u>系指</u>市场上流通的货币不足，购买力下降，进而造成物价下跌。(L8-1)
  国家 ... 按照法律规定的标准，对组织或个人无偿征收实物或货币，<u>即为</u>"征税"。(L9-1)

- Listing items and viewpoints 罗列
  企业管理经历了三个阶段：经验管理阶段，科学管理阶段及文化管理阶段。(L5-1)
  4P营销理论...把营销要素分为四类，<u>即</u>产品、价格、渠道和促销。(L3-1)
  [通胀的原因] <u>一个</u>是全球新兴市场的需求增加，造成了物资短缺；<u>另一个</u>是国家发行了过量的货币。(L8-2)
  跨国经营的发展主要经历以下三个阶段。<u>第一</u>，建立国外营销网点 ...。<u>第二</u>，在国外投资设厂 ...。<u>第三</u>，...实现企业内部的国际性分工。(L6-1)
  那么，2007年12月开始的这次衰退会给未来10年造成什么样的影响呢？<u>首先</u>，...。<u>其次</u>，...。<u>最后</u>，...。(L8, Ex7)

QUESTION 1: You can find two more cases of 第一, 第二, 第三 in Lesson 9 and Lesson 11 respectively. How are they different in usage from the one quoted here?

- Making a contrast 对比
  汇率下降要引起进口商品在国内的价格上涨。<u>相反</u>，本币升值则有可能降低进口商品的价格。(L2-1)
  如出口额大于进口额，叫做"贸易顺差"；<u>反之</u>，则为"贸易逆差"。(L4-1)
  这件事之所以引起社会关注，...。<u>以前</u>，...。<u>现在</u>，...。(L9, Ex7)
  影响市场营销的因素很多。<u>微观的如</u>...。<u>从宏观来看</u>，...。(L3-1)

- Citing examples 举例
  财政收入的种类很多，<u>如</u>税收、货币、国债、收费、罚没等。(L9-1)
  <u>例如</u>在2009年，立邦携手杜邦公司，启动了"为爱上色"项目。(L12, Ex7)
  各种智力创造，<u>比如</u>发明，文学和艺术作品，...，都可被认为是某一个人或组织所拥有的知识产权。(L11-1)
  您好像还谈到了计划经济的一些别的好处，<u>比如</u>...，等等。(L7-2)
  还有很多新的市场没有充分开发，<u>比如说</u>农村市场、老年市场、...等等。(L3-2)
  人民币升值也确实带来了一些好处。<u>比方说</u>，进口的汽车...比以前便宜了。(L2-2)
  资金，信誉，...有没有特殊要求<u>什么的</u>，都必须做到心中有底。(L4-2)

QUESTION 2: How are the underlined expressions different in levels of formality?

- Changing the topic 转换话题
  ...，收入也归地方财政所有。<u>至于</u>它的用途，今后会慢慢明确的。(L9-2)
  ...，所以我们面对的可是财富的缩水啊。<u>哎</u>，我来考你一下，...(L8-2)
  这就叫做"有理走遍天下"。<u>哦，对了</u>，马可，你过几天就要...。(L11-2)
  ...等我们班上讨论以后咱们再聊吧。<u>对了</u>，说了半天，你还没...。(L12-2)

  马　可：照您这么说，人民币升值，坏处比好处还多呢。
  张永安：不过，<u>再把话说回来</u>，现在很多中国企业多少有一些问题。(L2-2)

  王静文：对，...事实证明，对社会责任和环境责任的投资是不会赔本的。
  马　可：那么<u>把话再说回来</u>，刚才新闻里说，...。(L12-2)

QUESTION 3: How do the last two cases differ from the first four? Among the first four cases, how does the first one differ from the rest?

PRACTICE: Match each expression with its English definition, check the context in which it occurs, and see how it helps to organize and express thoughts.

a 同时(L7-2)/   e 因此 (L5-1)   k 一般来说 (L2-1)

   与此同时(L12-1)   f 正因为如此 (L3-1)   l 从长远来说 (L12-2)

b 其实 (L3-2)/   g 然而 (L12-1)   m 在这种情况下 (L9, Ex7)

   实际上(L4, Ex7)   h 再说 (L7-2)   n 由此可见 (L6, Ex7)

c 这样 (L5-1)   i 这就是说 (L6-2)

d 那么 (L4-2)   j 所有这些 (L12-1)

1 however ____   8 all these ____

2 as a matter of fact; in fact ____   9 it is because of this that ____

3 meanwhile, at the same time ____   10 therefore ____

4 in the long run ____   11 in that case ____

5 generally speaking ____   12 so; in this way ____

6 this is to say ____   13 it can be seen from this that ____

7 under the circumstances ____   14 moreover ____

REVIEW PRACTICE: Write out the short forms of the following phrases. (Refer to L3's learning guide if necessary.)

1 欧洲联盟 _____ (L7, Ex7)

2 通货膨胀 _____ (L8-1)

3 美国联邦储备系统 _____ (L8-2)

4 中央银行 _____ (L8-2)

5 科学技术 _____ (L11-2)

6 人寿保险 _____ (L10, Ex7)

7 欧洲和美国 _____ (L12-2)

8 环境保护 _____ (L12, Ex7)

第十二课 商业道德与社会责任

Lesson 12 *Business ethics and social responsibility*

课文一 Text 1

与商业政策及规章制度不同，商业道德不具有强制性，它主要是借助于传统习惯、社会舆论和从业者内心的信念来实现的。千百年来，在历史演变中形成了"先义后利"、"买卖公平"、"诚信无欺"等商业道德观念。正是这些道德观念制约着商人的行为。

然而，在计划经济时期的中国，"利"与"义"被极端地对立起来，追求利益被看成是资本主义的本质，通过经营取得利润的方式得不到社会的认可。政府的统一供应，使很多商品成为"皇帝的女儿不愁嫁"，因而商业服务态度不佳，顾客得不到应有的尊重。所有这些严重地制约了经济的发展。

市场经济发展的初期，有些企业为了追求自身的经济利益，运用不正当手段损害消费者的利益。一时间，盗版猖獗，假冒伪劣商品泛滥，各类欺诈现象纷纷出笼。更为严重的是，为了追求短期利益，一些生产活动破坏环境，影响了人们的生活和生存。

随着商品经济的发展，越来越多的企业认识到诚信对自身长远利益的重要性，它们处处遵契守法，注重信誉。与此同时，许多企业也增强了使命感与责任感，它们通过赞助或主办各种公益活动来回馈社会。

與商業政策及規章制度不同，商業道德不具有強制性，它主要是借助於傳統習慣、社會輿論和從業者內心的信念來實現的。

千百年來，在歷史演變中形成了"先義後利"、"買賣公平"、"誠信無欺"等商業道德觀念。正是這些道德觀念制約著商人的行為。

然而，在計劃經濟時期的中國，"利"與"義"被極端地對立起來，追求利益被看成是資本主義的本質，通過經營取得利潤的方式得不到社會的認可。政府的統一供應，使很多商品成為"皇帝的女兒不愁嫁"，因而商業服務態度不佳，顧客得不到應有的尊重。所有這些嚴重地制約了經濟的發展。

市場經濟發展的初期，有些企業為了追求自身的經濟利益，運用不正當手段損害消費者的利益。一時間，盜版猖獗，假冒偽劣商品氾濫，各類欺詐現象紛紛出籠。更為嚴重的是，為了追求短期利益，一些生產活動破壞環境，影響了人們的生活和生存。

隨著商品經濟的發展，越來越多的企業認識到誠信對自身長遠利益的重要性，它們處處遵契守法，注重信譽。與此同時，許多企業也增強了使命感與責任感，它們通過贊助或主辦各種公益活動來回饋社會。

词语表 Words and expressions

(* Refer to notes or language tips following the word list.)

1	借助*		jièzhù	*draw support from; with the help of*
2	传统	傳統	chuántǒng	*tradition*
3	舆论	輿論	yúlùn	*public opinion*
4	从业者	從業者	cóngyèzhě	*employees of commercial and service industries*
5	信念		xìnniàn	*conviction; belief*
6	演变	演變	yǎnbiàn	*evolve*
7	义	義	yì	*justice; righteousness*
8	利		lì	*profit; interest*
9	诚信	誠信	chéngxìn	*honesty; credit;* 诚实

10	无欺	無欺	wúqī	*no cheating; without cheating*
11	极端	極端	jíduān	*extreme; radical*
12	对立	對立	duìlì	*conflict*
13	追求		zhuīqiú	*seek; pursue*
14	利益		lìyì	*interest; profit*
15	资本主义	資本主義	zīběn zhǔyì	*capitalism*
16	本质	本質	běnzhì	*nature; essence*
17	认可	認可	rènkě	*endorsement*
18	统一	統一	tǒngyī	*unified*
19	态度	態度	tàidù	*attitude*
20	损害	損害	sǔnhài	*damage; harm*
21	盗版	盜版	dàobǎn	*piracy*
22	猖獗		chāngjué	*rampant*
23	假冒		jiǎmào	*fake; bogus; counterfeit*
24	伪劣	偽劣	wěiliè	*fake; shoddy*
25	泛滥	氾濫	fànlàn	*(of evil things) run unchecked*
26	欺诈	欺詐	qīzhà	*swindle; fraudulence*
27	纷纷	紛紛	fēnfēn	*one after another; in succession*
28	出笼	出籠	chūlóng	*(of evil things, shoddy goods, etc.) come forth*
29	生存		shēngcún	*existence*
30	长远	長遠	chángyuǎn	*long-term; long-range*
31	遵契守法		zūnqì shǒufǎ	*abide by contracts and laws*
32	注重		zhùzhòng	*attach importance to; emphasize; 重视*
33	使命		shǐmìng	*mission*
34	赞助	贊助	zànzhù	*provide monetary or material support*
35	主办	主辦	zhǔbàn	*sponsor; host*
36	公益		gōngyì	*public welfare*
37	回馈	回饋	huíkuì	*requite*

俗语 Common sayings

皇帝的女儿 不愁嫁*	皇帝的女兒 不愁嫁	huángdì de nǚér bù chóu jià	*(See notes.)*

理解考核 Comprehension check

对错选择 True or false

		True	False
1	商业政策具有强制性，商业道德不具有强制性。	☐	☐
2	在计划经济时期的中国，追求利益是不被社会认可的。	☐	☐
3	在计划经济时期的中国，人们追求"义"，不追求"利"，所以商业服务态度很好。	☐	☐
4	在市场经济初期，有些企业过分追求利益，不重视商业道德。	☐	☐
5	随着商品经济的发展，企业的商业道德意识越来越强。	☐	☐

注释 Notes

1　皇帝的女儿不愁嫁

"An emperor's daughter never has to worry about her marriage." The implication in the saying is that a princess, good or bad, will be taken by somebody as wife no matter what. In the context of text 1, the saying means that, in a planned economy with the government's monopoly over supply, commodities are guaranteed to have buyers regardless of their quality.

语言提示 Language tips

1　借助于: have the aid of; draw support from

- 商业道德主要…是借助于传统习惯…和从业者内心的信念来实现的。

  商家要宣传好自己的产品，就得借助于电视广告。
  该公司借助于技术方面的优势打败了所有的竞争对手。

2　V1 来 V2: When 来 is used between two verbs or verbal phrases, V1 indicates the way of doing things and V2 indicates the purpose.

■ ...借助于传统习惯...和从业者内心的信念<u>来</u>实现〔商业道德〕...。

世界各国都颁布了法律<u>来</u>保护知识产权。
多半的人得靠退休储蓄<u>来</u>安度晚年。

3 正: 正 can be used for emphasis, meaning "just that and nothing else." Besides in 正是, this usage is commonly seen in expressions such as 正要, 正像, 正如, and 正因为.

■ <u>正是</u>这些道德观念制约着商人的行为。
■ <u>正是</u>这一点确保了他们的成功。(L5-2)
■ <u>正因为</u>如此，市场营销是以满足顾客的需求为出发点的。(L3-1)
■ <u>正因为</u>这样，计划经济反而容易造成供不应求或供过于求。(L7-2)

<u>正是</u>中国的经济发展吸引了外商来华投资。
<u>正因为</u>税收是国家财政收入的重要来源，政府非做好征税工作不可。

4 一时间: This expression is used for a fast-emerging dominant phenomenon that spreads out in a short period of time.

■ 市场经济发展的初期....。<u>一时间</u>，盗版猖獗，假冒伪劣商品泛滥...。

iPhone一推出就非常流行，<u>一时间</u>，差不多每个人都用上了它。
央行刚刚宣布提高利率，<u>一时间</u>，大家都赶着 (gǎnzhe, hurry) 往银行存钱。

5 更为 Adj 的是 ...: What is more Adj is ...
特别 Adj 的是 ...: What is especially Adj is ...

■ <u>更为</u>严重<u>的是</u>，为了追求短期利益，一些生产活动破坏环境...。
■ <u>特别</u>有意思<u>的是</u>，通领集团...的胜诉，居然把...推翻了。(L11-2)

保险是一种个人理财的手段，<u>更为</u>重要<u>的是</u>，它能增强社会抵御风险的能力。
昨天的聚会参加的人不多，<u>特别</u>可惜<u>的是</u>王总没到。

课文二 Text 2

马可这次在上海的经历，特别是在咨询公司的实习，用他自己的话来说，是"胜读十年书"。现在他已经回到了美国，今天跟王静文约好了在商学院的大厅见面。王静文过来时，他正在看墙上的大屏幕电视新闻。

王静文： 你好，马可。在看什么呢？

马　可：这段新闻很有意思，说的是中国的一个调查结果，发现外资企业的社会责任心比不上国有和民营企业。

王静文：哦，是这个呀。我们班刚才就在讨论，觉得这个结论的依据不像是真实的绩效表现，而像是公司对信息的披露程度。

马　可：我也正在奇怪，欧美的大公司一般都具有很强的社会责任感，大部分是优秀的社会公民，怎么可能到了中国就成了"铁公鸡"了呢？

王静文：这正是布朗教授的问题。我们刚好在上"企业社会责任"（CSR）这一章。

马　可：是吗？那严格地说，什么是CSR？

王静文：CSR是指企业的行为会对人类、社区和环境造成影响，而企业必须对这些影响承担责任。这就是说，企业需要考虑的不只是"股份持有者"的权益，他们也得要关注"利益相关者"的权益，像消费者、社区居民、生态环境，等等。

马　可：这听起来很有道理。从长远来说，一个企业再大、再成功，要是只顾赚钱，不关心社会，到头来一定会失败。

王静文：对，这就是"责任的铁律"。西方的企业家在卡内基和亨利·福特的带动下，很早就树立了所谓的"慈善原则"，后来提供非盈利和慈善项目的企业就越来越多了。事实证明，对社会责任和环境责任的投资是不会赔本的。

马　可：那么把话再说回来，刚才新闻里说，中国的外资企业对公益捐赠披露得比较多，可是却不太愿意披露其他有关的财务指标。那是为什么？

王静文：这个问题，等我们班上讨论以后咱们再聊吧。对了，说了半天，你还没把我舅舅让你捎的东西拿出来呢。

馬可這次在上海的經歷，特別是在諮詢公司的實習，用他自己的話來說，是"勝讀十年書"。現在他已經回到了美國，今天跟王靜文約好了在商學院的大廳見面。王靜文過來時，他正在看牆上的大屏幕電視新聞。

王靜文：你好，馬可。在看什麼呢？

馬　可：這段新聞很有意思，說的是中國的一個調查結果，發現外資企業的社會責任心比不上國有和民營企業。

王靜文：哦，是這個呀。我們班剛才就在討論，覺得這個結論的依據不像是真實的績效表現，而像是公司對信息的披露程度。

馬　可：我也正在奇怪，歐美的大公司一般都具有很強的社會責任感，大部分是優秀的社會公民，怎麼可能到了中國就成了"鐵公雞"了呢？

王靜文：這正是布朗教授的問題。我們剛好在上"企業社會責任"（CSR）這一章。

馬　可：是嗎？那嚴格地說，什麼是CSR？

王靜文：CSR是指企業的行為會對人類、社區和環境造成影響，而企業必須對這些影響承擔責任。這就是說，企業需要考慮的不只是"股份持有者"的權益，他們也得要關注"利益相關者"的權益，像消費者、社區居民、生態環境，等等。

馬　可：這聽起來很有道理。從長遠來說，一個企業再大、再成功，要是只顧賺錢，不關心社會，到頭來一定會失敗。

王靜文：對，這就是"責任的鐵律"。西方的企業家在卡內基和亨利·福特的帶動下，很早就樹立了所謂的"慈善原則"，後來提供非盈利和慈善項目的企業就越來越多了。事實證明，對社會責任和環境責任的投資是不會賠本的。

馬　可：那麼把話再說回來，剛才新聞裡說，中國的外資企業對公益捐贈披露得比較多，可是卻不太願意披露其他有關的財務指標。那是為什麼？

王靜文：這個問題，等我們班上討論以後咱們再聊吧。對了，說了半天，你還沒把我舅舅讓你捎的東西拿出來呢。

词语表 Words and expressions

(* Refer to notes or language tips following the word list.)

1	胜*	勝	shèng	*be superior to*
2	约好	約好	yuēhǎo	*with an appointment scheduled*
3	大厅	大廳	dàtīng	*hall; lobby*
4	段		duàn	*classifier for length or distance*
5	依据	依據	yījù	*basis; things to go by;* 根据
6	真实	真實	zhēnshí	*true; real*
7	绩效	績效	jìxiào	*performance and results*
8	披露		pīlù	*reveal; announce*
9	优秀	優秀	yōuxiù	*outstanding; excellent*
10	公民		gōngmín	*citizen*
11	铁*	鐵	tiě	*iron*
12	刚好	剛好	gānghǎo	*by chance; by coincidence*
13	人类	人類	rénlèi	*mankind*
14	社区	社區	shèqū	*community*

15	考虑	考慮	kǎolǜ	*think over; consider*
16	持有		chíyǒu	*hold; possess;* 有
17	权益	權益	quányì	*rights and interests*
18	生态	生態	shēngtài	*ecology; ecological*
19	顾	顧	gù	*attend to*
20	失败	失敗	shībài	*fail; lose*
21	铁律*	鐵律	tiělǜ	*iron law*
22	树立	樹立	shùlì	*establish; erect*
23	所谓*	所謂	suǒwèi	*so-called*
24	慈善*		císhàn	*charity*
25	原则*	原則	yuánzé	*principle*
26	项目	項目	xiàngmù	*project; program*
27	事实	事實	shìshí	*fact*
28	证明	證明	zhèngmíng	*prove; testify; verify*
29	赔本	賠本	péiběn	*lose money in doing business;* 赔钱
30	捐赠	捐贈	juānzèng	*donation*
31	指标	指標	zhǐbiāo	*indicator*
32	捎		shāo	*take along sth to or for sb*

专有名词 Proper nouns

卡内基		Kǎnèijī	*Andrew Carnegie*
亨利·福特		Hēnglì·Fútè	*Henry Ford*

俗语 Common sayings

胜读十年书	勝讀十年書	shèng dú shínián shū	*better than reading books for ten years*
铁公鸡	鐵公雞	tiěgōngjī	*"iron rooster"; stingy person; miser*

理解考核 Comprehension check

回答问题 Answer the following questions

1　马可觉得这次在上海的经历怎么样？

2　马可看的电视新闻在说什么？

3　马可和王静文对新闻里的结论有什么看法？

4　什么是 CSR？

5　什么是"责任的铁律"？

注释 Notes

1　胜读十年书

This saying comes from 听君一席话，胜读十年书, which means "talking with you for one moment is much better than reading books for ten years" (a translation by a Chinese scholar) or "a single conversation [across a table] with a wise man is worth a month's study of books" (a translation by a Westerner).

2　铁公鸡

This is from 一毛不拔——铁公鸡, a two-part allegorical saying. In a saying like this, the first part is descriptive and always stated, while the second part carries the message and is sometimes unstated. In his conversation with Wang Jingwen, Mark comes straight to the point without having to give the first part of the saying because 铁公鸡, from which obviously no feathers can be plucked, is descriptive and complete in meaning by itself.

3　责任的铁律

The term "Iron Law of Responsibility" first appears in the textbook *Business and Its Environment* (Davis and Blomstrom, 1966). It recognizes that avoiding social responsibility leads to the gradual erosion of power. The essential message here is that, in the long run, those who do not use power in ways that society considers responsible will tend to lose it. Carroll (1998) summarizes CSR in terms of "the four faces of corporate citizenship" as follows: "economic responsibilities" that pertain to the necessity for corporations to be profitable; "legal responsibilities" that require business to operate within the boundaries of laws and national policies; "ethical responsibilities" that demand firms to operate morally, fairly, and justly; and "philanthropic responsibilities" that oblige companies to contribute financial and other resources for the welfare and betterment of society and the community.

4　慈善原则

The Charity Principle, developed along with the Stewardship Principle (管家原则) by Lawrence, Weber and Post in 2005, urges business firms to give voluntary aid to society's unfortunate or needy groups. Much like the "philanthropic responsibilities" mentioned above, the Charity Principle is reminiscent of the historical times when rulers and royalty provided for the poor citizenry. At the beginning of the twentieth century, wealthy industrialists in the United States such as Andrew Carnegie and John D. Rockefeller contributed large sums of money to charitable organizations, educational institutions, and other community groups. In contrast, the Stewardship Principle requires companies to be keepers, stewards, or trustees in the public interest. Companies must ensure that society benefits or does not suffer from their business decisions and actions. Implicit in the Stewardship Principle is the interdependence of business and society. While companies act according to their self-interests, they are obligated to balance the interests and desires of various stakeholders, some of whom look for support for various specific causes.

语言提示 Language tips

1　从 . . . 来说/看: (speaking/judging) from the aspect or angle of

- 从长远来说，一个企业再大、再成功，要是 . . .，到头来一定会失败。
- 从宏观来看，人口、 . . .，等等，都会对 . . . 市场营销产生 . . . 影响。
(L3-1)

从个人来说，是要理一生的财。
从历史来看，计划经济制约了经济的发展。
从发展的角度来看，这种全球性的眼光非常重要。

2　到头来: in the end; eventually

- . . . 一个企业再大、再成功，要是 . . . 不关心社会，到头来一定会失败。

发展经济要是不注意保护环境，到头来生活质量非下降不可。
逃税的人到头来会受到法律的制裁 (zhìcái, punishment)。

3　在 . . . 的 . . . 下: with (care, help, encouragement, etc.) from . . .

- 西方的企业家在 . . . 的带动下，很早就树立了所谓的"慈善原则"。

在方总的关心和大家的帮助下，马可的实习进行得很顺利。
在林教授的鼓励 (gǔlì, encouragement) 下，马可为经济课准备了一个发言。

4　所谓的: so-called

- 西方的企业家 . . . 很早就树立了所谓的"慈善原则"。

在4P的基础上增加政治力量与公共关系，这就形成了所谓的6P理论。
所谓的"沪市"和"深市"，是指现在大陆的两家证券交易所。

练习 Exercises

1 将左栏的数量词和右栏的名词配对（每个词语只能用一次）。Match each classifier in the left column with an appropriate noun in the right column. Each item can be used only once.

1) 一位 _____   a) 公司
2) 一条 _____   b) 经济课
3) 一家 _____   c) 蛋糕
4) 一门 _____   d) 副局长
5) 一番 _____   e) 短信
6) 一份 _____   f) 房子
7) 一套 _____   g) 投资
8) 一件 _____   h) 计划书
9) 一块 _____   i) 好事
10) 一项 _____   j) 功夫

2 听写并用汉语解释下列词组。Complete a dictation of the following phrases and explain them in Chinese.

1) 先义后利
2) 诚信无欺
3) 皇帝的女儿不愁嫁
4) 盗版猎獭
5) 欺诈现象纷纷出笼
6) 遵契守法
7) 胜读十年书
8) 铁公鸡
9) 企业社会责任
10) 利益相关者
11) 责任的铁律
12) 慈善原则

3 选词填空。Fill in the blanks with the provided words and expressions.

1) 一时间，借助于，所谓的，更为

_____商业道德不同于商业政策及规章制度，不具有强制性。它主要是_____ 传统习惯、社会舆论和从业者的内心信念来实现的。随着商品经济的发展，中国企业的商业道德意识越来越强，_____ 重要的是，许多企业增强了使命感和责任感，_____，各大企业纷纷赞助或主办公益活动来回馈社会。

2) 假冒伪劣，诚信无欺，遵契守法，社会责任

　　　在经济活动中，任何企业都必须处处_____，对消费者_____，不生产经营_____产品。随着商品经济的发展，企业还应该增强_____感，努力回馈社会。

4　用指定的表达方式完成句子或对话。Complete the following sentences with the provided words or expressions.

1) 正是/正因为

a) _____使"百度"很快就发展成了全球最大的中文搜索引擎。

b) _____，中国的房地产市场开始降温了。

2) 一时间

a) Google 突然宣布退出中国，_____。

b) 2010年底，中国取消了对外资企业的税收优惠政策，_____
_____。

3) 从...来说/看

a) _____，经济衰退也有好处。

b) _____，人民币升值对中国经济利大于弊。

4) 到头来

a) 企业如果运用不正当手段损害消费者的利益，_____
_____。

b) 跨国经营如果不重视本土化，_____。

5) 在...的...下

a) _____，这家公司的股票成功上市。

b) _____，这次的贸易洽谈进行得非常顺利。

6) 所谓的

a) 所谓的按揭，_____。

b) _____，就是企业的社会责任。

5　把下面的句子改成不太正式的语体。Paraphrase the following sentences in a less formal style, paying special attention to the underlined words and phrases.

1) 商业道德不具有强制性，它主要借助于传统习惯、社会舆论和从业者内心的信念来实现。

_____

_____。

2) 政府的统一供应使<u>大量商品成为</u>"<u>皇帝的女儿不愁嫁</u>",<u>因而</u>商业服务态度<u>不佳</u>,顾客得不到<u>应有的</u>尊重。

_____

_____。

3) <u>某些</u>企业为了追求自身的<u>经济利益</u>,运用不正当手段损害消费者。<u>一时间</u>,盗版<u>猖獗</u>,假冒伪劣商品泛滥,各类欺诈现象纷纷<u>出笼</u>。<u>更为</u>严重的是,对环境的破坏影响了人们的生活和生存。

_____

_____

_____。

6 自行查找参考资料,解释与本课话题有关的词语。Using available resources as a reference, explain the following terms, which are related to this lesson's topic.

1) 企业伦理　　　　5) 窃取商业机密

2) 行为准则　　　　6) 恶性竞争

3) 员工敬业度　　　7) CAUX 圆桌会议

4) 商业贿赂　　　　8) 《反海外腐败法》

7 阅读理解与讨论。Reading comprehension and discussion.

立邦的"ECOLOR"计划

2010年,中国涂料行业的领导者立邦公司(Nippon Paint)在上海启动了以"ECOLOR"为主旨的企业社会责任(CSR)计划。ECOLOR是立邦的企业社会责任标识,由ECO(绿色、生态)与COLOR(色彩)组成,用以体现企业的价值。根据这一计划,立邦拟与战略伙伴巴斯夫(BASF)公司及杜邦(DuPont)公司一起,开发低碳环保涂料,致力环境生态平衡,创造可持续发展的未来。与此同时,立邦还本着社会各界互助互惠的精神启动了"绿色银行"平台,把所有利益攸关者串连起来,让它们与立邦一起身体力行企业社会责任,为环保贡献力量。

立邦对企业社会责任的重视由来已久,曾先后推出过多个项目。例如在2009年,立邦携手杜邦公司,启动了"为爱上色"项目,计划在三年内免费涂刷100所希望小学的外墙,美化校园外观,改善教学环境。除了免费涂刷计划以外,"为爱上色"项目还包括立邦与中国青少年发展基金会共同设立的"立邦色彩希望工程基金"。两年来,立邦已经在全中国捐建了超过20所立邦希望小学,45间以上的立邦快乐美术教室。这一项目对在全社会形成关注公益、关注希望小学的氛围作出了重要贡献。

涂料	túliào	paint; coating	重视	zhòngshì	attach importance to
启动	qǐdòng	start up	由来已久	yóulái yǐ jiǔ	long-standing
主旨	zhǔzhǐ	purport; keynote	推出	tuīchū	launch
标识	biāozhì	logo; emblem	携手	xiéshǒu	hand in hand
拟	nǐ	plan; be going to	免费	miǎnfèi	free of charge
战略	zhànlüè	strategy; strategic	涂刷	túshuā	paint; brush
低碳	dītàn	low-carbon	希望小学	Xīwàng Xiǎoxué	Hope Primary School
环保	huánbǎo	environmental protection			
致力	zhìlì	be devoted to; strive for	外墙	wàiqiáng	external wall
本着	běnzhe	in line with	美化	měihuà	beautify; prettify
各界	gèjiè	all walks of life; all circles	外观	wàiguān	outward appearance
互助	hùzhù	mutual help; mutual aid	基金会	jījīnhuì	foundation
互惠	hùhuì	mutual benefit	设立	shèlì	establish; set up
精神	jīngshén	spirit	希望工程	Xīwàng Gōngchéng	Hope Program (a project launched in China to help poor kids to go to school)
平台	píngtái	platform			
攸关	yōuguān	at stake; be affected	捐建	juānjiàn	donate and build
串连	chuànlián	link one by one	超过	chāoguò	surpass
身体力行	shēn tǐ lì xíng	practice what one advocates	美术	měishù	fine arts
			氛围	fēnwéi	atmosphere
贡献	gòngxiàn	contribute; contribution			

<u>选择填空</u> Select the correct answer for each blank.

1) 立邦公司在2009年启动的是 ＿＿＿＿。

   a) ECOLOR 计划

   b) "为爱上色" 项目

   c) "绿色银行" 平台

2) 关于 ECOLOR 计划<u>不正确</u>的是 ＿＿＿＿。

   a) ECOLOR 是立邦的企业社会责任标识

   b) ECOLOR 指的是 "绿色、生态" 和 "色彩"

   c) 立邦早已跟杜邦和巴斯夫合作开发低碳环保涂料

3) "绿色银行" 平台 ＿＿＿＿。

   a) 把所有利益攸关者串连起来

   b) 是立邦和杜邦公司联合发起的

   c) 比 ECOLOR 计划开始得早

4) "为爱上色" 项目<u>不包括</u> ＿＿＿＿。

   a) 免费涂刷100所希望小学的外墙

   b) 设立 "立邦色彩希望工程基金"

   c) 致力于环境保护

讨论 Discussion.

什么是立邦的"ECOLOR"计划？根据你了解的情况或所查的资料，介绍一下立邦公司在另一个国家的一项社会公益活动。What is Nippon Paint's ECOLOR Program? According to what you know or what you have found from research, talk about a Nippon Paint event for public welfare in a different country.

8 实践活动。Tasks.

1) 查阅资料，列出美国钢铁大王卡内基（1835–1919）对慈善事业的两个最重要的贡献。Conduct research to find out US steel magnate Andrew Carnegie's two most important contributions to charities.

2) 做一个10分钟的口头报告，介绍一家重视企业社会责任、热中公益活动的中国或美国企业。在报告中请说明这家企业的具体做法和效果，并发表自己的意见。先查看最近六个月之内的资料，然后根据老师的要求为自己准备一个简单的提纲。Give a ten-minute oral report about a US or Chinese enterprise that values CSR and cares about public welfare. Explain what it does and how it works, and provide your own comments. You should base your report on information from within the past six months and, following your teacher's instructions, prepare a brief outline.

3) 写一篇短文（不要超过一页），用事实和例子证明你对中国（或美国）目前的商业道德的看法，并提出自己的建议。Write a short essay (limited to one page) supporting your viewpoint about business ethics in present-day China (or the United States) with facts and examples. You may also want to offer suggestions.

4) 如果你对一个不同的任务有兴趣，请结合本课的主题向老师提出建议，然后在老师的指导下完成这个任务。If you are interested in a different kind of task, you are encouraged to suggest your proposal and complete it under your teacher's guidance.

学习指导 Learning guide

礼貌语 Polite language

Modesty and circumspection are important virtues in Chinese culture. You will be appreciated if you humble yourself in speaking to or about others, especially to or about a senior, a superior, or whoever deserves special public respect. Polite language is even more desirable and expected on formal occasions, whether it is in the form of speech or writing. This feature is not quite obvious in the article texts in this course because, as introductions to common knowledge, the language has to be plain and objective in the first place. In the dialogue texts, however, there are quite a few cases that deserve your interest and attention.

马可, the main character in the dialogues, converses with a few people of varying degrees of familiarity. One of them is 方海明, his boss at the consulting company. Although he may know 方海明 very well since she is his father's former student, he still addresses her as 方总 in public. When 马可 talks to 林汉华, his professor at the university, he could have addressed him as 林教授 or 林先生 to show reverence, but he calls him 林老师 instead, which still shows respect but brings the two of them closer. As for 张永安, 王静文's uncle and a school teacher, 马可 chose not to call him 舅舅 as 王静文 does, but addresses him as 张老师. This helps him to show more respect than intimacy. Besides, in his interactions with all three people, 马可 uses 您, while he uses 你 to address his young friends, colleagues, and classmates. From 马可's usage, we can tell that he addresses Chinese people in a most appropriate manner.

Some good examples of 马可's polite language can be found in his conversation with 方海明 at a company event (L3-2):

方总您<u>过奖</u>了。
这次我参加了对中国市场的调查和分析，<u>应该说学到了不少才是</u>。
今天有机会，正好想<u>请教</u>一下方总对中国市场的看法。

There are also good examples in 马可's conversations with Professor 林汉华 (L7-2 and L9-2), where he shows humility by suggesting a sense of uncertainty on his part:

您<u>好像</u>在课上说了一<u>些</u>计划经济的好话，我<u>不知道是不是听错了</u>。
您<u>好像</u>还谈到了计划经济的一<u>些</u>别的好处，比如 . . .
<u>我想</u>您说了， . . .
所以您的结论是，计划经济不适合搞现代化<u>？</u>
听您这么说，<u>好像</u>房地产税的问题现在还有很多东西不清楚。

As a matter of fact, in his conversations with others 马可 also humbles himself by showing uncertainty, modesty, and appreciation:

<u>我听说</u>人民币升值对中国的外贸出口影响很大。(with 张永安 in L2-2)
你比较有经验，<u>有什么要提醒我的吗</u>？ (with 王静文 in L4-2)
你对洽谈<u>有什么建议吗</u>？ (Ibid.)
跟中国公司谈判<u>要特别注意什么呢</u>？ (Ibid.)
我看到过一<u>些</u>报道，<u>好像</u>不少人在担心通胀失控。(with 李瑛瑛 in L8-2)
我可不是理财专家，<u>只是听说过一些皮毛罢了</u>。(with 张永安 in L10-2)
<u>这好像</u>也是投资理财的一个热点。(Ibid.)
<u>真感谢</u>方总给我安排了这样一个机会。(with 钱亮 in L11-2)
<u>我原来以为</u> . . .。<u>没想到现在</u> . . . (Ibid.)

PRACTICE: Seek advice about your academic major and/or career opportunities from a Chinese-speaking senior like 张永安 or 林汉华, with whom you are not quite familiar. Try to follow 马可's example and make appropriate use of polite language.

REVIEW PRACTICE: Make sense of the likenesses in meaning in the following three-character compounds. (Refer to Lı's learning guide if necessary.)

1 积极<u>性</u>, 创造<u>性</u>, 随机<u>性</u>, 时间<u>性</u>, 重要<u>性</u> ＿＿＿＿＿＿＿

2 成就<u>感</u>, 使命<u>感</u>, 责任<u>感</u> ＿＿＿＿＿＿＿

3 劳动<u>者</u>, 从业<u>者</u>, 消费<u>者</u> ＿＿＿＿＿＿＿

4 经营<u>权</u>, 所有<u>权</u>, 使用<u>权</u> ＿＿＿＿＿＿＿

REVIEW PRACTICE: Match the four-character expressions with their definitions.

a 一举两得   b 一无是处   c 力不从心   d 大有可为   e 遵契守法
f 家喻户晓   g 专款专用   h 宾至如归   i 与时俱进   j 原来如此

1 Unable to do as much as one wishes to ＿＿＿

2 Abide by contracts and observe laws ＿＿＿

3 Killing two birds with one stone ＿＿＿

4 Special fund being used for its earmarked purpose ＿＿＿

5 Advance with each passing day ＿＿＿

6 Devoid of any merit ＿＿＿

7 So that's how it is ＿＿＿

8 Guests arriving with the feeling of returning home ＿＿＿

9 Known to every household ＿＿＿

10 Having good prospects ＿＿＿

附录一 汉英词语总表

Appendix A: *Chinese–English glossary of words and expressions*

本表系以词语的拼音字母顺序及声调顺序排列
Words and phrases in this list appear in order of the *pinyin* alphabet and tones.

A

安度		āndù	*spend (time) in peace and safety*	10-2
安排		ānpái	*arrange*	6-1
案件		ànjiàn	*legal case*	11-2
按揭		ànjiē	*mortgage*	1-2
案例		ànlì	*case*	11-2
案情		ànqíng	*details of a legal case*	11-2
按照		ànzhào	*according to;* 根据	9-1

B

把握		bǎwò	*grasp; seize (an opportunity)*	5-2
罢了	罷了	bàle	*only; nothing else*	10-2
拜访	拜訪	bàifǎng	*pay sb a visit*	1-2
拜托	拜託	bàituō	*entrust sth to sb; request a favor*	5-2
颁布	頒佈	bānbù	*promulgate; issue*	11-1
包括		bāokuò	*include*	10-1
包装		bāozhuāng	*packaging*	4-2
保护	保護	bǎohù	*protect; guard*	11-1
保险	保險	bǎoxiǎn	*insurance*	4-2
保险金	保險金	bǎoxiǎnjīn	*insured amount*	10-1
保障		bǎozhàng	*ensure; protect*	7-2
保证	保證	bǎozhèng	*guarantee*	4-2
报酬	報酬	bàochóu	*pay; remuneration; rewards*	9-1
报道	報道	bàodào	*report*	8-2
报价	報價	bàojià	*quote*	4-2
本币	本幣	běnbì	*basic unit of a currency;* 本位货币	2-1
本土		běntǔ	*local;* 本地	6-2
本质	本質	běnzhì	*nature; essence*	12-1
崩溃	崩潰	bēngkuì	*collapse*	8-1
比较	比較	bǐjiào	*relative; relatively*	6-1
比例		bǐlì	*ratio; proportion*	10-1
比率		bǐlǜ	*ratio; rate*	2-1
弊病		bìbìng	*defect*	7-2
必定		bìdìng	*be bound to; be sure to;* 一定	3-2
毕竟	畢竟	bìjìng	*after all*	9-2
避开	避開	bìkāi	*avoid*	6-2
避免		bìmiǎn	*avoid*	7-1
贬值	貶值	biǎnzhí	*depreciation*	2-1
便		biàn	*thereupon;* 就	8-1

变现	變現	biànxiàn	cash (a check, etc.); turn sth into cash	10-2
标明	標明	biāomíng	mark; indicate	1-1
标志	標誌	biāozhì	symbol; sign	11-1
表示		biǎoshì	indicate	2-1
表现	表現	biǎoxiàn	show; display	2-1
宾至如归	賓至如歸	bīn zhì rú guī	Guests arrive as if they had returned home.	6-2
并存	並存	bìngcún	coexist	3-2
补偿	補償	bǔcháng	compensate; make up for	10-1
不得		bùdé	must not; not be allowed; 不准; 不可以	11-1
不动产	不動產	bùdòngchǎn	immovable property; real estate	10-2
不断	不斷	bùduàn	continuously	6-1
布局	佈局	bùjú	overall arrangement; layout	6-2
部门	部門	bùmén	department of an organization	5-1
不亦乐乎	不亦樂乎	bù yì lè hū	awfully; extremely	4-2
不止		bùzhǐ	exceed; not limited to; 不只	4-2
布置	佈置	bùzhì	arrangement and decoration	6-2
不至于	不至於	bùzhìyú	cannot go so far; be unlikely	8-2

C

财产	財產	cáichǎn	property; fortune	10-1
裁定		cáidìng	ruling	11-2
财富	財富	cáifù	wealth; fortune	8-2
财力	財力	cáilì	financial capability; financial resources	7-2
财务	財務	cáiwù	finance; financial affair	5-1
财政	財政	cáizhèng	finance	9-1
采购	採購	cǎigòu	purchase (for an organization or enterprise); 买; 购买	5-1
采取	採取	cǎiqǔ	select and adopt (a measure, plan, etc.)	6-2
菜单	菜單	càidān	menu	6-2
参观	參觀	cānguān	visit (a place); have a look around	1-2
参考	參考	cānkǎo	refer to (resources)	2-1
参与	參與	cānyù	participate in	4-1
策略		cèlüè	tactics	3-1
差额	差額	chā'é	difference; margin	4-1
差距		chājù	gap	7-2
差异	差異	chāyì	difference; 不同	4-1
产品	產品	chǎnpǐn	product	3-1
产权	產權	chǎnquán	property rights; ownership of property	11-1
产生	產生	chǎnshēng	come into being; emerge	3-1
产业	產業	chǎnyè	industry	1-2
猖獗		chāngjué	rampant	12-1
长远	長遠	chángyuǎn	long-term; long-range	12-1
厂	廠	chǎng	factory	6-1
彻底	徹底	chèdǐ	thoroughgoing; thorough	6-2
称	稱	chēng	call; be called;(被)叫做	1-1
承担	承擔	chéngdān	bear; undertake; assume	10-1
程度		chéngdù	degree; extent	5-1
惩罚	懲罰	chéngfá	punish; punishment	5-1
成分		chéngfèn	element	7-1
成功		chénggōng	success; successful	3-2
成果		chéngguǒ	achievement; positive result	11-1
成就		chéngjiù	achievement	4-2
成立		chénglì	establish; set up	1-1
承诺	承諾	chéngnuò	promise; 答应	11-1
承受		chéngshòu	bear; endure	10-2

成熟		chéngshú	*ripe; mature*	5-2
呈现	呈現	chéngxiàn	*show; display;* 表现	10-1
诚信	誠信	chéngxìn	*honesty; credit;* 诚实	12-1
成员	成員	chéngyuán	*member*	4-1
城镇	城鎮	chéngzhèn	*cities and towns*	9-2
吃亏	吃虧	chīkuī	*suffer losses*	10-2
持续	持續	chíxù	*continuous*	8-1
持有		chíyǒu	*hold; possess;* 有	12-2
充分		chōngfèn	*adequate; ample*	3-2
冲击	衝擊	chōngjī	*attack; strike against*	2-2
出发	出發	chūfā	*set out; start*	3-1
出笼	出籠	chūlóng	*(of evil things, shoddy goods, etc.) come forth*	12-1
初期		chūqī	*beginning period*	5-1
出洋相		chū yángxiàng	*make a fool of oneself*	4-2
厨房	廚房	chúfáng	*kitchen*	2-2
处理	處理	chǔlǐ	*process; deal with; handle*	7-2
储蓄	儲蓄	chǔxù	*save; savings deposit;* 存钱	10-2
传统	傳統	chuántǒng	*tradition*	12-1
创立	創立	chuànglì	*found; form*	5-2
创新	創新	chuàngxīn	*innovate; innovation*	6-1
创业	創業	chuàngyè	*start an enterprise*	5-2
创造	創造	chuàngzào	*create; initiate*	7-2
创作	創作	chuàngzuò	*create literary and art works*	11-1
慈善		císhàn	*charity*	12-2
刺激		cìjī	*stimulate*	8-1
从事	從事	cóngshì	*engage in; deal with;* 做	1-2
从业者	從業者	cóngyèzhě	*employees of commercial and service industries*	12-1
促进	促進	cùjìn	*promote*	4-1
促销	促銷	cùxiāo	*promotion*	3-1
存		cún	*deposit*	8-2
存货	存貨	cúnhuò	*goods in stock*	8-1
存款		cúnkuǎn	*savings deposits*	8-2
存在		cúnzài	*exist;* 有	4-1
错误	錯誤	cuòwù	*mistake; error; erroneous*	11-2

D

答应	答應	dāyìng	*promise*	4-2
达	達	dá	*reach (a place or a figure);* 达到	8-1
达到	達到	dádào	*reach (a figure)*	1-1
答疑		dáyí	*answer questions;* 回答疑问	7-2
大幅		dàfú	*substantially*	8-1
大户型		dàhùxíng	*large dwelling-size (house; apartment)*	9-2
大厅	大廳	dàtīng	*hall; lobby*	12-2
大意		dàyi	*be careless*	4-2
大有可为	大有可為	dà yǒu kě wéi	*promising*	3-2
带动	帶動	dàidòng	*bring along*	8-1
贷款	貸款	dàikuǎn	*loan;* 借钱	1-2
单子	單子	dānzi	*list*	4-2
蛋糕		dàngāo	*cake*	3-2
当前	當前	dāngqián	*present; current;* 目前	5-1
当事人	當事人	dāngshìrén	*person or party concerned; litigant*	10-1
倒闭	倒閉	dǎobì	*go out of business*	2-2
导致	導致	dǎozhì	*lead to; result in*	4-1
倒		dào	*contrary to an expectation*	2-2
盗版	盜版	dàobǎn	*piracy*	12-1

道德		dàodé	morals; ethics	5-2
得意门生	得意門生	déyì ménshēng	favorite pupil	11-2
低度		dīdù	low grade	8-1
底线	底線	dǐxiàn	baseline; bottom line	4-2
抵御	抵禦	dǐyù	resist; withstand	10-1
地区	地區	dìqū	region	4-1
地域		dìyù	region; area	9-1
点	點	diǎn	point; spot; dot; often as a suffix	3-1
点子	點子	diǎnzi	idea; key point; 想法; 主意	3-2
调查	調查	diàochá	investigation	3-1
调动	調動	diàodòng	bring into play; arouse	11-1
顶不住	頂不住	dǐng bu zhù	cannot stand	2-2
订立	訂立	dìnglì	conclude or make (a treaty, agreement, etc.)	10-1
定义	定義	dìngyì	define	8-1
动荡	動盪	dòngdàng	turbulence; upheaval	8-1
动力	動力	dònglì	motivational power; driving force	7-1
动身	動身	dòngshēn	set out (for a place)	1-2
动摇	動搖	dòngyáo	waver; fluctuate	8-1
独立	獨立	dúlì	independent	4-1
度量衡		dùliànghéng	length, capacity, and weight	4-1
短缺		duǎnquē	shortage; 缺少; 缺乏	8-2
短信		duǎnxìn	short message	8-2
段		duàn	classifier for length or distance	12-2
兑换	兌換	duìhuàn	exchange; convert (currencies)	2-1
对立	對立	duìlì	conflict	12-1
对手	對手	duìshǒu	opponent; competitor	6-2
对象	對象	duìxiàng	object; target; subject	9-1
多元		duōyuán	multi-element; multi-variant	10-1

E

耳目		ěrmù	ears and eyes	3-1

F

发布	發佈	fābù	issue; release	11-2
发达	發達	fādá	developed	7-2
发放	發放	fāfàng	(of a government or organization) distribute (money or goods)	8-2
发挥	發揮	fāhuī	bring (skill, talent, etc.) into play	9-1
发明	發明	fāmíng	invention	11-1
发起	發起	fāqǐ	originate	11-2
发生	發生	fāshēng	occur; take place	8-1
发行	發行	fāxíng	issue	1-1
发言	發言	fāyán	make a statement or speech	9-2
发展	發展	fāzhǎn	develop; development	1-1
罚没	罰沒	fámò	confiscate; confiscation	9-1
法令		fǎlìng	laws and decrees	9-1
法律		fǎlǜ	law	4-1
法院		fǎyuàn	court	11-2
番		fān	(measure word) time, as in 一番功夫	3-2
反义	反義	fǎnyì	antonym	8-1
泛滥	氾濫	fànlàn	(of evil things) run unchecked	12-1
范围	範圍	fànwéi	range	4-1
方案		fāng'àn	plan	4-2
方法		fāngfǎ	method; way; 做法	9-2
方面		fāngmiàn	aspect	2-1

方式		fāngshì	*way (of doing sth)*	4-2
方针	方針	fāngzhēn	*guiding principle*	7-1
房地产	房地產	fángdìchǎn	*real estate; real property;* 房产和地产	1-1
非		fēi	*not-, un-; non-; often as a prefix*	9-2
分别		fēnbié	*respectively*	1-1
纷纷	紛紛	fēnfēn	*one after another; in succession*	12-1
分工		fēngōng	*division of work*	6-1
分离	分離	fēnlí	*separate; segregate;* 分开	7-1
分配		fēnpèi	*allot; distribute*	7-1
分期		fēnqī	*(pay) by installment*	1-2
分析		fēnxī	*analyze; analysis*	3-2
分支		fēnzhī	*branch; division*	6-1
丰富	豐富	fēngfù	*abundant; plentiful;* 很多	3-1
风俗习惯	風俗習慣	fēngsú xíguàn	*customs and habits*	4-1
风险	風險	fēngxiǎn	*risk*	4-1
浮动	浮動	fúdòng	*float; fluctuate*	2-1
符合		fúhé	*conform to; tally with*	7-2
福利		fúlì	*welfare*	8-2
服务	服務	fúwù	*service*	3-1
付		fù	*pay*	1-2
负	負	fù	*minus; negative*	8-1
副		fù	*vice; deputy; associate*	11-2
付还	付還	fùhuán	*pay back*	1-2
附近		fùjìn	*vicinity; nearby*	6-2
付清		fùqīng	*pay off; clear (a bill)*	1-2
复杂	複雜	fùzá	*complicated*	4-1
负责	負責	fùzé	*be in charge of*	4-1

G

该	該	gāi	*this; that; the above-mentioned*	1-1
改称	改稱	gǎichēng	*be renamed as*	7-1
改革		gǎigé	*reform*	7-1
改善		gǎishàn	*improve*	1-2
赶巧	趕巧	gǎnqiǎo	*it so happened that*	5-2
感情		gǎnqíng	*emotion; sentiment*	5-1
刚好	剛好	gānghǎo	*by chance; by coincidence*	12-2
岗位	崗位	gǎngwèi	*post; position*	10-1
高档	高檔	gāodàng	*top grade*	2-2
高度		gāodù	*elevation above a specified level*	9-1
高速		gāosù	*high speed*	7-2
搞		gǎo	*do; carry on;* 做	6-2
各		gè	*each; every*	3-1
个体	個體	gètǐ	*individual; individuality*	7-1
各自		gèzì	*respective; respectively*	6-2
根据	根據	gēnjù	*according to*	1-1
供		gōng	*provide sb with the convenience of doing sth*	1-1
供不应求	供不應求	gōng bù yìng qiú	*supply falls short of demand*	7-2
功夫		gōngfu	*time devoted to a task; same as* 工夫	3-2
公关	公關	gōngguān	*public relations*	6-2
供过于求	供過於求	gōng guò yú qiú	*supply exceeds demand*	7-2
供给	供給	gōngjǐ	*supply*	8-1
工具		gōngjù	*tool*	2-1
公民		gōngmín	*citizen*	12-2
功能		gōngnéng	*function*	10-1
供求		gōngqiú	*supply and demand;* 供给和需求	2-1

公益		gōngyì	public welfare	12-1
供应	供應	gōngyìng	supply; provide	3-1
公有		gōngyǒu	publicly owned; 公共所有	7-1
公约	公約	gōngyuē	convention; pact	11-1
共同		gòngtóng	together; 一起	6-1
购买力	購買力	gòumǎilì	purchasing power	8-1
股份		gǔfèn	share; stock	1-1
股民		gǔmín	stock investor	1-1
股票		gǔpiào	share; stock; a certificate of these	1-1
股市		gǔshì	stock market; 股票市场	1-1
故		gù	so; therefore; 所以	4-1
顾	顧	gù	attend to	12-2
固定		gùdìng	fixed; immobile	9-1
顾客	顧客	gùkè	customer	3-1
关闭	關閉	guānbì	close; shut down	1-1
关键	關鍵	guānjiàn	key point; the key (to sth)	3-1
观念	觀念	guānniàn	concept; idea; 看法	3-1
关系	關係	guānxi	relationship; relation	2-1
关注	關注	guānzhù	pay close attention to	9-2
管理		guǎnlǐ	manage; control	2-1
广	廣	guǎng	extensive; wide	10-2
广告	廣告	guǎnggào	advertisement; commercial	6-2
广阔	廣闊	guǎngkuò	vast; wide	9-1
归	歸	guī	belong to; be attributed to	9-2
规定	規定	guīdìng	regulate; regulation	9-1
规范	規範	guīfàn	standard; norm	5-2
归根到底	歸根到底	guī gēn dào dǐ	in the final analysis	2-1
规模	規模	guīmó	scale; scope	2-2
规章	規章	guīzhāng	rules; regulations	5-1
国际	國際	guójì	international	1-1
国界	國界	guójiè	national boundary or border	6-1
国企	國企	guóqǐ	state-owned enterprise; 国有企业	1-1
国情	國情	guóqíng	conditions of a country	5-1
国有	國有	guóyǒu	state-owned; 国家所有	7-1
国债	國債	guózhài	national debt	9-1
过程	過程	guòchéng	process; course	5-1
过奖	過獎	guòjiǎng	(in response to a compliment) overpraise	3-2
过量	過量	guòliàng	excess; excessive; 太多	8-1
过头	過頭	guòtóu	go beyond the limit	8-2
过硬	過硬	guòyìng	be well up to standard	11-2

H

海关	海關	hǎiguān	customs; customhouse	4-1
行业	行業	hángyè	industry; trade	9-1
合理		hélǐ	reasonable	10-2
合同		hétong	contract	4-2
合资	合資	hézī	joint venture	6-2
宏观	宏觀	hóngguān	macroscopic	3-1
护钱	護錢	hùqián	protect (one's own) money	10-2
化		huà	verb suffix –ize or –ify	1-2
坏处	壞處	huàichu	harm; disadvantage	2-2
欢迎	歡迎	huānyíng	welcome	2-2
环节	環節	huánjié	link	4-2
环境	環境	huánjìng	environment	3-1
患病		huànbìng	fall ill; 生病	10-1

换钱	換錢	huànqián	change money	2-2
黄金		huángjīn	gold	10-1
黄金周	黃金週	Huángjīnzhōu	Golden Week	2-2
回馈	回饋	huíkuì	requite	12-1
毁灭	毀滅	huǐmiè	destructive	8-1
汇率	匯率	huìlǜ	exchange rate	2-1
混合		hùnhé	mix; mingle	7-1
伙伴	夥伴	huǒbàn	partners	4-2
货币	貨幣	huòbì	money; currency	2-1
获得	獲得	huòdé	obtain; acquire; 得到	3-1
祸福相依	禍福相依	huò fú xiāng yī	mixed blessing	2-2

J

基本		jīběn	basic; essential	5-1
基础	基礎	jīchǔ	foundation; base	2-1
基地		jīdì	base of operations	6-1
机构	機構	jīgòu	organization; institution	1-1
积极	積極	jījí	active; positive	5-1
基金		jījīn	fund; treasury	10-1
积累	積累	jīlěi	accumulate; accumulation	8-1
机制	機制	jīzhì	mechanism	7-1
极端	極端	jíduān	extreme; radical	12-1
集体	集體	jítǐ	collective	7-1
集团	集團	jítuán	group	11-2
集中		jízhōng	centralize; gather up	7-2
给付	給付	jǐfù	give; pay; 支付	10-1
季度		jìdù	quarter of a year	8-1
计划	計劃	jìhuà	plan; 打算	2-2
技术	技術	jìshù	technology	4-1
计算机	計算機	jìsuànjī	computer; calculating machine; 电脑	7-2
绩效	績效	jìxiào	performance and results	12-2
计征	計征	jìzhēng	calculation and levy	9-2
佳		jiā	good; superior; 好	6-1
家电	家電	jiādiàn	home appliance; 家用电器	2-2
加强	加強	jiāqiáng	strengthen; enhance	6-2
加入		jiārù	join	2-1
加速		jiāsù	speed up; accelerate	6-1
加息		jiāxī	raise interest rates	8-2
家喻户晓	家喻戶曉	jiā yù hù xiǎo	known to every family and household; widely known	5-2
假冒		jiǎmào	fake; bogus; counterfeit	12-1
价格	價格	jiàgé	price; 价钱	1-1
价值	價值	jiàzhí	value	5-1
监督	監督	jiāndū	supervise; watch over	5-1
监管	監管	jiānguǎn	supervision and control; 监督和管理	9-1
简称	簡稱	jiǎnchēng	be called for short; abbreviation	1-1
减少	減少	jiǎnshǎo	reduce; decrease	8-1
建立		jiànlì	build up; establish	5-2
建议	建議	jiànyì	suggest; suggestion	4-2
奖励	獎勵	jiǎnglì	award; reward with honor or money	5-1
讲义	講義	jiǎngyì	lecture handout; teaching material	7-2
讲座	講座	jiǎngzuò	lecture	5-2
降温		jiàngwēn	lower the temperature; 降低温度	1-2
焦点	焦點	jiāodiǎn	focal point; focus	9-2
交换	交換	jiāohuàn	exchange	4-1

交货	交貨	jiāohuò	*delivery of goods*	4-2
交流		jiāoliú	*exchange*	11-1
郊区	郊區	jiāoqū	*suburbs*	1-2
交易		jiāoyì	*business transaction; deal;* (做)买卖	1-1
角度		jiǎodù	*perspective; angle*	4-1
缴纳	繳納	jiǎonà	*pay*	9-1
叫苦连天	叫苦連天	jiào kǔ lián tiān	*complain incessantly and bitterly*	8-2
阶段	階段	jiēduàn	*phase; stage*	5-1
结构	結構	jiégòu	*structure*	6-1
结合	結合	jiéhé	*combine; combination*	5-1
结论	結論	jiélùn	*conclusion*	7-2
节省	節省	jiéshěng	*save*	7-2
解决		jiějué	*settle; solve*	10-2
界		jiè	*boundary*	5-2
借助		jièzhù	*draw support from; with the help of*	12-1
金融		jīnróng	*finance*	2-1
津津有味		jīnjīn yǒu wèi	*(to eat) with appetite and relish; (to read or listen) with great interest*	5-2
谨慎	謹慎	jǐnshèn	*prudent; careful; cautious;* 小心	8-2
紧缩	緊縮	jǐnsuō	*retrench*	8-1
进出口	進出口	jìnchūkǒu	*import and export;* 进口和出口	2-1
进而	進而	jìn'ér	*and then; after that*	8-1
进行	進行	jìnxíng	*proceed; carry out*	1-2
经	經	jīng	*as a result of; through*	11-1
经济	經濟	jīngjì	*economy*	1-2
经历	經歷	jīnglì	*go through; undergo an experience*	5-1
经验	經驗	jīngyàn	*experience*	4-2
经营	經營	jīngyíng	*run (a business)*	3-1
境外		jìngwài	*outside of a border; overseas*	1-1
竞争	競爭	jìngzhēng	*competitive*	2-2
纠纷	糾紛	jiūfēn	*dispute; issue*	4-1
就业	就業	jiùyè	*obtain employment*	2-2
居民		jūmín	*resident; inhabitant*	1-1
居然		jūrán	*unexpectedly; to one's surprise*	11-2
居住		jūzhù	*live; living*	1-2
局		jú	*bureau; office*	11-2
局长	局長	júzhǎng	*bureau chief*	11-2
举足轻重	舉足輕重	jǔ zú qīng zhòng	*play a decisive role*	9-1
俱		jù	*all; complete*	10-1
聚		jù	*assemble; get together*	3-2
具体	具體	jùtǐ	*concrete; specific*	5-1
具有		jùyǒu	*have;* 有	4-1
捐赠	捐贈	juānzèng	*donation*	12-2

K

开发	開發	kāifā	*open up and develop*	5-2
开放	開放	kāifàng	*open up*	1-1
看望		kànwàng	*call on; visit*	10-2
考虑	考慮	kǎolù	*think over; consider*	12-2
靠		kào	*depend on*	2-1
科技		kējì	*science and technology;* 科学技术	11-2
科学	科學	kēxué	*science; scientific*	5-1
客观	客觀	kèguān	*objective*	8-1
客户		kèhù	*client; customer*	3-2
课税	課稅	kèshuì	*levy a tax;* 征税	9-1

客厅	客廳	kètīng	*sitting room*	2-2
控制		kòngzhì	*control*	5-1
垮台	垮臺	kuǎtái	*collapse; fall from power*	8-1
跨国	跨國	kuàguó	*transnational*	6-1
款		kuǎn	*fund; a sum of money*	1-2
扩大	擴大	kuòdà	*expand; broaden the scope*	6-1

L

劳动	勞動	láodòng	*labor*	7-1
劳动力	勞動力	láodònglì	*labor; labor force*	4-1
老百姓		lǎobǎixìng	*ordinary people*	1-2
老总	老總	lǎozǒng	*general manager*	5-2
类	類	lèi	*type; category*	2-1
理财	理財	lǐcái	*manage financial affairs*	10-1
理解		lǐjiě	*understand; comprehend;* 懂	7-2
理论	理論	lǐlùn	*theory*	3-1
理念		lǐniàn	*concept*	5-1
力		lì	*power; often as a suffix*	2-2
利		lì	*profit; interest*	12-1
力不从心	力不從心	lì bù cóng xīn	*ability falling short of one's wishes*	5-1
厉害	厲害	lìhai	*power to develop; momentum*	6-2
力量		lìliàng	*force; power*	3-1
利率		lìlù	*interest rate*	8-2
利润	利潤	lìrùn	*profit*	3-1
利益		lìyì	*interest; profit*	12-1
例子		lìzi	*example; instance*	5-2
连	連	lián	*linked; connected*	9-2
联合	聯合	liánhé	*unite; ally*	6-1
连结	連結	liánjié	*connect*	2-1
联系	聯繫	liánxì	*establish contact*	6-2
连续	連續	liánxù	*continuously; successively*	8-1
两位数	兩位數	liǎngwèishù	*double-digit*	8-1
聊		liáo	*chat*	2-2
了解	瞭解	liǎojiě	*understand; know about*	3-1
零售		língshòu	*retail sale*	6-2
流动	流動	liúdòng	*flow*	2-1
流量	流量	liúliàng	*rate or volume of flow*	10-2
流通		liútōng	*circulate; flow*	8-1
垄断	壟斷	lǒngduàn	*monopolize; monopolization*	6-1
漏电	漏電	lòudiàn	*electric leakage*	11-2
路子		lùzi	*way*	11-2
履行		lǚxíng	*perform; fulfill*	10-1
率		lù	*rate; often as a suffix*	8-1

M

马路	馬路	mǎlù	*street; road*	6-2
卖场	賣場	màichǎng	*marketplace*	6-2
满足	滿足	mǎnzú	*satisfy*	3-1
盲目		mángmù	*blind*	7-1
贸易	貿易	màoyì	*trade*	2-1
免征		miǎnzhēng	*exemption*	9-2
面积	面積	miànjī	*measure of area; square measure*	9-2
面临	面臨	miànlín	*face;* 面对	6-2
面值		miànzhí	*face value*	1-1
面子		miànzi	*face; feeling*	4-2

民事		mínshì	civil; relating to civil law	10-1
民营	民營	mínyíng	privately operated; private; 私营	7-1
民主		mínzhǔ	democracy	7-2
名称	名稱	míngchēng	name of a thing or organization	11-1
明确	明確	míngquè	clear and definite; 清楚	9-2
模式		móshì	mode	5-1
某		mǒu	certain; some	4-1
目标	目標	mùbiāo	target	3-1
目的		mùdì	purpose	2-1
目前		mùqián	now; presently; 现在	1-2

N

纳税	納稅	nàshuì	pay tax; 交税	9-1
闹	鬧	nào	charivari	1-2
内地		nèidì	inland; interior (of a country)	1-1
内流		nèiliú	inflow	2-1
能源		néngyuán	energy resources	8-2
逆差		nìchā	(in foreign trade) deficit	4-1
年纪	年紀	niánjì	age; 年龄	10-2
年龄	年齡	niánlíng	age	10-1
农产品	農產品	nóngchǎnpǐn	agricultural product	4-2
农村	農村	nóngcūn	countryside	3-2
弄清		nòngqīng	make clear; find out	4-2

O

| 偶然 | | ǒurán | accidental; by chance | 5-2 |

P

排斥		páichì	exclude; reject	5-1
判定		pàndìng	determine; judge	11-2
抛		pāo	throw; fling	6-2
陪		péi	accompany	11-2
赔本	賠本	péiběn	lose money in doing business; 赔钱	12-2
赔偿	賠償	péicháng	compensate	10-1
佩服		pèifú	admire	5-2
膨胀	膨脹	péngzhàng	inflate; inflation	8-1
披露		pīlù	reveal; announce	12-2
皮毛		pímáo	(fig.) superficial knowledge	10-2
贫富	貧富	pínfù	the poor and the rich	7-2
品牌		pǐnpái	brand	5-2
品种	品種	pǐnzhǒng	variety; breed	10-2
评估	評估	pínggū	assessment; evaluation	9-2
平衡		pínghéng	balance	4-1
凭借	憑藉	píngjiè	rely on; depend on; 靠; 依靠	9-1
屏幕		píngmù	computer, TV, or hanging screen	10-2
破产	破產	pòchǎn	go bankrupt; bankruptcy	2-2
破坏	破壞	pòhuài	destroy	8-1

Q

期间	期間	qījiān	time; period	9-1
期限		qīxiàn	deadline	10-1
欺诈	欺詐	qīzhà	swindle; fraudulence	12-1
其		qí	its; it	3-1
起诉	起訴	qǐsù	sue; prosecute	11-2
企业	企業	qǐyè	enterprise	3-1

洽谈	洽談	qiàtán	negotiate; negotiation	4-2
签约	簽約	qiānyuē	sign a contract	4-2
前途		qiántú	future; prospect	7-2
欠		qiàn	owe	8-2
抢得	搶得	qiǎngdé	vie for and win	3-2
强制	強制	qiǎngzhì	force; compel	9-1
巧妙		qiǎomiào	ingenious; clever	6-2
切		qiē	cut	3-2
侵犯		qīnfàn	violate; infringe upon	11-2
侵权	侵權	qīnquán	tort; infringe upon others' rights; 侵犯权利	11-2
请教	請教	qǐngjiào	ask for advice; consult	3-2
庆祝	慶祝	qìngzhù	celebrate	3-2
趋势	趨勢	qūshì	trend; tendency	2-1
渠道		qúdào	channel	3-1
取消		qǔxiāo	cancel	9-1
权	權	quán	right; 权利; power; 权力	7-1
全部		quánbù	all	1-1
权力	權力	quánlì	power; authority	7-2
权利	權利	quánlì	right	11-1
全民		quánmín	all the people (within a country)	7-1
权威	權威	quánwēi	authority	4-1
权益	權益	quányì	rights and interests	12-2
缺点	缺點	quēdiǎn	shortcoming; defect; weakness	7-2
缺乏		quēfá	lack; be short of; 缺少	7-1
缺少		quēshǎo	lack; be short of	10-2
确保	確保	quèbǎo	ensure; assure	5-2
确定	確定	quèdìng	decide; confirm	3-1
确实	確實	quèshí	indeed; 真的	2-2

R

让步	讓步	ràngbù	concede	4-2
热点	熱點	rèdiǎn	hot spot; center of attention	2-1
热烈	熱烈	rèliè	enthusiastic; ardent	7-2
热情	熱情	rèqíng	warmhearted and hospitable	2-2
人才		réncái	person of talent	5-2
人类	人類	rénlèi	mankind	12-2
人力		rénlì	manpower	5-1
人民币	人民幣	rénmínbì	Renminbi (RMB)	1-1
人心惶惶		rénxīn huánghuáng	public disquiet	8-2
人性		rénxìng	human nature; humanity	5-1
人治		rénzhì	rule by men	5-1
认购	認購	rèngòu	offer to buy; subscribe	1-1
任何		rènhé	any	11-1
认可	認可	rènkě	endorsement	12-1
日用品		rìyòngpǐn	daily commodities	8-2
入门	入門	rùmén	introductory guide; introduction	10-2
润滑	潤滑	rùnhuá	lubricate	8-1
若		ruò	if; 如果; 要是	2-1

S

丧失	喪失	sàngshī	lose; 失去	10-1
商		shāng	merchant; businessman; dealer; often as a suffix	3-1
商标	商標	shāngbiāo	trademark	11-1
伤残	傷殘	shāngcán	wounded and disabled	10-1

商务	商務	shāngwù	business affairs	3-2
商业	商業	shāngyè	commerce; trade; business	4-1
上升		shàngshēng	rise	2-1
上市		shàngshì	go on the market	1-1
上涨	上漲	shàngzhǎng	rise; go up	1-2
捎		shāo	take along sth to or for sb	12-2
设	設	shè	establish; set up; 办	6-1
社会	社會	shèhuì	society	7-1
设计	設計	shèjì	design	3-2
社区	社區	shèqū	community	12-2
涉外		shèwài	concerning foreign affairs; 涉及外事	11-2
深受启发	深受啟發	shēn shòu qǐfā	be greatly inspired	5-2
生产	生產	shēngchǎn	produce; production	4-1
生存		shēngcún	existence	12-1
生态	生態	shēngtài	ecology; ecological	12-2
升值		shēngzhí	appreciation	2-1
省钱	省錢	shěngqián	save money	2-2
胜	勝	shèng	be superior to	12-2
胜诉	勝訴	shèngsù	win a lawsuit	11-2
失败	失敗	shībài	fail; lose	12-2
失控		shīkòng	out of control; 失去控制	8-2
失去		shīqù	lose	2-2
失业	失業	shīyè	unemployment	8-1
实际	實際	shíjì	reality	7-2
实践	實踐	shíjiàn	practice; put into practice	7-1
实力	實力	shílì	actual strength	2-2
食品		shípǐn	food	8-2
实时	實時	shíshí	real time	2-1
实体	實體	shítǐ	entity	6-1
实物	實物	shíwù	material object	9-1
实习	實習	shíxí	intern; internship	1-2
实现	實現	shíxiàn	realize; realization	1-1
实行	實行	shíxíng	put into practice	5-2
使命		shǐmìng	mission	12-1
使用		shǐyòng	use; 用	9-2
市场	市場	shìchǎng	market	1-1
事故		shìgù	accident	10-1
适合	適合	shìhé	be fit for; suit	7-2
事实	事實	shìshí	fact	12-2
事先		shìxiān	in advance; beforehand	7-1
适用	適用	shìyòng	applicable	9-1
市值		shìzhí	market value; 市场价值	1-1
收集		shōují	collect; gather	7-2
收入		shōurù	income; revenue	8-2
收益		shōuyì	income; profit; earnings; 收入	10-2
收支		shōuzhī	income and expense; 收入和支出	10-1
手段		shǒuduàn	means; measure; 方法; 办法	7-1
首付		shǒufù	down payment; first payment	1-2
首先		shǒuxiān	before all others; first	2-1
售后	售後	shòuhòu	after-sale	6-2
熟人		shúrén	acquaintance	5-2
熟悉		shúxī	be familiar with	3-2
数据	數據	shùjù	data	7-2
树立	樹立	shùlì	establish; erect	12-2
衰退		shuāituì	decay; recession	5-2

双方	雙方	shuāngfāng	*both sides; both parties;* 两方	2-1
双刃剑	雙刃劍	shuāngrènjiàn	*double-edged sword*	2-2
水平		shuǐpíng	*level*	3-1
税款		shuìkuǎn	*tax payment; taxation*	9-1
税收		shuìshōu	*taxation; tax revenue*	9-1
顺差	順差	shùnchā	*(in foreign trade) surplus*	4-1
顺利	順利	shùnlì	*smooth; without a hitch*	3-2
私人		sīrén	*private*	9-2
私营	私營	sīyíng	*privately operated; private*	7-1
搜索		sōusuǒ	*search*	5-2
速度		sùdù	*speed*	1-1
诉讼	訴訟	sùsòng	*litigation; lawsuit*	11-2
算是		suànshì	*at last;* 总算	11-2
随机	隨機	suíjī	*random*	8-1
随机应变	隨機應變	suí jī yìng biàn	*adapt oneself quickly to changing conditions*	4-2
损害	損害	sǔnhài	*damage; harm*	12-1
损失	損失	sǔnshī	*loss*	10-1
缩水	縮水	suōshuǐ	*shrink;* 变少	8-2
所		suǒ	*place; office; often as a suffix*	1-1
索赔	索賠	suǒpéi	*claim*	4-2
所谓	所謂	suǒwèi	*so-called*	12-2
所有		suǒyǒu	*ownership*	7-1

T

抬头	抬頭	táitóu	*raise one's head*	8-2
态度	態度	tàidù	*attitude*	12-1
谈判	談判	tánpàn	*negotiate; negotiation*	4-2
讨价还价	討價還價	tǎojià huánjià	*bargain*	4-2
讨论	討論	tǎolùn	*discuss*	7-2
套		tào	*classifier indicating a series or set of things*	1-2
特定		tèdìng	*specific*	4-1
特殊		tèshū	*exceptional; special;* 特别	3-2
特性		tèxìng	*characteristic; special property*	5-1
特征	特徵	tèzhēng	*characteristic; feature; trait*	9-1
提到		tídào	*mention;* 说到	7-2
提供		tígōng	*provide; supply*	3-1
提升		tíshēng	*upgrade*	5-2
提醒		tíxǐng	*remind*	4-2
体会	體會	tǐhuì	*knowledge from experience; realize*	3-2
体系	體系	tǐxì	*system*	8-1
体现	體現	tǐxiàn	*embody; incarnate*	9-1
条件	條件	tiáojiàn	*condition*	1-2
调节	調節	tiáojié	*adjust; regulate*	2-1
调解	調解	tiáojiě	*mediate*	4-1
调控	調控	tiáokòng	*regulation and control*	1-2
调整	調整	tiáozhěng	*adjust; regulate*	6-1
挑战	挑戰	tiǎozhàn	*challenge*	3-2
铁	鐵	tiě	*iron*	12-2
铁律	鐵律	tiělù	*iron law*	12-2
停滞		tíngzhì	*cease moving or making progress*	8-1
挺		tǐng	*quite; very;* 非常	7-2
通常		tōngcháng	*generally*	1-1
通过	通過	tōngguò	*by means of*	2-2
通货	通貨	tōnghuò	*currency*	8-1
通讯	通訊	tōngxùn	*communication*	2-1

同事		tóngshì	co-worker; colleague	4-2
统一	統一	tǒngyī	unified	12-1
投保		tóubǎo	buy insurance; 购买保险	10-1
投机	投機	tóujī	speculate in a risky adventure	2-1
投资	投資	tóuzī	invest	1-1
突出		tūchū	outstanding; obvious	1-2
图像	圖像	túxiàng	picture; produced image	11-1
团队	團隊	tuánduì	team	3-2
推		tuī	push forward	5-2
推动	推動	tuīdòng	push forward	6-1
推翻		tuīfān	overthrow; overturn	11-2
推广	推廣	tuīguǎng	popularize; expand the use of	6-1
推进	推進	tuījìn	promote	4-1
退休		tuìxiū	retire; retirement	10-2
脱节	脫節	tuōjié	be disconnected	7-1

W

外币	外幣	wàibì	foreign currency; 外国货币	1-1
外观	外觀	wàiguān	appearance; exterior; 外表	11-1
外汇	外匯	wàihuì	foreign exchange	2-1
外流		wàiliú	outflow	2-1
外资	外資	wàizī	foreign capital; 外国资本	1-1
完美		wánměi	perfect; flawless	5-1
完善		wánshàn	perfect; flawless; 完美	9-2
晚年		wǎnnián	old age; one's later years	10-2
网点	網點	wǎngdiǎn	network point	6-1
往往		wǎngwǎng	often; frequently; 常常	3-2
微观	微觀	wēiguān	microscopic	3-1
伪劣	偽劣	wěiliè	fake; shoddy	12-1
委员会	委員會	wěiyuánhuì	committee; commission	11-2
未必		wèibì	not necessarily; 不一定	2-2
位于	位於	wèiyú	be located at; 在	1-1
文件		wénjiàn	document; paper	9-2
稳定	穩定	wěndìng	stable; steady	9-1
无偿	無償	wúcháng	gratuitously; free; gratis	9-1
无欺	無欺	wúqī	no cheating; without cheating	12-1
无形	無形	wúxíng	invisible; intangible	11-1
武器		wǔqì	arms; weapon	11-2
物价	物價	wùjià	price of goods	2-1
物力		wùlì	material resources	7-2
物资	物資	wùzī	goods and materials	8-2

X

吸引		xīyǐn	attract	3-2
系		xì	be; 是	8-1
下跌		xiàdiē	(price, etc.) drop; decline	2-1
下降		xiàjiàng	descend; decrease	2-1
先机	先機	xiānjī	preemptive opportunity	3-2
显得	顯得	xiǎnde	look; seem; appear; 看起来	5-1
险种	險種	xiǎnzhǒng	insurance type; 保险的种类	10-2
现金	現金	xiànjīn	cash	10-2
现象	現象	xiànxiàng	phenomenon	8-1
限制		xiànzhì	limit; restriction	6-2
现状	現狀	xiànzhuàng	current situation	3-1
相当	相當	xiāngdāng	match; be about equal to	4-1

相对	相對	xiāngduì	*relatively; comparatively*	9-1
相反		xiāngfǎn	*on the contrary*	2-1
相关	相關	xiāngguān	*related;* 有关	9-1
享受		xiǎngshòu	*enjoy*	6-2
享有		xiǎngyǒu	*possess; enjoy (prestige, right, etc.)*	11-1
项	項	xiàng	*classifier for itemized things*	1-2
项目	項目	xiàngmù	*project; program*	12-2
消费	消費	xiāofèi	*consume*	3-2
销售	銷售	xiāoshòu	*sell; sale;* 卖	6-1
萧条	蕭條	xiāotiáo	*depression*	8-1
效力		xiàolì	*effect; favorable function*	11-1
效率		xiàolǜ	*efficiency; effectiveness*	7-1
协助	協助	xiézhù	*help;* 帮助	4-2
新房		xīnfáng	*bridal chamber*	1-2
新居		xīnjū	*new residence*	1-2
心理		xīnlǐ	*psychology; psychological*	5-1
新兴	新興	xīnxīng	*burgeoning; newly risen*	8-2
心中有底		xīnzhōng yǒu dǐ	*know what to expect;* 心中有数	4-2
信贷	信貸	xìndài	*financial credit; usually bank loans*	10-1
信念		xìnniàn	*conviction; belief*	12-1
信息		xìnxī	*information*	3-1
信誉	信譽	xìnyù	*reputation*	4-2
形成		xíngchéng	*form; take shape*	1-1
形式		xíngshì	*form; style*	9-1
行为	行為	xíngwéi	*behavior; act*	5-1
性		xìng	*suffix designating a specified quality, property, etc.*	1-2
性质	性質	xìngzhì	*nature; character*	6-1
雄厚		xiónghòu	*solid; abundant*	6-1
修		xiū	*study (a course)*	3-2
需求		xūqiú	*demand*	3-1
选修	選修	xuǎnxiū	*take an elective or optional course*	1-2
选择	選擇	xuǎnzé	*choose; select*	8-2
学术	學術	xuéshù	*systematic learning; academic*	5-2
询价	詢價	xúnjià	*inquire; inquiry;* 问价	4-2

Y

压力	壓力	yālì	*pressure; stress*	2-2
研发	研發	yánfā	*research and development;* 研究开发	5-2
严格	嚴格	yángé	*strict; rigorous, rigid*	11-1
研究		yánjiū	*research*	3-2
严重	嚴重	yánzhòng	*serious; seriously*	7-1
演变	演變	yǎnbiàn	*evolve*	12-1
眼前		yǎnqián	*at present;* 当前; 现在	10-2
央行		yāngháng	*central bank;* 中央银行	8-2
养老	養老	yǎnglǎo	*live out one's life in retirement*	10-1
要素		yàosù	*essential factor; key element*	3-1
业	業	yè	*business; industry; often as a suffix*	6-2
业务	業務	yèwù	*business*	5-1
一次		yīcì	*one time*	1-2
一旦		yīdàn	*once; in case*	8-1
医疗	醫療	yīliáo	*medical treatment*	10-1
依据	依據	yījù	*basis; things to go by;* 根据	12-2
一举两得	一舉兩得	yī jǔ liǎng dé	*obtain two benefits with one move*	1-2
一生		yīshēng	*all one's life; a lifetime;* 一辈子	10-2

一无是处	一無是處	yī wú shì chù	without a single redeeming feature	7-2
一向		yīxiàng	always; all the time	10-2
依照		yīzhào	according to; in light of; 按照	9-1
以茶代酒		yǐ chá dài jiǔ	drink tea instead of wine	4-2
以人为本	以人為本	yǐ rén wéi běn	people-oriented; person-centered	5-1
以至		yǐzhì	to such an extent as to	8-1
亿	億	yì	a hundred million	1-1
义	義	yì	justice; righteousness	12-1
亦		yì	also; too; 也	4-1
意识	意識	yìshí	consciousness; awareness	10-2
艺术	藝術	yìshù	art	11-1
意义	意義	yìyì	sense; meaning; significance	5-2
抑制		yìzhì	restrain; control	8-1
因素		yīnsù	factor	2-1
引导	引導	yǐndǎo	guide; lead	7-1
引进	引進	yǐnjìn	introduce from elsewhere; import	5-1
引起		yǐnqǐ	bring about; cause	2-1
引擎		yǐnqíng	engine	5-2
引入		yǐnrù	introduce from elsewhere; 引进	5-2
英明		yīngmíng	wise; brilliant	5-2
赢	贏	yíng	win; gain	11-2
盈利		yínglì	earn a profit; profit; 赚钱	3-1
营利	營利	yínglì	seek profits	10-1
赢利	贏利	yínglì	earn a profit; 盈利; 赚钱	6-1
营销	營銷	yíngxiāo	marketing	3-1
应邀而来	應邀而來	yìng yāo ér lái	come as invited	2-2
应用	應用	yìngyòng	apply; put in use	11-1
佣金	傭金	yòngjīn	commission	4-2
拥有	擁有	yōngyǒu	possess; have; 有	9-2
永久		yǒngjiǔ	permanent	4-1
用途		yòngtú	use; application; 用处	9-2
优惠	優惠	yōuhuì	benefits; favorable treatment	9-1
优势	優勢	yōushì	advantage	2-2
优秀	優秀	yōuxiù	outstanding; excellent	12-2
尤其		yóuqí	especially; particularly; 特别	5-1
有关	有關	yǒuguān	be related to	8-1
有效		yǒuxiào	effective; valid	11-1
有助于	有助於	yǒuzhùyú	contribute to; be conducive to; 有利于	11-1
舆论	輿論	yúlùn	public opinion	12-1
与日俱增	與日俱增	yǔ rì jù zēng	grow with each passing day	10-1
与时俱进	與時俱進	yǔ shí jù jìn	advance with the times	5-2
预先	預先	yùxiān	in advance; beforehand; 事先	9-1
员工	員工	yuángōng	staff; personnel	5-1
原材料		yuáncáiliào	raw material	6-1
原来如此	原來如此	yuánlái rúcǐ	so that's how it is	11-2
原料		yuánliào	raw materials	8-2
原则	原則	yuánzé	principle	12-2
约定	約定	yuēdìng	agree on	10-1
约好	約好	yuēhǎo	with an appointment scheduled	12-2
运输	運輸	yùnshū	transportation	4-2
运营	運營	yùnyíng	operate	10-1
运用	運用	yùnyòng	make use of; 使用	7-1

Z

暂时	暫時	zànshí	temporary; for the moment	10-1
赞助	贊助	zànzhù	provide monetary or material support	12-1

则	則	zé	*then; in that case;* 那么	2-1
责任	責任	zérèn	*duty; responsibility*	10-1
增强	增強	zēngqiáng	*strengthen; enhance*	2-2
增长	增長	zēngzhǎng	*grow; growth*	4-1
债券	債券	zhàiquàn	*bond; debenture*	10-1
债务	債務	zhàiwù	*debt*	8-2
展开	展開	zhǎnkāi	*unfold; carry out;* 开展	6-1
占		zhàn	*hold (a certain status)*	7-1
占领	佔領	zhànlǐng	*occupy*	6-1
章		zhāng	*chapter*	9-2
掌握		zhǎngwò	*master*	3-1
障碍	障礙	zhàng'ài	*obstacle*	6-2
招呼		zhāohu	*greet; say hello*	10-2
照		zhào	*in accordance with;* 按照	2-2
折扣		zhékòu	*discount*	8-2
者		zhě	*person (of a category); often as a suffix*	1-1
真实	真實	zhēnshí	*true; real*	12-2
争端	爭端	zhēngduān	*controversial issue; conflict*	4-1
征收	徵收	zhēngshōu	*levy; collect*	9-1
整合		zhěnghé	*integrate*	3-1
整体	整體	zhěngtǐ	*overall; whole; entirety*	6-1
政策		zhèngcè	*policy*	4-1
政府		zhèngfǔ	*government*	1-2
证明	證明	zhèngmíng	*prove; testify; verify*	12-2
证券	證券	zhèngquàn	*security; bond*	1-1
正确	正確	zhèngquè	*correct; correctly;* 对	3-1
正式		zhèngshì	*officially*	4-1
政治		zhèngzhì	*politics; political*	3-1
支付		zhīfù	*pay (money);* 付	10-1
知识	知識	zhīshi	*knowledge*	5-1
支柱		zhīzhù	*pillar*	1-2
值		zhí	*value; often as a suffix*	9-2
直接		zhíjiē	*direct; directly*	6-1
职能	職能	zhínéng	*function*	5-1
值钱	值錢	zhíqián	*valuable*	2-2
职业	職業	zhíyè	*profession; professional*	5-2
指		zhǐ	*refer to*	1-1
指标	指標	zhǐbiāo	*indicator*	12-2
指挥	指揮	zhǐhuī	*direct; command*	5-1
指数	指數	zhǐshù	*index*	8-2
制		zhì	*system;* 制度; *often as a suffix*	7-1
治安		zhì'ān	*public security; public order*	9-2
制定		zhìdìng	*set up; institute*	9-2
制度		zhìdù	*system*	2-1
智力		zhìlì	*intelligence*	11-1
至少		zhìshǎo	*at least*	8-2
秩序		zhìxù	*order*	4-1
至于	至於	zhìyú	*as for; as to*	9-2
制约	制約	zhìyuē	*restrict*	7-1
中间商	中間商	zhōngjiānshāng	*middleman*	3-1
种类	種類	zhǒnglèi	*kind; type*	9-1
仲裁		zhòngcái	*arbitrate*	4-2
重大		zhòngdà	*great; significant;* 重要	7-2
重点	重點	zhòngdiǎn	*emphasis; the focal (or key) point*	5-2
逐步		zhúbù	*gradually; step by step*	3-1
主办	主辦	zhǔbàn	*sponsor; host*	12-1

主导	主導	zhǔdǎo	leading; predominant	7-1
主体	主體	zhǔtǐ	main body	7-1
主义	主義	zhǔyì	-ism; doctrine	7-1
注册	註冊	zhùcè	register; registration	1-1
祝贺	祝賀	zhùhè	congratulate; congratulation	3-2
住宅		zhùzhái	residence	9-2
注重		zhùzhòng	attach importance to; emphasize; 重视	12-1
著作		zhùzuò	writing; work	11-1
专家	專家	zhuānjiā	expert	10-2
专款专用	專款專用	zhuānkuǎn zhuānyòng	earmark a fund for a specified purpose	9-2
专利	專利	zhuānlì	patent; 专有权利	11-1
专门	專門	zhuānmén	special; specially; specialized	5-1
专有	專有	zhuānyǒu	proprietary	11-1
转变	轉變	zhuǎnbiàn	change; transform	7-1
赚钱	賺錢	zhuànqián	make a profit; earn money; 挣钱	10-2
装修	裝修	zhuāngxiū	decorate; decoration	1-2
追求		zhuīqiú	seek; pursue	12-1
资本	資本	zīběn	capital	1-1
资本主义	資本主義	zīběn zhǔyì	capitalism	12-1
资产	資產	zīchǎn	assets; property	7-1
资料	資料	zīliào	data; information	4-2
咨询	諮詢	zīxún	consult; consultation	1-2
资源	資源	zīyuán	resource	5-1
子公司		zǐgōngsī	subsidiary company	6-1
自豪		zìháo	proud of sth	2-2
自然		zìrán	naturally	2-2
自营	自營	zìyíng	self-run	6-2
自愿	自願	zìyuàn	voluntarily; willingly; 自己愿意	10-1
自主		zìzhǔ	autonomy; act on one's own	7-1
自助游	自助遊	zìzhùyóu	self-guided tour	2-2
总	總	zǒng	overall	1-1
总	總	zǒng	chief; short for "general manager"	3-2
总称	總稱	zǒngchēng	general term	5-1
总额	總額	zǒng'é	total (amount or value)	4-1
足		zú	sufficient; plentiful	7-1
组成	組成	zǔchéng	form; make up	1-2
组织	組織	zǔzhī	organization	1-1
最终	最終	zuìzhōng	finally; eventually; 最后	8-1
遵契守法		zūnqì shǒufǎ	abide by contracts and laws	12-1
尊重		zūnzhòng	respect	5-1
遵守		zūnshǒu	abide by; comply with	11-1
作品		zuòpǐn	works (of literature and art)	11-1
作用		zuòyòng	effect; role	4-1

附录二 语言提示索引

Appendix B: *Index of language tips*

反而	on the contrary; instead	7-2
反之	a connective meaning "on the contrary; whereas; or otherwise"	4-1
非	不是, just like non-, in-, and un- in English	9-2
非(得)...不可	must do sth; have to do sth	3-2
分为 A 和 B 两种	be divided into two types such as A and B, 分为 being the same as 分成	10-1

G

该	this; that; the above-mentioned	1-1
A 跟 B 并存	A and B coexist	3-2
更为 Adj 的是	What is more Adj is . . .	12-1
供	for (sb to do sth)	1-1
故	same as 所以, but formal	4-1
关系到	relate to; have a bearing on	10-2

H

好不容易	not at all easy	6-2
好容易	not at all easy; the same as 好不容易	6-2
...化	verb suffix –ize or –ify	1-2

J

即	namely; the same as; (也)就是	3-1
既...又..., 一举两得	both . . . and . . ., gaining two things in one move	1-2
(被)简称为	be called sth for short; 简称: abbreviated form of a name	1-1
借助于	have the aid of; draw support from	12-1
进而	and then; after that	8-1
进行	carry out; execute; conduct	7-1
经	When used as a preposition with a "subject + predicate" structure as its object, what follows is the result of the action.	11-1
就是	introduces an afterthought that is usually incongruous with the previous statement	9-2
具有...的地位	have a . . . status or position	9-1
具有...的优势	have advantage in	6-1
(对...)具有...作用	have a . . . impact (on . . .)	9-1

L

| V1 来 V2 | When 来 is used between two verbs or verbal phrases, V1 indicates the way of doing things and V2 indicates the purpose. | 12-1 |

M

| 某 | used for an indefinite person or thing, but can also be used to avoid naming a known person or thing | 4-1 |

Q

其	As a pronoun, 其 can mean "his, her, its, or their," or "he, she, it, or they." It represents the afore-mentioned noun.	3-1
(对...)起...作用	affect (. . .) in the capacity of	9-1
(对...)起...作用	play a . . . role (in . . .)	7-1
(在...中)起...作用	play a . . . role (in . . .)	7-1
确定...的方针	determine the guiding principle of	7-1

R

| 如...等 | such as; for instance | 9-1 |
| 若..., 则... | same as 如果 . . ., 那么 . . ., but more formal | 2-1 |

S

| 是由...决定的 | be decided by | 2-1 |

234

附录三 注释索引

Appendix C: *Index of notes*